Twayne's United States Authors Series

EDITOR OF THIS VOLUME

Lewis Leary

University of North Carolina

Washington Irving

TUSAS 379

Washington Irving

WASHINGTON IRVING

By MARY WEATHERSPOON BOWDEN

TWAYNE PUBLISHERS
A DIVISION OF G. K. HALL & CO., BOSTON

Copyright © 1981 by G. K. Hall & Co.

Published in 1981 by Twayne Publishers,
A Division of G. K. Hall & Co.
All Rights Reserved

Printed on permanent/durable acid-free paper and bound
in the United States of America

First Printing

FRONTISPIECE

Portrait of Washington Irving (age c. 45–47)

A pencil on paper sketch c. 1828–1830 by
Sir Thomas Lawrence (1769–1830) or possibly Sir David Wilkie.
London, England.

Reproduction courtesy of Sleepy Hollow Restorations.

Library of Congress Cataloging in Publication Data

Bowden, Mary Weatherspoon.
Washington Irving.

(Twayne's United States authors series ; TUSAS 379)
Bibliography: p. 190–94
Includes index.
1. Irving, Washington, 1783–1859—Criticism and
interpretation.
PS2088.B66   818′.209   80–21364
ISBN 0–8057–7314–2

TO THE

NEW YORK

HISTORICAL SOCIETY

This Work is respectfully Dedi-
cated, as a humble and unworthy
Testimony of the profound venera-
tion and exalted esteem of the
Society's
Sincere Well wisher
and
Devoted Servant

MARY WEATHERSPOON BOWDEN.

Contents

About the Author

Mary Weatherspoon Bowden was born and raised in Johnston, Iowa, and received her B.A. from the University of Nebraska. She held a teaching assistantship at the University of Texas, from which she received an M.A. and Ph.D. During this time she developed an interest in the influence of politics on literature, an interest which continues in this book.

The author was an assistant professor at Indiana University at Fort Wayne, and has taught at the University of Texas. Her research interests include Philip Freneau, Washington Irving, and the events of the year 1832. She wrote *Philip Freneau* for Twayne and has published articles on Freneau and Irving.

Preface

Today, few readers know more than one or two stories by Washington Irving, probably "Rip Van Winkle" and "The Legend of Sleepy Hollow," possibly "The German Student" or "The Spectre Bridegroom." While admiring these jewels, the readers do not realize that they are but a small portion of a large treasure chest. In his own day, Irving's many works were very popular, but even then Irving complained that most did not understand him. Those who did fully appreciate his artistry (and who were influenced by him) were fellow authors— Hawthorne, Melville, Poe, Dickens, Mark Twain, Henry James.

It is not the intention of this work to insist that all readers should read all of Irving, but to present to them most of Irving's works. (Because of space limitations, this work does not deal with Irving's later contributions to periodicals, nor with his dramatic works, nor with works recently attributed to him.) It is the intention of this work to show that all Irving's books are readable today, that many are worth reading, and that a few demand reading and rereading. It is also its intent to demonstrate that Irving was not a short-story writer, but a composer of books: thus, a story in one of his books is more than that story alone, for it gains meaning from what came before and gives meaning to what will follow.

In my study, I have prefaced each chapter with a short biographical sketch of Irving during the time of the composition of the works discussed. There are two reasons for this. The first is that Irving's works are very personal in tone; his mood during composition is reflected in the work and, in some instances, dictates its content. The second reason is perhaps equally important: Irving's beliefs are reflected in his works. Modern readers have a vague image of a gentle Irving, conservative, disgusted by political brawls, enamored of the glory of royalty. This image is largely derived from his nephew's biography of him, written in a time of Victorian sensibility, and chiefly dependent upon

Irving's "public" letters, letters written with the consciousness that they would be published either immediately or in the future. If, as this study hopes to suggest, Irving was throughout his life a staunch Jeffersonian—disgusted by the monarchical governments of Europe and who loved being knowledgeable of behind-the-scenes political maneuvering—we can read his works with a different attitude; and we will then find that they confirm all these assertions about the "real" Irving.

In order to show the development of Irving's artistry, I have discussed his books chronologically and refer, in most cases, to the text of the first edition. (The quoted texts are listed under "Primary Sources" in the Bibliography.) The reader must be aware, however, that Irving revised his works frequently, adding to them, altering the tone, changing the intention of the work and the impression it gives. Since my study, in its limited amount of space, cannot examine all the different revisions, I will discuss the earlier versions of the works, and rely on the reader to be aware of the later revisions.

I must thank a number of scholars who have directly or indirectly helped me with this work. First, thanks go to my husband, Edwin T. Bowden, a constant reference source of Irving bibliography and a captive reader of this manuscript. Thanks also go to Ralph Aderman, who furnished me freely with transcripts of Irving letters; to Richard Rust for his work on Irving's "American Essays"; to Earl Harbert for his comments on *Granada*; to Bruce Granger and Lewis Leary and Sylvia Bowman for their encouragement; to C. L. Cline for his advice on the first chapter; and most of all to all the editors of the Twayne Irving edition, from whose extensive labors I have profited.

MARY WEATHERSPOON BOWDEN

Chronology

1783	Washington Irving born on April 3.
1802–1804	Begins writing for *The Morning Chronicle*.
1806–1807	First tour of Europe.
1808	Publishes *Salmagundi* (with William Irving and James Kirke Paulding).
1809–1812	Knickerbocker's *A History of New York*.
1814	Edits *The Analectic*.
1814–1815	Colonel in the New York Militia and aide-de-camp to Governor Daniel Tompkins.
1815	May 25, sails for Europe.
1818	Offered position of undersecretary of the Navy.
1819	First installments of *The Sketch Book* published in America.
1820	*The Sketch Book* published in England. Leaves England for the Continent.
1822	*Bracebridge Hall*.
1824	*Tales of a Traveller*.
1826	Goes to Spain to translate Navarette's *Columbus*.
1828	*The Life and Voyages of Christopher Columbus*.
1829	Fray Antonio Agapida's *The Conquest of Granada*. Appointed secretary of the legation at London.
1831	*Voyages and Discoveries of the Companions of Columbus*.
1832	*The Alhambra*. May 21, arrives in New York. September–October, accompanies Ellsworth to the Indian hunting grounds.
1835	*The Crayon Miscellany*.
1836	*Astoria*.

1837   *The Rocky Mountains, (The Adventures of Captain Bonneville).*

1840   Offered position of secretary of the Navy.

1841–   *Biography of Margaret Miller Davidson.*
1842

1846   Ambassador to Spain.

1849   *Goldsmith, Mahomet.*

1850   *Mahomet's Successors.*

1855   *Wolfert's Roost.*

1855–   *Life of Washington.*
1859

1859   Washington Irving dies on November 28.

CHAPTER 1

Early Works

I *Family Background and Early Education*

WASHINGTON Irving, the eleventh child of Sarah and William Irving, was born on April 3, 1783, in New York City. For the first thirty-two years of his life New York was his home, his education, his inspiration, his material. Here he won his reputation, first as a casual humorist, later as the city's best-known literary figure. In these years, Irving worked for his brother's hardware business, joined another brother in a law firm, politicked, wrote for newspapers, visited the frontiers on land deals, was a lobbyist in Washington, and edited at least one magazine. But all was not work; he toured Europe, visited friends in Montreal, Virginia, Baltimore, Washington, and Philadelphia, and was twice disappointed in love. In 1815, when he left the United States, he was admired by many, and disliked by a number. In 1815, his family was solidly established in the city, having been successful in business, politics, and law. But, that spring, Washington Irving gave up this life, his family, and friends, to go to Europe to linger until 1832. Although he won greater fame as an author while in Europe, he was never to recapture the *joie de vivre* of his first works, written for his hometown audience.

Irving maintained close ties with his family his entire life. Although he says little about his father, he had great affection for his mother and sisters. But it was his brothers who were the early dominant influence. William, the eldest, Peter, Ebenezer, and John Treat, the lawyer, all counseled him, aided him, and warned him. They may have, as he grew older, chosen his education. From ages six to fourteen he was a student of Benjamin Romaine, then graduated to the seminary of Josiah Henderson. Although the seminary was geared to prepare its students for college, Irving learned little Latin, less Greek, some science, and, of course, the three *R*'s and geography. He did not impress any of his teachers as being outstanding. It was outside school that his interests were developed: these interests were the fine arts. He was encouraged in art by a sister's suitor: his fascination with art is evident in his works, in which he composes paintings in words that he could not achieve with paint. Music, too, drew response from him, although he attempted to practice only the flute. But above music, above art, was his devotion to the theater, at which he was probably a familiar figure while in his teens.

Although affluent enough not to have to apprentice the boys, William Irving nevertheless expected each son to support himself. So, in 1801, Washington began the study of law with Brockholst Livingston and continued it in 1802 with Josiah Ogden Hoffman. Also in 1802, Peter established the *Morning Chronicle*, and the town's and nation's concerns became grist for the family. The *Morning Chronicle*, like most New York papers, was partisan in politics, and the politics it favored were those of the Burrite faction of the Anti-Federalist party. The Burrites were followers of Aaron Burr, and formed the radical wing of the Jeffersonian party. They tended to be suspicious of the landed families who embraced Anti-Federalism as well as the Federalists who controlled the banks which dispensed economic favors on political bases. Never a majority party, the Burrite faction achieved its successes by allying itself with one of the other parties, this election with the Federalists, that with the Jeffersonians. The Irving family, like Peter's paper, was Burrite, either from personal attraction to Burr or from economic circumstances—and Washington was no exception. He knew Burr, he admired Burr, he worked for the party's principles even after Burr disappeared from the party scene.

But, except for a solid core of families, no faction drew consistently on loyal adherents. The Kings and Hamiltons were Federalists, the Livingstons were now Federalist, then Jeffersonians, the Clintons were now Jeffersonians, then anti-Jeffersonians (although never Federalist), the Hoffmans were Federalist, although once supporting the Jeffersonian Morgan Lewis. Politics in New York seem to have changed from day to day, from event to event. What was true in 1804 was no longer true in 1807. Despite all this movement between and among parties, social life went on smoothly. One could lampoon a political opponent vilely one day, and dine with him the next. New York was still essentially a small town, just beginning to feel big: one met one's political opponents at meetings of societies, and came to know that they had certain mitigating virtues, despite their politics.

New Yorkers were also tolerant; William Hedges quotes a Philadelphia reviewer as complaining, in 1821, of the New Yorkers: "'a propensity to satire and burlesque has been their besetting sin . . . and they have laughed at their own caricature in every variety of shape.'"[1] New York, fortunately, was a fluid enough society to be able to tolerate such jokes. Although Irving and the other Salmagundians, in 1807, pictured the old landed families as sneering at the *nouveau-riche*, nevertheless, families of taste and sufficient wealth did meet socially.

During the social season, Irving attended balls, the theater, and the concerts—and ridiculed them all, either in his published writings or in letters to his friends. The best of Irving's early correspondence that still remains is with Mary Fairlie, a witty, bright girl. In his letters to her, Irving tries out his style, his puns, his excursions in wit, many of which, in more polished form, were later to appear in print. Somewhat different was his relationship with Matilda Hoffman, young daughter of Josiah Ogden Hoffman under whom Irving studied law. Irving became a close friend of the Hoffman family, admired the young wife of Hoffman, and took care of the family in the lawyer's absence. But Matilda died, on April 26, 1808. The most sentimental account of his love for Matilda was written by Irving himself,[2] but written in much later years. That summer he was at William Van Ness's country seat, writing to his friends Henry Brevoort and James Kirke Paulding for the news of the town and sending them sheets of Knickerbocker's *History* to edit.

Once Knickerbocker's *History* appeared, Irving became famous —in his own town—pointed out on the streets, accused of every satirical extravaganza that appeared in print. But, despite this success, literature was still only a means of expression, not a profession. While he may have written for the lively *Mirror of Taste* in 1810–1811, he continued as his brother's law partner and helped in the hardware business, roistered with the bachelors, and gallanted the ladies and enjoyed himself. When he was offered the editorship of the *Analectic Magazine*, he took it, for it paid well and he anticipated it would cost him little effort. The first volume or two, indeed, show little effort. But soon the *Analectic* began reflecting the War of 1812; indeed, it carried on the war on a literary battlefront—unlike the publications of the Federalists, who opposed the war.

Perhaps inspired by the *Analectic's* laudatory biographies of heroes of the war, Irving resigned the editorship to become aide-de-camp to Governor Tompkins, military governor of New York, and during the next two years enjoyed issuing orders, riding helter-skelter from here to there, and coordinating the New York war effort. Although he wrote mockingly, he was in good spirits until the spring of 1815, when he became greatly depressed. Irving revealed one reason for his depression in a letter to Brevoort, written at sea, as he was on his way to England. In it, he reminds Brevoort that Henry (Black Horse) Lee had told Irving of his engagement to Serena Livingston, and tells Brevoort that Lee had given him a letter, to be opened at sea. In Lee's letter, Lee had confessed that there was no engagement after all. Had Irving known this sooner, he says, he would have been more particular in his visits to the Livingstons. Irving is outraged with Lee's lie, and urges Brevoort to convey his regards to the lady— regards he could not give in person, for, arriving in England, he discovered the Irving brothers were in financial trouble.[3] It was many years before he would feel financially secure again. Thus did Irving leave the United States: a name in his region, with a modicum of wealth—but his fame did not extend to Europe, and the wealth soon vanished.

II *Contributions to the* Morning Chronicle *and* The Corrector

In October 1802, Peter Irving established the *Morning Chronicle*, a daily paper that opposed Federalism and supported Aaron Burr, then vice-president of the United States. The paper also supported the rights of the citizens of the United States to use the Mississippi and the port of New Orleans for their trade: indeed, at one point, it called for a system of militia to be established whereby the Floridas and New Orleans could be seized by force. Except for dramatic reviews, there are few lighter articles, and these appear when Washington Irving is in the city, and all but disappear when he is not, as in the late summer and fall of 1803 and after he left for his European tour in May 1804. On November 15, 1802, Washington Irving began the series of letters to the *Morning Chronicle* by which he is best known, his "Letters of Jonathan Oldstyle." They criticized the theater building, the audience, the entire corps of actors, and the orchestra. But these letters appear innocuous today; the persona seems but a weak rendering of a *Spectator* bachelor, inconsistently presented, and the theatrical criticisms seem petty and ill-natured. Although in these letters Irving may have been parodying another theatrical critic, they demonstrate that Irving was, in 1802 and 1803, but an apprentice in the field of literature.

Letter 7 is one of the best, for while presenting his observations on the theater, Oldstyle gives us the fullest insight into his personality. He muses upon the crowd's eating habits, the smells of the green room, the loss of dignity of the actors in the afterpiece. He is shocked when one of the actors proclaims, "and as to *Oldstyle*, I wish him to old nick." Oldstyle objects to this: "I suppose we are now to have the stage a vehicle for lampoons and slanders; on which, our fellow citizens are to be caricatured by the clumsy hand of every dauber who can hold a brush!" The letter presents a whole range of Oldstyle's personality; his mind wandering on the subject of food, his old-fashioned dress, his testy reaction to modern manners, his sentimental chivalry of old ladies, and his objection to lampoons of private citizens. There is irony here: a created character observing other created characters, and a lampoon objecting to lampoons.

The inspiration for the last Oldstyle letter was twofold: one was an act, passed by the New York legislature, excluding both those who dueled and those who acted as go-betweens from holding office or from exercising the vote. The other was the presentation of the drama, "The Tournament," which contained a finely staged medieval duel. The news of the act, brought by Quoz, surprises Oldstyle, Jack Stylish, and Oldstyle's sister Dorothy. Dorothy, "deep read in all the volumes of ancient romance," "mourned to see the last spark of chivalric fire thus rudely extinguished." Oldstyle, while thinking the modern gun duels "blunt unceremonious affairs," seems to have nothing against dueling itself. He romantically describes one recent affair:

how, on a fair summer's morning, the knight of the Golden Goose met the knight of the Fiery Fiddle; how the knight of the Fiery Fiddle exclaimed in lofty tones, "whoever denies that Donna Fiddleosa is the most peerless beauty in the universe, must brave the strength of this arm!" how they both engaged with dreadful fury; and, after fighting till sunset, the knight of the Fiery Fiddle fell a martyr to his constancy; mummuring in melodious accents, with his latest breath, the beloved name of Fiddleosa.

The group, loath to see such romance depart from the world, seeks a way around the act. Quoz suggests the duelists draw lots to see which would drop a brick on the other's head. Stylish suggests that duelists apply for a license for a duel from the Blood and Thunder Office, give proper notice of the event, and allow all to attend, thus mimicking gladiator combats. Oldstyle finds some merit in this, since the duelists "fight to please the world, the world being thus interested in their encounter, should be permitted to attend and judge in person of their conduct."

Irving, in this letter, has greatly improved his handling of character. Each of the four reacts characteristically: Oldstyle preferring the old style, his novel-read sister preferring chivalry, Quoz seeking a way around the order, and Stylish finding a thoroughly modern solution. New Yorkers must have enjoyed the timing of the piece, and they would certainly have snickered at Oldstyle's description of the knightly duel—not a reference to the duel of the play, but to one that had occurred the previous summer, between the Knight of the Fiery Fiddle, Burrite Samuel Swartwout, and DeWitt Clinton. The engagement seemed unending (the duelists fired five times), but was finally broken off when Swartwout was injured in the leg.[4]

Irving described the duel again in *The Corrector*, and his second version shows the difference between that campaign paper and the more staid *Morning Chronicle*. It appears in "The Aristidean Gallery of Portraits," done by "An Amateur," one of Irving's *Morning Chronicle* pen names. It begins with this declaration: "the amateurs of the fine arts, will find in this collection a rich fund of amusement. The moralist may here contemplate the vanity and short lived greatness of an imbecile, arrogant and wicked faction."[5] The high tone of this beginning quickly degenerates into name calling, and prepares the reader for the crudity of the portrait of Clinton, during his duel:

NUMBER I, Is the portrait of Captain Skunk, as he was dubbed by a wag of the day; it arose from the following circumstances: This gallant gentleman went once a privateering, and fell in with an enemy

of equal force, they exchanged five broadsides; his antagonist be-
haved with cool bravery, and shewed a determination to continue
the fight, although disabled in his lower timbers—Our hero took advantage of this circumstance, and determined to sheer off—he immediately put before the wind, and fired from his stern ports such
discharges as effectually secured his retreat.

In other portraits, Irving makes clear the objects of his abuse by
use of puns on their names, or, as in this first portrait, by the use
of some well-known incident from their past to characterize and
embarrass them.

Another character sketch, hardly more lovely, is also probably
by Irving who did, in later life, admit to writing for this "stinging
little sheet," as it was described by Martin Van Buren.[6] It is
"Billy Luscious," which anticipates Irving's "On Greatness" of
Salmagundi. Irving makes clear from the beginning sentence that
this is a portrait of William L. Rose, a minor politician of the
Clintonian camp: "as every movement of a *great man* is interesting, I cannot but notice the important biography of *Billy
Luscious* '—*A Rose by any other name would smell as sweet.*'"
Luscious, we are told, began as a lawyer, soliciting custom from
every ship that docked, until the sailors became weary of him
and sought to dunk him. Luscious, "having a heavy head, he
would doubtless for once in his life, have descended below the
surface of things, had not a dungboat fortunately laid along side
of the vessel, and received him on the kindly soil from whence
he sprang." [7]

In a later contribution, Irving uses an ancient literary device,
the discovery of a diary of a traveler. This time the diary is that
of Morgan Lewis, a candidate for governor opposing Burr. Perhaps the most damning of all *The Corrector* contributions,
Irving's diary presents Lewis as an incompetent judge, uneasy
with the Clinton alliance, too aristocratic in manner to feel free
to shake the hands of the common people, and a womanizer.
Here, too, Irving has recourse to bodily humor, as Lewis writes,
"*snuffed* up my nose when I passed D—W——t, couldn't help it,
must have some fun, he got in a passion." [8] But, despite all the
Irvings's efforts, Morgan Lewis defeated Burr for the governorship.

In his contributions to the *Morning Chronicle* and *The Corrector,* Washington Irving experimented with a variety of styles,

poses, and comic effects. His writing improved tremendously in the two years, especially in his control of his persona and his use of the whimsically turned phrase. In his *Corrector* contributions, he experimented with broader humor, burlesque, and invective. While, especially in his later contributions, there is discernible the hand that wrote Knickerbocker's *History*, he still, in 1804, admitted himself "An Amateur."

III   Salmagundi

In 1807, Washington Irving and James Paulding were in their early twenties, were in high spirits, were inclined to laugh at all the high and mighty, and had been accustomed to doing so in print. With the aid of William Irving they roasted New York for over a year. *Salmagundi* was written for the hometown New York audience, and it mocked that audience, generally, while it specifically mocked well-known men and women of New York society. Just as the objects of their satire were citizens of the town who could be clearly recognized, so the authors were easily recognized, despite their assumed names. While New York knew who was responsible, it could not pinpoint authorship of individual articles. Even today, attribution is uncertain:[9] the three freely shared pen names.

Salmagundi appeared twenty times, irregularly, apparently whenever the authors had sufficient material to make up an issue. While the bulk of the first issues consisted of material written in reaction to events or to criticism, as the series goes on there are more and more polished essays. Also, as the series continues, there are fewer "pot shots" taken at individuals; when individuals are satirized in the later numbers, the satire is less silly, more skillful, and consequently, more brutal. The last two numbers' genial tone shows either a mellowing in the authors' attitudes toward society, or lack of any inspiring event.

The first issue of *Salmagundi* is a parody of a short-lived periodical named *The Town*, which had announced that it intended to elevate the morals of the town, but which was chiefly devoted to theatrical criticism. It appeared irregularly (although its intention was to be regular) during the first weeks of January 1807. To Paulding and the Irvings, the idea of improving the morals of the age seems laughable; they prefer wisdom, who "is a plump, jolly dame, who sits in her arm chair, laughs right merrily at the farce of life—and takes the world as it goes." In the first issue, Editor Launcelot Langstaff presents the contributor in charge of fashions and society—Anthony Evergreen—as "a kind of patriarch in the fashionable world," who "seems a little prejudiced in favor of the dress and manners of the *old school*." Launcelot gives Will Wizard the department of theatrical criticism, for which he is well qualified, for "he has improved his taste by a long residence abroad, particularly at Canton, Calcutta, and the gay and polished court of Hayti."

These three eccentric bachelors of *Salmagundi* are more than derivative, pale imitations of the eccentric bachelors of Sterne, Addison, or even of Philadelphia's Joseph Dennie. Of the three bachelor-authors, Anthony Evergreen is the least lifelike. He is sketched in the first number, but is not developed in later numbers, nor does he seem to be connected intimately with the Cockloft family, as are Will Wizard and Launcelot Langstaff. His contributions, too, present an inconsistent persona, ranging from the mocking sketch of Langstaff in number 8 to the sentimental "Sketches from Nature" in number 15. Of the three original authors, he contributes the least to the series.

Of the three, Will Wizard is the most brilliantly conceived. From the very first number the Salmagundians probably intended him to be a caricature of Robert Fulton, who had recently returned to the United States after a long sojourn in England and France. Fulton was a painter who had studied with Benjamin West in England; he was also interested in printing and engraving, and bore part of the cost of Joel Barlow's *Columbiad* in the spring of 1807. Also in 1807, he demonstrated his torpedo at Washington and New York, and was busy constructing, with the financial aid of Robert R. Livingston, the steamboat, whose first successful voyage was made on August 17.[10] Perhaps as reward for this success, Robert Livingston, on August 18, announced Fulton's engagement to Harriet Livingston. They were married on January 8, 1808.[11] (Washington Irving, late in life, regretted the ending of *Salmagundi* in January 1808, just when "he had designed, among other plans in embryo, a marriage of William Wizard with one of the Miss Cocklofts, and had amused himself in idea with a description of their queer nuptials.")[12]

While the presentation of Fulton is not as vicious as some of the caricatures in *Salmagundi*, the authors do find him a comic figure. Unlike Evergreen, Will Wizard is socially inept. His dress is outmoded, he hates social occasions; to him a party was "equivalent to being stuck up for three hours in a steam-engine." He is intrigued with odd characters, whom he whisks around to be entertained at Christopher Cockloft's. He is "a universal busy-body," and a painter—the Salmagundians ascribe the portrait of Launcelot Langstaff which appeared in number 8 to him. In number 13 he submits to Launcelot his "Plans for Defending Our Harbour," which ridicule the torpedo. As he sits waiting for Launcelot's reaction, he becomes impatient:

[he] began to smoke like a steam-engine . . . . to puff away at his cygarr with such vigour, that in a few minutes he had entirely in-volved himself in smoke, except his nose and one foot which were just visible, the latter wagging with great velocity. . . . Will's nose is a very goodly nose; to which it may be as well to add, that in his voyages under the tropics, it has acquired a copper complexion, which renders it very brilliant and luminous. You may imagine what a sumptuous appearance it made, projecting boldly . . . and sur-rounded on all sides with smoke and vapour.

This is a true cartoon done in words. From the paddling foot to the copper boiler nose, to smoke and steam, Fulton is drawn as his invention, the steamboat.

While Wizard bustles eccentrically in and out of the pages of *Salmagundi*, it is Launcelot Langstaff who gives it its rich texture, for Langstaff is related to the Cockloft family, the members of which either, like Jeremy and Pindar, contribute regularly to *Salmagundi*, or, like Christopher, Uncle John, and Aunt Charity, are described in *Salmagundi's* essays. Until number 8, we know little of Launcelot except these relationships. With number 8, the Salmagundians pull their most audacious joke, for in it Anthony Evergreen describes Langstaff, and a portrait, sup-posedly by Will Wizard, appears at the front. Both portray Morgan Lewis,[13] then governor of New York, who was, within a few weeks of number 8, to lose the governorship to Daniel Tompkins. While on its surface Evergreen's sketch seems to be a traditional one about an eccentric old bachelor, those familiar with the details of the election campaign would have recognized the satire.

According to Evergreen, Launcelot "is, or pretends to be, ex-ceedingly proud of his personal independence . . . . whether he is sincere in these professions, or whether his present situation is owing to choice or disappointment, he only can tell." He has been disappointed, "his success was ruined by one for whom he had long cherished a warm friendship," but he "remembered his treachery 'more in sorrow than in anger.'" Launcelot "is a man of excessive irritability of nerve," for he "solemnly declares that the boasted month of May has become a perfect 'vagabond,'" fears a broom, "a household implement which he abominates above all others," and rarely appears at balls and assemblies "since the introduction of the drum, trumpet and tamborine, all of which he abhors on account of the rude attacks they make on his organs of hearing." All of these traits have reference to Lewis's election campaign.

Although in 1804 the Burrites and Federalists united, unsuccessfully, against the Clintons and Livingstons, who elected Lewis governor, in 1807 the coalitions had changed. DeWitt Clinton, possibly disappointed by the amount of patronage given his faction, broke with Lewis (the treachery), and sought an alliance with the Burrites, nominating for governor Daniel Tompkins, the lawyer who had initiated Burr's suit against James Cheetham in 1804. The Federalists, seeking broader support by naming themselves the American party, sought to be neutral. The Clintonians accused Lewis of seeking Federalist support; this he denied (thus asserting his personal independence) since he, too, was seeking Burrite support. The election results would be known the first part of May; the name of the Clintonian candidate for lieutenant-governor was John Broome; and the drum, trumpet, and tamborine bother him because the Clintonians greatly mocked Lewis's speech to the legislature in which he underlined "the importance of having in the militia, musicians skilled in the various branches of military music." [14] In number 10, Launcelot resumes *Salmagundi* after a lapse, chiefly, he says, to "raise the spirits of the poor federalists, who, in truth, seem to be in a sad taking, ever since the American Ticket met with the accident of being so unhappily *dished*." This is the last specific connection of Langstaff to Lewis. For the rest of the issues he reverts to his character of whimsical editor and relative of the eccentric Cocklofts.

But, like Langstaff and Wizard, the Cocklofts are also caricatures of New Yorkers. Pindar Cockloft is the first to be introduced, in number 2, and thereafter appears irregularly to fill the "poetry corner" of *Salmagundi*. Pindar is a caricature of Thomas Green Fessenden,[15] Federalist editor of *The Weekly Inspector*, and his poetry is a parody of Fessenden's. In number 4, Pindar (and the Salmagundians) make the caricature clear with the publication of "Flummery . . . in the manner of Doctor Christopher Costive." (Caustic was Fessenden's *nom de plume*.) The remaining contributions by Pindar are not so pointedly satiric, although traces appear in number 7 and in number 12. Pindar's works are generally ascribed to William Irving and are, to a modern reader unacquainted with the town at the time, generally uninteresting and overly sentimental. That the sentimentality is a pose, that the poetry is intended as parody, does not relieve its dullness.

Launcelot introduces Jeremy Cockloft, the Younger, in number 4, and mentions there also, necessarily, Christopher Cockloft, for Jeremy is his "only son and darling pride." Jeremy was a prodigy, was educated at "our university," where "no student made better squibs and crackers to blow up the chemical professor." Evidently doomed to be a scientist, "he once shook down the ash-house by an artificial earthquake, and nearly blew his sister Barbara and her cat, out of the window with thundering powder." Wanting to see foreign lands upon graduating, he applied to his father, who sent him to spend "some few days at the splendid metropolis' of Albany and Philadelphia." His education complete, Jeremy decided to turn travel-writer, and his manuscripts, discovered by Launcelot, appear in *Salmagundi* as "The Stranger in New Jersey," "The Stranger in Philadelphia," and "The Stranger at Home."

As with Pindar, so with Jeremy. In this intial sketch of Jeremy, the Salmagundians present a caricature of Dr. Samuel Latham Mitchill, junior, professor of Columbia University, researcher of gunpowder, state assemblyman (Albany), U.S. representative (Philadelphia), and, in 1807, U.S. senator. Mitchill was a fine example of the enlightened scholar, for he was interested in everything from fish to fossils; his special project, however, in 1807 was *A Picture of New York*, portions of which are mocked in "The Stranger in New Jersey."

The New Yorker, having enjoyed the earlier caricatures of the Federalist Fessenden and the Jeffersonian Mitchill, might have been surprised, or shocked, or amazed by number 6, which describes the Cockloft family as a whole:

From time immemorial, it has been the rule for the Cocklofts to marry one of their own name; and as they always bred like rabbits, the family has increased and multiplied like that of Adam and Eve. In truth their number is almost incredible, and you can hardly go into any part of the country without starting a warren of genuine Cocklofts.

While this might seem only comic over-exaggeration, the description, coupled as it is with a description of Christopher Cockloft, would have sent the average New Yorker either to chuckling or to snorting with fury, for the Cocklofts are the Livingstons, and Christopher, the head of the Cocklofts, is none other than a caricature of chancellor and former minister to France, Robert R. Livingston. To make these identifications, New Yorkers would not need the information, given in the last number, "that the Cocklofts were a real family dwelling in the city—paying scot and lot, entitled to the right of suffrage, and holding several respectable offices in the corporation," for there were twenty-three fourth generation Livingstons: they sired eighty-three children. Christopher is Robert Livingston, for his home was decorated "with enormous china punch-bowls . . . in which a projector might with great satisfaction practice his experiments on fleets, diving-bells, and submarine boats," a clear reference to Livingston's and Fulton's experiments. The Methodism of Aunt Charity Cockloft, who died of curiosity about a Frenchman, marks her as a caricature of Catherine Livingston Garretson, wife of a Methodist minister. Uncle John's Federalism, his relationship to the Cocklofts and to Launcelot Langstaff, and his estate in Westchester County mark him as John Jay, who had married into the Livingston family.

While the satire contained in the Cockloft essays holds the real-life counterparts up to ridicule, it is usually the ridicule of an easygoing observer who tolerates eccentricities. But there are sketches in *Salmagundi* that are not easygoing, indeed, that may be said to be vicious. One of these is Will Wizard's characterization of Ding-dong. Another is "On Style," which heaps abuse on the Giblet family. Like Ding-dong, the Giblets belong to the social, rather than the political, world. Because of this, their counterparts are uncertain (although the Goelets were then becoming important).[16] But it is "On Greatness" that most resembles the abuse of *The Corrector*—not surprisingly, since it is

a revision of the sketch of Billy Luscious. Although "On Greatness" concerns itself with that little great man, Timothy Dabble,
and although the *Salmagundi* sketch is prefaced by the quotation
"The Hero Rose," instead of *The Corrector*'s quotation, "A Rose
by any other name," the butt is still the same, the Clintonian
partisan, William L. Rose.

Even "the tiresome Mustapha" [17] occasionally turns vicious,
especially when this citizen of the world deals with Jefferson and
the lack of national defense. While Mustapha describes the
United States' system of government as a logocracy, or government of words, he sees Jefferson as "a man of superlative ven-
tosity, and comparable to nothing but a huge bladder of wind,"
who is capable of little but making speeches and issuing proclamations—especially against Burr and his western adventure. But
Jefferson is not the only recipient of Mustapha's observations.
In number 5 he comments satirically on the Battery, "defended
with formidable *wooden* bulwarks, which in the course of a hard
winter were *thriftily* pulled to pieces by an *economic* corporation, to be distributed for fire-wood among the poor; this was
done at the hint of a cunning old engineer, who assured them it
was the only way in which their fortifications would ever be able
to keep up a *warm fire*." But we soon grow weary with Mustapha,
his harem, and his slave-driver.

Other references to national affairs occur in "The Little Man
in Black," often reprinted as a sentimental, moral, *Spectator*-like
piece. It tells a most pathetic story of a village's reaction to a
stranger, a little man in black who carries with him the large
folio of Linkum Fidelius. At first the village ignores him, then
fears him, and finally stones him. His forebearance was taken as
"the gloomy sullenness of a wizard, who restrained himself for
the present, in hopes of mid-night vengeance." Finally, one night,
with Lemuel Cockloft in attendance, he proclaims himself "the
last descendant of the renowned Linkum Fidelius," turns to the
east, and dies of starvation. Who furnished the original for
Lemuel Cockloft is unknown; Linkum Fidelius, elsewhere described in *Salmagundi*, is pretty clearly DeWitt Clinton, who had
forged the 1807 Burrite-Clintonian alliance, and the little man in
black portrays the little Burr,[18] who often wore black, who had
been termed a magician by his troops during the Revolutionary
War, and who escaped stoning in Baltimore after being acquitted

for treason. In his letters, Irving speaks scathingly of the lack of Christian virtue in those who condemned him without a hearing.[19] After his trial this fall of 1807, Burr moved about New York incognito, preparing to sail east, to Europe. Again, in this, Irving uses the form of the *Spectator* essay to cover his un-*Spectator*-like intentions.

There are good-humored and lighthearted essays in *Salmagundi*, and most of them seem to be by Washington Irving. One, by "Demy Semiquaver," presents his masterpiece of music, "The Breaking up of the Ice in the North-river." In the course of the description, Irving is enabled by the form to joke and pun about the state Assembly, its members, the "North River Society," the Society's attempts to set the river on fire (the building of the steamboat), the nation's lack of defense, and Tom Paine's drinking habits ("apply to 'common Sense,' for his lantern—Air—'Nose, nose, jolly red nose'"). Part 2, entitled "Great Thaw," is described as consisting "of the most *melting* strains, flowing so smoothly, as to occasion a great overflowing of scientific rapture." The sheer enjoyment of the author with his creation of this essay is easily passed on to the reader.

Irving's evident predilection for punning continues in "The Stranger in Pennsylvania," by Jeremy Cockloft. On his arrival in Philadelphia, Jeremy is "confined to my bed with a violent fit of the *pun* mania—strangers always experience an attack of the kind on their first arrival." After giving a whole catalog of puns, Jeremy next considers the etymology of Philadelphia, as put forth by his learned friend, Linkum Fidelius, is rendered homesick for New York by Philadelphia's only crooked street, and comments on its fine buildings. Finally, he asserts, "Philadelphia is a place of great trade and commerce—not but that it would have been much more so, that is had it been built on the scite of New-York: but as New York has engrossed its present situation, I think Philadelphia must be content to stand where it does at present—at any rate it is not Philadelphia's fault nor is it any concern of mine." This sort of logic is just what made *Salmagundi* loved by New Yorkers—this sophisticated assumption of being central to the world and unconcerned about any other place.

In this lighthearted category also belongs "Of the Chronicles of the Renowned and Antient City of Gotham," found in number 17. Will had found and translated an ancient manuscript of New

Amsterdam which recounts the capture of the city by the formidable Hoppingtots. Led by the warriors Pirouet and Rigadoon, the Hoppingtots, armed with fiddles, invest the city, now assaulting with a contradance, now with cotillions, "but truly their most cunning and devilish craft, and subtilty, was made manifest in their strenuous endeavours to corrupt the garrison, by a most insidious and pestilent dance called the *Waltz*." Having broken down, by these means, the town's fortifications, they carried the town by means of a Grand Ball. Needless to say, the Hoppingtots have certain similarities to Frenchmen; their battle song is the *Ca Ira*, and it is Linkum Fidelius's opinion that they are condemned to dance because of their offenses against frogs. All of this is pure froth and frivolity.

Will Wizard concludes *Salmagundi* by advising his readers "to live honestly and soberly . . . reading diligently the bible, the almanack, the newspaper and Salmagundi—which is all the reading an honest citizen has occasion for—and eschewing all spirit of faction, discontent, irreligion and criticism." His non– New York readers apparently took him seriously, for they apparently never imagined any spirit of party faction, or discontent or criticism in *Salmagundi*. In 1821, *The Port Folio* observed that *Salmagundi* "was seasoned with learning and gentleness, while good humour, playfulness and wit sparkled around it." [20] That New Yorkers made little public comment on the nature of *Salmagundi* is not surprising. Fessenden, in his *Weekly Inspector*, damned *Salmagundi*'s early issues and was thoroughly satirized by it for his pains. It is probable that the objects of its humor, recognizing the cloak of gentility that surrounded its caricatures, preferred not to remove that cloak; it is more probable that they responded in kind.

Salmagundi is, in truth, a veritable stew of humors, including puns, parodies, caricatures, burlesques, satires, invective, mock history, irony, and sarcasm. All the range of comedy is here. Not every word is a jewel, but every issue managed to irritate some New Yorker in his tenderest part—and the rest of New York laughed. *Salmagundi* is not genial; the objects of its humor are meant to feel the hurt, and undoubtedly did. But *Salmagundi* succeeded because its authors had the intelligence to hide its true faction-loving, discontented, probably irreligious, critical self underneath the costume of the gentle, genial, *Spectator*-like essay.

IV *Knickerbocker's* History

Knickerbocker's *History* is also a salmagundi, a mixture of humors dished up for Irving's New York audience. Like *Salmagundi*, it shows Irving feeling confidently free of any restraints. He apparently cared not what critics would say, cared not whether any section of the country was angered, cared not whether the English would like the book, and cared not that the history it contained was inaccurate. Indeed, the authentic history seems more of a frame to enclose Irving's jests and jibes than the ostensible purport of the work. Because of this, it is the grandfather of all United States' local color and local humor. In it Irving created, rather than recorded, history. The traits he gave to his three Dutch governors are more believed than the traits possessed by the real governors. Although he constantly reads the present into the past, he does it so persuasively that the present and past are confounded. Like *Salmagundi*, the first, 1809 edition is brash, audacious, cheeky, irreverent—qualities which Irving toned down in his later revisions. While the later revisions made the work more artistic and genteel, the first edition is far more representative of American humor.

Much of the success of Knickerbocker's *History* is due to Irving's creation of the character of the supposed author, Diedrich Knickerbocker. Knickerbocker first appears as if real. A series of newspaper squibs, run by Seth Handaside, proprietor of the Independant Columbian Hotel, announced that his lodger, Knickerbocker, had disappeared, leaving behind only a manuscript, which Handaside intended to publish in lieu of his rent. New Yorkers, probably undeceived by this hoary device, would nevertheless have been curious to examine the *History*, first advertised for sale on December 6, 1809.

The serious student of history, rejoicing that such a long-needed work had been published, would not have been made suspicious by the title page, with its Dutch quotation, nor by its dedication to the New-York Historical Society, which had called for such a book. The "Account of the Author," written by Seth Handaside, and giving a fuller description of the author than the advertisements had done, would have assured the reader that the author was a true scholar. The reader would then have proceeded to "To the Public" and would have found this preface by Knickerbocker little different from any other preface to a

serious work of the time. Indeed, it is only toward the end of
the preface that Knickerbocker shows himself to be at all eccentric. When he declares, "thrice happy therefore, is this our
renowned city, in having incidents worthy of swelling the theme
of history; and doubly thrice happy is it in having such an historian as myself, to relate them," he passes from the usual into
the extravagant.

Knickerbocker further inflates his importance by asserting
that "cities *of themselves*, and in fact empires *of themselves*, are
nothing without an historian." This statement he explains with a
comparison: "Like the great projector of inland lock navigation,
who asserted that rivers, lakes and oceans were only formed to
feed canals; so I affirm that cities, empires, plots, conspiracies,
wars, havock and desolation, are ordained by providence only
as food for the historian." This is the first of Knickerbocker's
comparisons in which Irving uses the present to explain one of
Knickerbocker's concepts, and in which the present situation is
mocked as much as is Knickerbocker himself. Thus Knickerbocker's claim that the world exists only for the historian also
ridicules the claim of "the great projector of inland lock navigation." The last paragraph of the preface confirms Knickerbocker
in his role as eccentric author and kinsman of *Salmagundi*'s
bachelors. After asking "ye mighty Whales, ye Grampuses and
Sharks of criticism" to be gentle with his craft, he threatens "ye
great little fish! ye tadpoles, ye sprats, ye minnows, ye chubbs,
ye grubs, ye barnacles, and all you small fry of literature" with
retaliation if they insult the new work.

Irving keeps the reader aware of the eccentric nature of
Knickerbocker by having him address the reader in asides, inter-
jections, and even in book and chapter subtitles. Book 1, we are
told, is "like all introductions to American histories, very learned,
sagacious, and nothing at all to the purpose; containing divers
profound theories and philosophic speculations, which the idle
reader may totally overlook, and begin at the next book." This
seeming unconcern is repeated in chapter 2, when he advises the
serious reader to "take fast hold of my skirts, and keep close at
my heels, venturing neither to the right hand nor to the left,
least they get bemired in a slough of unintelligible learning." In
book 6, Knickerbocker laughs at those readers who have quit the
book and congratulates the persevering readers, giving his friendship to "those who undauntedly bore me company," and promises

"to stand by you to the last; and to conduct you . . . triumphantly to the end of this our stupendous undertaking."

Thus pictured as caring little for any but the most dedicated reader, and unwilling to cater to any reader, Knickerbocker's true concern is the method of writing history and with the subject of his history. He seems to feel the need to explain and defend his methods. Irving uses these defenses as a means of mocking New York situations. He uses the refurbishing of the Park Theater, recently bought by John Jacob Astor, as the basis for Knickerbocker's defense for having begun his history with an account of the creation and existence of the world:

Had not the foundation, the body, and the roof of the theatre first been built, the cupola could not have had existence as a cupola— it might have been a centry-box—or a watchman's box—or it might have been placed in the rear of the Manager's house and have formed —a temple;—but it could never have been considered a cupola. As therefore the building of the theatre was necessary to the existence of the cupola, as a cupola—so the formation of the globe and its internal construction, were first necessary to the existence of this island, as an island—and thus the necessity and importance of this part of my history, which in a manner is no part of my history, is logically proved.

No matter that Knickerbocker's logic is faulty, Irving has thus managed to include his comments on the cupola. Knickerbocker's defense, in book 2, of having begun the work so slowly, is similar in construction. Here the work is likened to a church built slowly by his grandfather. Knickerbocker declares the time well spent, for "the church came out of my grandfather's hands, one of the most sumptuous, goodly and glorious edifices in the known world —excepting, that, like our transcendant capital at Washington, it was begun on such a grand scale, the good folks could not afford to finish more than the wing of it."

While in these instances Knickerbocker compares his work to solid, carefully constructed buildings, a more frequent metaphor is that of the pilgrimage, of a long slow walk passing by sloughs as well as pleasant valleys. The metaphor is made concrete in one of Knickerbocker's most famous digressions, his walk on the Battery in book 3. Knickerbocker defends this central digression by asserting that it was given "to gratify the reader with a correct description of that celebrated place." A storm intrudes, he claims, "to give a little bustle and life to this tranquil part of my work, and to keep my drowsy readers from falling asleep." These reasons certainly establish Knickerbocker as a whim-whamsical scholar, but, as in *Salmagundi*, the whim-whams allow apparent eccentricity to cover serious satire. What Irving has Knickerbocker see on the Battery is, primarily, no battery: "our sagacious corporation, in a spasm of economical philanthropy" had pulled apart the ramparts to distribute to the poor as firewood, what guns there are are quaker guns, and Governor's Island, though "covered with fortifications," has a garrison armed only with shovels, the evening gun sounds, but only as a signal "for all the regular, well meaning poultry throughout the country, to go to roost." The Battery, which ought to be one, is not; the seeming digression is central to Irving's thesis of the *History*, that the United States needed to strengthen its defense.

Irving endows Knickerbocker with all true scholarly traits: love of his profession, untidiness in keeping his papers, a disposition to discuss methodology, a lack of concern for any of his readers but those who are in his own field, and a tendency to long-winded irrelevant digressions. But Knickerbocker still lacks one trait characteristic of the scholar, and this Irving endows him in the last part of the book, where Knickerbocker falls in love with his subject. The culmination of this particular character trait occurs in book 6, when Knickerbocker records a charge by the New Englanders against Peter Stuyvesant for his enlisting the aid of the Indians by supplying them with liquor. This charge, some two hundred years remote as it was, arouses Knickerbocker's deepest feelings: "this wanton, wicked and unparalleled attack . . . has overset, with a single puff, the patience of the historian and the forebearance of the Dutchman." Then follows one of the most eloquent of all of Knickerbocker's addresses to the reader: "Oh reader it was false!—I swear to thee for it was false!—if thou hast any respect for my word—if the undeviating and unimpeached character for veracity, which I have hitherto borne throughout this work, has its due weight with thee, thou wilt not give thy faith to this tale of slander." Such passion is, of course, misspent, since by this time no reader would have believed the *History* to be so veracious.

Irving's mockery of the scholarship of his time finds its fullest expression in book 1, in which he presents various theories of the creation of the earth, the discovery of America, the origin of the Indians, and the claims of the Europeans to the Americas. All this, as Knickerbocker justly observes, has nothing to do with the history of New York, but it does provide Irving with the opportunity to parody philosophical speculations. In most instances, having "battered" the reader with hosts of varying opinions, Knickerbocker will refuse to decide among them, contenting himself simply with the commonsense statements that the world does exist, America was discovered, that the Indians do exist in America. Of all the philosophers, Irving is most astounded by Charlevoix, who put forth the thesis that America was populated by accident. Irving is indebted to Charlevoix for more than just this theory, for chapters 3 and 4, on the discovery and peopling of America, are parodies of Pierre Charlevoix's "Preliminary Discourse on the Origin of the Americans," prefaced to his *Journal of a Voyage to North-America* (1744).

This first book is not easy reading; the catalogs of theories are too infrequently relieved by touches of humor. The reader wishes there were more digressions like the description of Professor Von Poddingcraft's head being soused by a bucket of water as his illustration of the cosmic forces of attraction and repulsion failed, or Knickerbocker's protest against Plato, "who threw the cold water of philosophy on the form of sexual intercourse, and inculcated the doctrine of Platonic affection, or the art of making love without making children." Fortunately, by the fifth chapter, Irving wearies of his extensive documentation and theories, changes tone and style, and discusses the right of Europeans to claim the new land while thoroughly condemning their treatment of the Indians.

Although Irving, in book 2, begins the history of New York with historically accurate information, and ends the Dutch dynasty with the same, much of the intervening "history" is purely Irving's filling in the arcana of history with pseudohistory that he had extrapolated from the present state of affairs in New York City. Hudson did sail on the Hudson, with Juet as his mate; and there were three Dutch governors named Van Twiller, Kieft, and Stuyvesant (and three more, whom Irving neglects to mention). But the names of the people surrounding these governors date from nineteenth-century New York, not seventeenth-century New Amsterdam, and their quarrels, and deeds, and means of government are those of the nineteenth century. Irving confessed to this in the preface he wrote for the 1824 Paris edition of

Salmagundi: "KNICKERBOCKER'S NEW-YORK, is a whimsical and satirical work, in which the peculiarities and follies of the present day are humorously depicted in the persons, and arrayed . . . in the grostesque costume of the ancient Dutch colonists." Thus, in Irving's history of Dutch New York we have a satire (once more) of his city and its people.

Irving begins book 2 with a fairly straightforward account of Hudson's voyage to the New World, following the journal kept by Robert Juet, the first mate. Irving adds flourishes, to be sure ("Hudson had laid in abundance of gin and sour crout, and every man was allowed to sleep quietly at his post, unless the wind blew"), but these merely enrich the facts. The striking exception to his adaptation of the journal is his picture of Hudson's first view of New York—and it is a painting, rather romantically composed. It is no wonder that this prose painting has remained in the national consciousness:

The island of Manna-hata, spread wide before them, like some sweet vision of fancy, or some fair creation of industrious magic. Its hills of smiling green swelled gently one above another. . . . On the gentle declivities of the hills were scattered in gay profusion, the dog wood, the sumach, and the wild briar, whose scarlet berries and white blossoms glowed brightly among the deep green of the surrounding foliage; and here and there, a curling column of smoke rising from little glens that opened along the shore, seemed to promise the weary voyagers, a welcome at the hands of their fellow creatures. As they stood gazing with entranced attention on the scene before them, a red man crowned with feathers, issued from one of these glens, and after contemplating in silent wonder, the gallant ship, as she sat like a stately swan swimming on a silver lake, sounded the war-whoop, and bounded into the woods.

Such is Irving's pictorial power, that one can clearly envision the composition of such a painting, even to its ornate gilt frame.

Having been so faithful to historical sources for his beginning chapter, Irving, either by necessity or desire, thenceforward deviates from them. Sober history records that the first ship bearing settlers was the *New Netherland* full of French-speaking Walloons, captained by the first governor, Cornelius May.[21] But Irving will have it that the ship was the *Goede Vrouw*, "full in the bows, with a pair of enormous cat-heads, a copper bottom, and withal, a most prodigious poop!" Irving has the first settlers settle in the mud at Communipaw on the Jersey shore, whereas the first settlers really established themselves on Nutten Island. At Communipaw, Irving asserts, some still vegetate, drinking "to the success of admiral Von Tromp, who they imagine is still sweeping the British channel, with a broom at his masthead"—a most atrocious pun, but neither the first, nor the last, in the *History*.

After a time (as Irving and history tell us), the first settlers felt the need to move to more spacious quarters. According to sober history, the move was led by Cryn Frederickz; according to Irving, it was led by Oloffe Van Kortlandt, Abraham Hardenbroek, Jacobus Van Zandt, and Weinant Ten Broek. Since Irving furnishes us circumstantial details about these men, it seems that we ought to believe him. Among these details are Irving's derivations of the names. Van Kortlandt, he says, comes from *lack land*, "from his landed estate, which lay somewhere in Terra incognita"; Van Zandt, we are told, "freely translated, signifies from the dirt"; Hardenbroek (or Tough Breeches) was "a sturdy, obstinate, burley, bustling little man"; while Ten Broek (either "tin breeches" or "ten breeches") was a "poor, but merry rogue."

It is somewhat to be wondered at, that although history includes none of these names among the founders of New York, all of them are to be found among the notables of New York of Irving's early years. Thus, Pierre Van Courtland had been chief member of a commission selling confiscated Tory lands, Wynant Van Zandt had been an alderman under Marinus Willet's mayoralty in 1807, Henry Ten Broeck was on the board of the Free School, and William Hardenbroek was elected assistant alderman of the ninth ward in November 1809. It is one thing to have one's great-grandfather being ridiculed, it is entirely another thing to realize that one's great-grandfather was nowhere near "the scene of the crime," and so the ridicule of the name must apply to oneself. No wonder the old Dutch families of New York were not pleased with Knickerbocker's *History*.

A colony having been established on Manhattan, and a fort built, the colony "took root and throve amazingly." The only event that disturbed the growth was "the first internal altercation on record among the new settlers." In trying to plan for the growth of the new town, Ten Broek wanted to cut up the ground with canals, but Hardenbroek argued instead for docks, wharves, and piles. The two argued bitterly: "Ten Breeches had, therefore, the most mettle, but Tough Breeches the best bottom." Although history does not record this altercation, the *Minutes of the Common Council* for the first decade of 1800 do record that extensive improvements to Canal Street were initiated during the first mayoralty of Clinton, and during Willet's mayoralty the Council was most industriously constructing piles. All of this activity on the part of Irving's Council is in sharp contrast to the inertness of the council of the infant colony. Viewing this inertness with approbation, Knickerbocker bewails his degenerate age, and exclaims, "return—return sweet days of simplicity and ease—dawn once more on the lovely island of Manna hata!" But such days had gone: the colony grew rich, the mother country grew interested, and sent out its first governor.

Book 3, "in which is recorded the golden reign of Wouter Van Twiller," is the least unified of all the books, perhaps because, as we are led to believe, so little happened during Wouter's reign. Instead of events the historian offers descriptions of Wouter's council, the old Dutch houses, tea parties, the Dutch dress, takes his walk on the Battery, describes the Yankees and only, in the last chapter, has an event to deal with, the surrounding of Fort Goed Hoop by the Yankees. Thus the book is really a series of separate sketches having no common theme or tone, with only Irving's wit and style in common.

True history describes Van Twiller, the fourth governor of the colony, as ambitious, grasping, and quarrelsome, but who, "despite his taste for whisky," [22] did accomplish a few things: he erected a fort near Hartford, another on the Delaware, and helped settle Long Island. Of these, Irving only includes the fort near Hartford, Goed Hoop. In Irving's hands the character of the governor undergoes a complete metamorphosis. According to Irving, Van Twiller was "descended from a long line of dutch burgomasters"; his name "is said to be a corruption of the original *Twister*, which in English means *doubter*." This name derivation is more farfetched than Irving's usually are.

In describing Wouter's physical appearance, Irving creates one of his cartoons. "He was exactly five feet six inches in height, and six feet five inches in circumference." His legs were short and stubby, "so that when erect, he had not a little the appearance of a robustious beer barrel, standing on skids." Wouter had an inordinate love of eating and sleeping (especially during council meetings), so it is no wonder that "so tranquil and benevolent was his reign, that I do not find throughout the whole of it, a single instance of any offender being brought to punishment." Not that there were no law suits; there was one, between Barent Bleeker and Wandle Schoonhoven, carefully adjudged by Twiller. He weighed the two books of accounts, found them equal in weight, "therefore it was the final opinion of the court that the accounts were equally balanced—therefore Wandle should give Barent a receipt, and Barent should give Wandle a receipt—and the constable should pay the costs." Needless to say, the result of this was that "not another law suit took place throughout the whole of his administration."

While Irving's Twiller has little in common with the historical Wouter, he has much in common with the historical Marinus Willet, mayor of New York in 1807. The similarity of the names must have been tempting. Willet, like Irving's Twiller, had the same name as a former New York mayor, or burgomaster; Thomas Willet was the first mayor under the English. Further, when Willet was appointed by Lewis, objections had been made because, as mayor, he would be expected to preside over the civil and criminal courts. At least one newspaper thought him incompetent to do this, for he was "a gentleman who had probably never looked into a law book in his life." [23] Willet, nevertheless, accepted and was "conscious of his limitations"; "not being a man of law, he could not judge cases with the cleverness which had characterized his predecessors . . . so a deputy mayor was sworn in to handle this part of the job." [24] Thus, it is doubtful whether Willet judged even one case, as Irving has Twiller do. Later, when Willet ran for lieutenant governor, a newspaper chronicled his many changes of parties and declared, "let him be dubbed Marinus the Twister," [25] thus using Irving's name derivation.

This confounding of Irving's present with the Dutch past is extended to the second chapter of book 3, in which Irving describes the grand council of New Amsterdam, consisting of five burgermeesters and five schepens. Since burgermeesters and schepens did not exist in the New World until Peter Stuyvesant's rule, it is pretty clear that here Irving is taking the opportunity to caricature and satirize his own Common Council, although he actually names only one member, Van Zandt, alderman during Willet's tenure. The criticism of the alderman and assistants is not much different from that contained in *The Corrector* and *Salmagundi*. The only difference between an alderman and his assistant, according to Irving, is his weight, schepens being eligible for the higher office only "when they had been fed and fattened into sufficient bulk of body and drowsiness of brain." With such a governor, and such a council, " 'the profoundest *tranquility* and *repose* reigned through the province.' "

But, as Irving shows when discussing the perilous situation of Fort Goed Hoop, such repose is not for the best. Jacobus Van Curlet, commander of the fort, no sooner was established than he was surrounded by Connecticut squatters who "extended those plantations of onions . . . under the very noses of the garrison of Fort Goed Hoop—insomuch that the honest dutchmen could not look toward that quarter, without tears in their eyes." "This crying injustice" was properly regarded by Van Curlet, who sent word of it to the council of New Amsterdam. The protest caused Wouter to fall into deep doubt, the council smoked on it, and his protests "were soon as completely beclouded and forgotten, as is a question of emergency swallowed up in the speeches and resolution of a modern session of congress." This but continues the criticism of this democratic fault begun in *Salmagundi*.

Having confounded the politics of the present and past, Irving does describe the old Dutch customs and dress soberly, though with touches of exaggeration, as, for instance, the tale of "the lady of Wouter Van Twiller, having occasion to empty her right pocket in search of a wooden ladle, the contents filled three corn baskets." But all is peaceful and calm, "when every thing was better than it has ever been since." The Dutch prosperity, serenity, and stolidity are in contrast to Irving's characterization of the Yankees. He enjoys himself describing bundling and the New Englander's habit of moving forever westward, bent on improving himself. He settles in a new spot, improves it for a while, then "reloads his cart, shoulders his axe, puts himself at the head of his family, and wanders away in search of new lands —again to fell trees—again to clear corn-fields—again to build a shingle palace, and again to sell off, and wander."

Such a life-style, according to Knickerbocker, greatly shocked the Dutch when they came into contact with the Yankees on their frontier. Fearing the reader might not completely understand their reaction, Knickerbocker offers one of his comparisons:

If they cannot, I would ask them, if they have ever known one of our regular, well organized antediluvian dutch families, whom it hath pleased heaven to afflict with the neighbourhood of a French boarding house. The honest old burgher . . . cannot sleep at night for the horrible melodies of some amateur, who chooses to serenade the moon, and display his terrible proficiency in *execution*, by playing demisemiquavers in alt on the clarionet, the hautboy, or some other soft toned instrument.

We have a wealth of allusion in this one comparison. The situation is the same as recorded in *Salmagundi*'s "Aunt Charity," and two of Irving's pen names, "An Amateur," and "Demisemiquaver," are included. Once more Irving is using the past to mock the recent present.

The end of Twiller may well be Irving's summation of Willet's mayoralty. A second courier from Fort Goed Hoop arrives at New Amsterdam and disturbs the council, but cannot "ruffle the tranquility of this most tranquil of rulers," for Wouter, "who had so often slumbered with his contemporaries, now slept with his fathers, and Wilhelmus Kieft governed in his stead." The chapters dealing with Wouter Van Twiller's rule are generally good-humored (if one excepts the satire directed at the Common Council), but while they, through the voice of Knickerbocker, proclaim this Dutch age to be the best of all tranquil worlds, Irving's own asides show that, though tranquil, the age has achieved nothing purposeful, that there is much that needs to be done. As Knickerbocker describes the past, Irving comments on the present.

Book 4, "Containing the Chronicles of the reign of William the Testy," has packed within it the greatest number of satiric squibs of any book in the *History*. While the satire is not organized, or directed at a single object, it covers most aspects of New York political life of 1808 and 1809. Here there are no leisurely digressions, no descriptions of the dress of former times. All at once, New Amsterdam seems greatly populated. In this book, we have more minor characters, more of Irving's contemporaries named. As the tranquillity of the previous book is said to have been derived from the character of its governor, so the energy of book 4 may be said to derive from the character of Governor William Kieft, "a brisk, waspish, little old gentleman," whose fiery soul incited him "to most valourous broils, altercations and misadventures."

Since 1825, when John Neal, a New England critic, declared

it so,[26] William Kieft has been accepted as a caricature of Thomas Jefferson, complete with proclamations, more proclamations when the first did not work, Non-Intercourse Acts, and philosophy. While Irving does endow Kieft with all these Jeffersonian traits, he probably intended to hit two birds with the same shotgun, for DeWitt Clinton, mayor of New York in 1808–1809, shared many of Jefferson's characteristics. According to Irving (but not history), Kieft was educated at an academy at The Hague (which Irving compares to one of "our American colleges") where he studied several of the sciences and also languages, especially Greek and Latin, "which he constantly paraded in conversation and writing" (a trait more characteristic of Clinton than Jefferson). He also studied logic and metaphysics, and was a universal genius, which genius only "entangled the government of the little province of Nieuw Nederlandts in more knots during his administration, than half a dozen successors could have untied."

As a governor, he is less than successful: Fort Goed Hoop was captured, but Kieft only swore valiantly at the Yankees, swore "that they might stay at Fort Goed Hoop and rot," and "ordered the new raised troops, to be marched forthwith into winter quarters, although it was not as yet quite mid summer." Further, "though no man could be more ready to stand forth in an hour of emergency, yet he was so intent upon guarding the national pocket, that he suffered the enemy to break its head— in other words, whatever precaution for public safety he adopted, he was so intent upon rendering it cheap, that he invariably rendered it ineffectual." Kieft bases this philosophy upon a cabalistic word learned at The Hague, "economy." By its influence "the mighty navy of America . . . dwindles into small craft, and shelters itself in a mill-pond!" This satire on "economy" is aimed at both the national and local governments, for in 1809, Clinton and the Common Council were debating the most economical way to fortify New York Harbor.

Kieft is constantly busy but his business has little concrete result. He garrisons the Battery, but with Quaker guns, a huge flagpole, and a windmill, "somewhat of a novelty in the art of fortification." As additional defense of the city, Kieft employed "one Anthony Van Corlear a jolly fat dutch trumpeter . . . . [who] strutted up and down the ramparts, fearlessly twanging his trumpet in the face of the whole world, like a thrice valorous editor daringly insulting all the principalities and powers—on the other side of the Atlantic." Irving is consistent in likening Corlear to a newspaper editor: if he had any one in mind it was probably Clinton's James Cheetham, previously attacked in *The Corrector.*

While Kieft seems incompetent to defend New Amsterdam, his efforts at internal affairs are also failures. He "conceived that the true policy of a legislator was to multiply laws, and thus secure the property, the persons and the morals of the people," but the result was "in time they became too numerous to be remembered, and remained like those of certain modern legislators, in a manner dead letters." One must remember that Clinton, at this time, was not only mayor of New York, but also a member of the state Assembly, and he was indeed busy securing the passage of many bills favorable to the city and the good morals of its inhabitants. While Irving records that Kieft was the first to introduce capital punishment, Clinton was a firm believer in it, and, in his capacity as a municipal judge, rigorously assessed it.[27]

After an abortive attempt to improve the morals of the people by banning tobacco, Kieft only succeeded in replacing the long pipes with short pipes, but this "rendered the people as vapourish and testy as their renowned little governor." But the worst effects of his intermeddling came from a right idea. Irving quotes directly Kieft (or Clinton, or Jefferson): " 'There is nothing more essential to the well management of a country, than education among the people; the basis of good government, should be laid in the public mind.' " (In these years, Clinton was collecting for the Free School, for which he had won financial assistance from the legislature in 1806.) But, according to Knickerbocker, the result of this right idea was disastrous: Kieft set up debating societies, the societies became enlightened, and dissatisfied, and began to hold public meetings. Eventually the New Amsterdamers "soberly settled down into two distinct parties." In later editions, Irving names these the long pipes and short pipes; in this first edition, however, he names them "Square head" and "Platter breech":

the former implying that the bearer was deficient in that rotundity of pericranium, which was considered as a token of true genius—the latter, that he was destitute of genuine courage, or *good bottom,* as it has since been technically termed—and I defy all the politicians of this great city to shew me where any two parties of the present day, have split upon more important and fundamental points.

Irving seems deliberately inviting us to remember his "Aristidean Gallery" of *The Corrector*, in which the author avers that the Clintonian Ambrose Spencer "wanted bottom," and even perhaps the portrait of Captain Skunk itself. Irving does compare Kieft to a captain, but in a far more refined manner than in *The Corrector*: "Kieft kept constantly firing off his proclamations and protests, like a sturdy little sea captain, firing off so many carronades and swivels, in order to break and disperse a water spout—but alas! they had no more effect than if they had been so many blank cartridges." While the firing of salvos is reminiscent of Captain Skunk/Clinton, the firing off of proclamations reminds us of Jefferson.

In his accounts of Kieft's relations with surrounding colonies, Irving interweaves names of his contemporaries so skillfully that we never know whether he is being historical or satirical. Since history tells us that the real Kieft's external troubles were only with the Indians, not with the other colonies, we must suspect Irving's inentions. In one of Van Curlet's messages to the Council during Kieft's time was the complaint that the Yankees " 'struck Ever Duckings a hole in his head, with a stick, soe that the blood ran downe very strongly downe upon his body!' " In a footnote, the editor assures us that the name is misspelt; in other manuscripts "we find the name of Evert Duyckingh, who is unquestionably the unfortunate hero above alluded to." While this could not refer to Evert Duyckinck, the Cyclopedist, a member of the previous generation may here be referred to, but what caused the blood, is unknown. Another of Curlet's grievances, that of the Yankees' stealing a pig, according to Irving, "awakened a grunt of sympathy from every bosom," as well it might. There are a great number of pigs in book 4, perhaps in reaction to a law passed by the Common Council in 1809 that regulated the running of pigs in the streets of New York.

Although he lost Fort Goed Hoop to the Yankees, Kieft is more successful in routing the Yankees from Oyster Bay, on Long Island, for he has a successful commander in Stoffel Brinkerhoff, "so called because he was a man of mighty deeds, famous throughout the whole extent of Nieuw Nederlandts for his skill at quarterstaff." (This sounds suspiciously like the description of Langstaff's ancestor.) Brinkerhoff was opposed "by a tumultuous host of valiant warriors, headed by Preserved Fish, and Habbakuk Nutter, and Return Strong, and Zerubbabel Fisk, and Jonathan Doolittle and Determined Cock!" While these, especially "Jonathan Doolittle," are Yankee names, they are also New York names: Selah Strong and Nicholas Fish were Federalist aldermen, Valentine Nutter was assessor and election inspector, and "Determined Cock" is probably a reference to Solomon Lang, Federalist editor of the *Morning Gazette*, whose paper, marked by a cock, had been satirized by the *Morning Chronicle*. Apparently, Stoffel finds they were "armed with no other weapons but their tongues," and put them to rout. Needless to say, New York rejoiced in this victory, and Kieft decreed a grand triumph for Stoffel. The picture of the triumphal entry is at once a mockery of all the New Yorker imagined a Yankee held dear, and one of those grand processions New Yorkers loved.

In book 4, Irving also makes merry with another region of the country, the South. The incident he records is somewhat confusing historically, since we know that the Dutch colony was beset, to the east, by the Puritans in Connecticut and, to the South, by the Swedes of Delaware. But now Irving introduces a third threat, the Marylanders. To combat them, Kieft sends out, economically, but thirty men, in two sloops, who seek "to drive the Marylanders from the Schuylkill," a river in Pennsylvania. Heading this expedition was the historically unknown Jan Jansen Alpendam: opposing him was a strange people:

who were represented as a gigantic gunpowder race of men, who lived on hoe cakes and bacon, drank mint juleps and brandy toddy, and were exceedingly expert at boxing, biting, gouging, tar and feathering, and a variety of other athletic accomplishments, which they had borrowed from their cousins german and prototypes the Virginians, to whom they have ever borne considerable resemblance.

Since Irving has, throughout the *History*, used the second half of one of Knickerbocker's explanations to indicate the true object being satirized, we may assume that here he is satirizing neither the Marylanders nor the Swedes of Delaware, but the Virginians. Alpendam attacks these strangers in a speech, "wherein he courteously commenced by calling them a pack of lazy, louting, dram

drinking, cock fighting, horse racing, slave driving, tavern haunt-
ing, sabbath breaking, mulatto breeding upstarts," and orders
them to leave the country. Their answer, "in plain English (as
was very natural for Swedes)" was "'they'd see him d——d
first.'" Upon hearing this, Alpendam retreated to New York,
where he "was unanimously called the deliverer of his country."
What incident Irving is here referring to is unclear; the major
event exacerbating the New York-Virginia rivalry in these years
was the New Yorkers' desire to see George Clinton in first place
on the Jeffersonian ticket in 1808, and the Virginians desire to see
James Madison there. The Virginians won. But whether this is
related to Alpendam, the thirty men, and the Schuylkill is con-
jectural. Certainly, however, this event did not occur during the
real Kieft's administration.

But all things must come to an end (or a good bottom), and
so must William Kieft. History records that he was lost at sea,
on his way to Holland to defend his administration. Knickerbocker favors a more miraculous end: "he at length became as
completely burnt out, as a dutch family pipe. . . . In this manner
did the choleric but magnanimous William the Testy undergo
a kind of animal combustion, consuming away like a farthing
rush light—so that when grim death finally snuffed him out, there
was scarce left enough of him to bury!" Irving's picture of Kieft,
whether intended primarily to mock Thomas Jefferson or DeWitt
Clinton, or both, satirizes the dilemma of the democratic intellectual who believes thoroughly in his theories, but who finds
that they, in practice, do not work as the theory predicted, who
discovers that, once given the proper vocabulary, "the mob" will
find grievances, no matter how happy its condition. Irving shows
further that the intellectual, while firmly believing that "honesty
is the best policy" in foreign affairs, is shocked to discover that
other nations profit in their disbelief of this tenet, and that
while promulgating disarmament, or only the cheapest armament, discovers his outlying colonies overrun by a superior and
craftier force.

The three books dealing with the governorship of Peter Stuyvesant are the most historically correct of the *History*. Irving does
faithfully record the major events of Stuyvesant's rule: the establishment of Fort Casimer and its consequent destruction by the
Swedes, Stuyvesant's retaliation and the surrender of the Swedish
governor, the Hartford treaty, and its consequent rejection by

Massachusetts and Connecticut. Even the account of the surrender of the city to the English is accurate, although somewhat embellished. Stuyvesant did tear a Winthrop letter to pieces when a burgomaster asked for a copy, the terms of surrender were generous, and the populace did refuse to take up arms. Unlike his pictures of the other two governors, Irving also followed history in his characterization of Peter, who "exhibited a hot temper, vitriolic language, and autocratic habits." [28] Though to some extent bound by history, Irving still takes liberties with it, especially in presenting his minor characters Van Corlear, Von Poffenburgh, Jan Risingh, and in book 7, the burgomeesters and political dignitaries.

From the beginning, Knickerbocker views Peter as a hero, and sees his faults as virtues. So inflated becomes his worship that his account of the taking of Fort Christina becomes mock heroic. The reader, ignoring Knickerbocker's bias, sees Peter at first as a welcome commonsense antidote for the philosophical Kieft, but, at the last, as a reactionary old gentleman unable to cope with democratic conditions, content to ignore the world and live on his domains in the old-fashioned manner. At the end, Peter is *Salmagundi's* Uncle John, or Christopher Cockloft, translated back to Dutch New York.

Peter, from the first, inspires awe in the New Yorkers, for "he possessed a sovereign contempt for the sovereign people, and an iron aspect, which was enough of itself to make the very bowels of his adversaries quake with terror and dismay." He "did not know Greek, and had never studied the ancients," and "had an unreasonable aversion to experiments, and was fond of governing his province after the simplest manner—but then he contrived to keep it in better order than did the erudite Kieft." In short, as Knickerbocker says, "if from all that I have said thou dost not gather, worthy reader, that Peter Stuyvesant was a tough, sturdy, valiant, weatherbeaten, mettlesome, obstinate, leathersided, lion hearted, generous spirited, obstinate, old 'seventy six' of a governor, thou art a very numscull at drawing conclusions." As with most of Irving's comparisons, the adjectives reflect equally upon any old "seventy-six" of a governor and Peter himself.

Peter's first actions as governor were to replace the short pipes with long ones, to replace Kieft's bustling aldermen with ones like Wouter, to uproot Kieft's windmill and flagstaff and quaker guns, and thus his whole system of defense. Despite Peter's believing that "to render a country respected abroad, it was necessary to make it formidable at home—and that a nation should place its reliance for peace and security, more upon its own strength, than on the justice or good will of its neighbors" (a good *Morning Chronicle*-Burrite statement), his means of defending New York were scarcely better than Kieft's. He erected "a substantial barrier from river to river, being the distance of full half a mile!" Although Knickerbocker compares this barrier to the Great Wall of China, he is "inclined to believe that it was a picket fence of especial good pine posts," and records that the public were thrown into a great panic one night by a drove of stray cows breaking through it. His other attempt at fortification fares little better: he "fortified the water edge with a formidable mud breast work, solidly faced, after the manner of the dutch ovens common in those days, with clam shells." This became the Battery, "which though ostensibly devoted to the purposes of war, has ever been consecrated to the sweet delights of peace."

Although, like a good Federalist, Peter "held the militia system in very considerable contempt," he nevertheless called it forth for inspection:

Here came men without officers, and officers without men—long fowling pieces, and short blunderbusses—muskets of all sorts and sizes, some without bayonets, others without locks, others without stocks, and many without lock, stock, or barrel.—Cartridge-boxes, shot belts, powder-horns, swords, hatchets, snicker-snees, crow-bars, and broomsticks, all mingled higgledy, piggledy—like one of our continental armies at the breaking out of the revolution.

Peter, after one night's rain melted away the troops, discarded the militia system, relying instead upon a standing army (not that it was much help either, for he had to go recruiting to win back Fort Casimer—the regular army there was incompetent).

But Knickerbocker, also being of the old school, approves of all that Peter does, especially applauding Peter's address to "an inspired cobbler," who was speaking to the enlightened mob, complaining about the government. Peter threatens, upon any further meddling, to have " 'your hides stretched for drum heads, that ye may henceforth make a noise to some purpose!' " Needless to say, although Peter's desired effect was achieved, he lost some popularity, for "many accused him of entertaining highly aristocatic sentiments, and of leaning too much in favour of the patricians." Mention of these patricians allows Irving to rail once more against families proud of the dignity of their ancestry and of the creeping inroads of luxury, as in *Salmagundi*. In fact, this is a most *Salmagundi*-like section, for in it we also have described the old Dutch festivals, the introduction of a new style of dance, and the ladies' fondness for shorter petticoats, which Peter wished to legislate against, but desisted, for he "plainly perceived, that if he attempted to push the matter any further, there was danger of their leaving off petticoats altogether."

The account of Peter's last days, after his surrender of New Amsterdam to the British, also has a *Salmagundi*-like tone. Peter departed the city for his bouwerie, where "he enjoyed that tranquillity of mind, which he had never known amid the distracting cares of government." He would never revisit the city, in fact, would never look in its direction until, like Christopher Cockloft, he had planted "a thick grove of trees . . . that effectually excluded it from the prospect." Like Christopher, he welcomed all in need, but, like Christopher, who was averse to Frenchmen and Democrats, so Peter, "in case the ill starred applicant was an Englishman or a Yankee . . . never could be brought to yield the rites of hospitality." Eventually Peter Stuyvesant died, "a valiant soldier—a loyal subject——an upright governor, and an honest Dutchman—who wanted only a few empires to desolate, to have been immortalized as a hero!" Unfortunately, the times of desolating empires had passed, and so only Knickerbocker remains, to proclaim him a true hero.

In fact, throughout the chapters of the *History*, Peter, even in his moments of apparent success, shows his weakness. He began well, succeeding in negotiating a treaty with the Yankees. But the treaty, like the Jay treaty with England, was deemed disastrous by Peter's contemporaries. Even faithful Knickerbocker deserts Peter on this matter, declaring that "the only time when two nations can be said to be in a state of perfect amity, is when a negociation is open, and a treaty pending." But "a treaty of peace is a great political evil and one of the most fruitful sources of war," for treaties "are virtually binding on the weaker party only, or in other words, they are not really binding at all." Therefore, in concluding the Hartford negotiations, did Peter make a great error. He is saved from the immediate consequences of it, however, by the supernatural. The colonies of the east were "horribly beleaguered and harrassed by the inroads of the prince of darkness, divers of whose liege subjects they detected, lurking within their camp, all of whom they incontinently roasted as so many spies, and dangerous enemies." Although this sounds like an Englishman's description of Napoleon and his legions, Irving is ostensibly satirizing New England, panicked by a witch scare.

Having digressed on New England, Irving turns his attention to the south, and back to the days of William Kieft, and tells us the history of Fort Casimer. The commander of the southern frontier was Jacobus Von Poffenburgh, who had managed to pass his brass off as solid gold to William Kieft, and who was retained by Peter. "Completely inflated with his own importance," when he felt the martial spirit rise in him, "if peradventure, he espied a colony of honest big bellied pumpkins quietly basking themselves in the sun . . . with one sweep of his sword, he would cleave the unhappy vegetables from their chins to their waistbands." His ardor satisfied, "he would return to his garrison with a full conviction, that he was a very miracle of military prowess." Von Poffenburgh's appearance, his disciplinary action against a soldier for refusing to cut his hair, and the rumour, later circulated, that he was in the pay of the Swedes, all make it evident that here, in this digression, Von Poffenburgh is a caricature of James Wilkinson, Burr's accuser.

Having paid off this old score, Irving moves on to book 6, perhaps the most unified and funniest of all the books. Knickerbocker presents the principal combatants of the epic struggle to come: Peter Stuyvesant, "one of the most commanding, bitter looking, and soldierlike figures, that ever strutted upon canvass," and Jan Risingh, "a gigantic Swede . . . who, had he not been rather in-kneed and splay-footed, might have served for the model of a Samson, or a Hercules." While there must, indeed, have been a Swedish commander, Irving apparently made up the name "Risingh" for his own purposes—further satire of New Yorkers. Risingh, judging the mettle of Von Poffenburgh, decides to take Fort Casimer by treachery. Accordingly, he pays a state visit to Von Poffenburgh, flatters him, admires his troops' evolutions, admires his planned "improvements," and then, with all his men, sits down to dinner:

Thus all was rout and revelry and hideous carousal within Fort Casimer, and so lustily did the great Von Poffenburgh ply the bottle, that in less than four short hours he made himself, and his whole garrison, who all sedulously emulated the deeds of their chieftain, dead drunk, in singing songs, quaffing bumpers, and drinking fourth of July toasts, not one of which, but was as long as a Welsh pedigree or a plea in chancery.

So far, all of this sounds like a satirical description of the militia review and public dinner on the Fourth of July in Irving's time. That Irving is mocking his contemporaries is supported by the description of Von Poffenburgh, who, when he awoke, "bore no little resemblance to a 'deboshed fish' or bloated sea monster, caught upon dry land," a description which, in *The Corrector*, was applied to the Long Island whale dealer, Benjamin Hunting.[29] It is also supported by another description of Jan Risingh wearing "a shirt which for a week, had longed in vain for the wash-tub." Remembering that *The Corrector's* dirty-shirt-clad Billy Luscious was identified as William Rose by the quotation "A Rose by any other name," that *Salmagundi's* sketch of the equally foul-clad Dabble was prefaced by "The Hero Rose," we realize that, in this history, the same man is now Risingh—surely one of Irving's funnier word-plays.

But Irving does not dwell upon his joke, and quickly moves on to other mockeries. The next is of the stereotyped backwoodsman, in this case Dirk Schuiler, a skulker about the fort, who guessed Risingh's intentions, and, "after wandering many days in the woods, toiling through swamps, fording brooks, swimming various rivers, and encountering a world of hardships that would have killed any other being, but an Indian, a back-wood-man, or the devil," reported the deed to Peter. Peter decided to retaliate, and ordered out recruiting parties: "but notwithstanding all his martial rout and invitation, the ranks of honour were but scantily supplied; so averse were the peaceful burghers of New Amsterdam to enlist in foreign broils, or stir beyond that home, which rounded all their earthly ideas." Whereupon Peter set sail up the Hudson, to recruit the backwoodsmen.

The minor, preparatory incidents past, Knickerbocker, now given an opportunity to show his worth, reviews the troops gathered for the mighty battle, each family, like the tribes of Tammany, marching under its own banner. The life guards of the governor, led by Brinkerhoff, displayed "a mighty beaver *rampant* on a field of orange"; to their right were the vassals of Communipaw, with their standard being "a huge oyster *recumbent* upon a sea-green field"; then come the Suy Dams and the Van Dams, the Brooklyn ferry men, and the troops recruited by Peter, the Van Brummels, the Van Vlotens, the Van Nests, the Van Grolls, the Gardeniers, the Van Hoesens, the Counhovens, the Van Winkles, the Knickerbockers, and many more, each described by their place and characteristic. The whole city turned out to view the troops as they embarked; the governor addressed the citizens from the ship: "he exhorted them, one and all, high and low, rich and poor, to conduct themselves *as well as they could.*"

Quickly taking Fort Casimer, Peter marched on to Fort Christina, where Risingh lay entrenched. After sending, by Van Corlear, a summons for surrender, which was refused, Peter prepared for battle. This battle, as recorded by Knickerbocker, is truly an epic one, complete with gods and goddesses: "Venus, swore by her chastity she'd patronize the Swedes, and in semblance of a blear eyed trull, paraded the battlements of Fort Christina, accompanied by Diana, as a serjeant's widow, of cracked reputation." The Dutch are protected by Juno, with two black eyes, Minerva, "as a brawny gin suttler," and Vulcan, "as a club-footed blacksmith, lately promoted to be a captain of militia." Peter addresses his troops; the Dutch then light their pipes and attack the fort. After the first volley, which killed no one, because the Swedes could not see their opponents' eyes for the smoke, the opponents came to close quarters, wherein ensued a great clamor.

Despite the confusion, our two heroes came face to face, and nearly killed each other several times. Once, Peter, stunned by a blow, "missing his footing, by reason of his wooden leg, down he came . . . and would infallibly have wracked his anatomical system, had he not been received into a cushion softer than velvet, which providence, or Minerva, or St. Nicholas, or some kindly cow, had benevolently prepared for his reception." Finally, Peter fired directly at Risingh "a little sturdy stone pottle, charged to the muzzle with a double dram of true dutch courage, which the knowing Van Corlear always carried about him by way of replenishing his valour." Risingh fell "with such tremendous violence, that old Pluto started with affright, lest he should have broken through the roof of his infernal palace," and "victory in the likeness of a gigantic ox fly, sat perched upon the little cocked hat of the gallant Stuyvesant."

Knickerbocker congratulates himself on so managing the battle that not a man was killed, which is, indeed, historically accurate, since no battle took place at all. Fortunately, Irving disregarded this historical fact, and gave us a fine example of the mock epic, the literary highlight of Knickerbocker's *History*. After this fine achievement, the last book seems anticlimactic. Irving sends Peter off to the east, with Corlear, to negotiate again at Hartford. But, instead of following his progress, and noting the perils and constraints Peter encountered in meeting the New Englanders, Irving instead leaves him in New England, and returns to New York, to satirize the Common Council and its attempts at defense —a subject he knew better than that of the New England character.

In his last chapters, Irving criticizes the Common Council, New York's rich men, and its politicians for not getting on with the defense of New York, and he holds up to them the effect if they do not do so: once before New York had been betrayed by its citizens' being unwilling to spend on defense, and it might well be again. Written at a time when the British had fired on the U.S.S. *Chesapeake*, and were daily impressing American seamen, when the French were regularly flouting the harbor laws of New York, this last book contains Irving's strongest satire of the New Yorkers' inaction in the face of these insolences. Politically, this last chapter contains the whole point of his book, voiced earlier: "to render a country respected abroad, it was necessary to make it formidable at home."

Irving satirically chronicles the deliberations of the council and the public meetings. All aspects of society felt inspired to govern, from "Coblers, Tinkers and Taylors" to "a number of superannuated, wrong headed old burghers, who had come over when boys, in the crew of the *Goede Vrouw*." Because they had discovered the country, it was thought that they knew how to govern it: Irving extends the observation to modern times with another comparison: "it would have been deemed as much a heresy, as at the present day to question the political talents, and universal infallibility of our old 'heroes of '76'—and to doubt that he who had fought for a government, however stupid he might naturally be, was not competent to fill any station under it." The council, made up primarily of Platter breeches, decides "that as the danger was imminent, there should no time be lost—which points being settled, they immediately fell to making long speeches and belabouring one another in endless and intemperate disputes." The Platter breeches "considered it their first duty to effect the downfall of the Square heads—their second, to elevate themselves, and their third, to consult the welfare of the country."

Like the Common Council of 1807–1809, the Dutch council considered a wide variety of projects for defense, "not one of which had ever been heard of before, nor has been heard of since, unless it be in very modern days." The major test of a project was that it be economical, true also of the modern Council, who favored a plan of DuBuc de Marentille, a plan "never before used," which would be economical, but which he would not reveal to the council until he had been paid for it. Despite this refusal, the council continued to spend many hours on this nonrevealed project. Irving's description is apt: "thus did this venerable assembly of *sages*, lavish away that time which the urgency of affairs rendered invaluable, in empty brawls and long winded arguments, without even agreeing, except on the point with which they started, namely, that there was no time to be lost, and delay was ruinous." The Dutch council's debates were finally ended by the British fleet entering the harbor: "thus was all further necessity of either fortifying or disputing completely obviated, and thus was the grand council saved a world of words, and the province a world of expense—a most absolute and glorious triumph of economy!"

If there is a near tragedy in this last book, it is not the death of Corlear, drowned on a mission to summon the men of the Hudson to Peter's aid, nor Peter's finally being forced to sign the papers of surrender; it is the behavior of the people of New York. They are word-valorous: their public meetings propose and pass the question, "whether it was not possible and politic to exterminate Great Britain?" and the council passed its affirmative into law. When the British do arrive, instead of turning to face the enemy, they hold another public meeting, chaired by Dofue Roerback (surely an allusion to yet another of Irving's contemporaries), which censured the conduct of the governor, and praised the British! As the British prepare to assault, "the whole party of Platter breeches in the course of a single night had changed into arrant old women—a metamorphosis only to be paralleled by the prodigies recorded by Livy." Book 7 is an account of the inability of democratic New York to act in a crisis, hampered as it was by the claims and counterclaims of party, and without a strong leader.

Knickerbocker's *History* is an anthology of humors and styles, ranging from sentiment and nostalgia to vicious satire, with random puns, cartoons, caricatures, burlesque, mock epic, wit, and irony. The objects of satire range from presidents to flagstaffs, with the Platter breeches of the Common Council receiving the majority of the satiric shots. The book is unified only by the faint outline of Dutch history, and the first book even escapes that outline. The persona of Knickerbocker is often forgotten by Irving; when he appears he is mocked as a scholar-intellectual of the old school with a great distaste, like Stuyvesant, for modern times. Not as high-spirited as *Salmagundi*, for Irving is serious in his satire of New York, it nevertheless possesses much of the freedom of the earlier work. It is a book that, with its expanse and its satiric irreverance, could only have been written by a New Yorker, and is the direct ancestor of Cooper's New York novels and Melville's *Moby Dick*. It is, despite its deficiencies and inconsistencies, the best of Irving's New York works.

CHAPTER 2

Early European Works

I *Laboring to be Successful*

WASHINGTON Irving arrived in England in 1815, having been effectively stopped from expressing his admiration for Serena Livingston by "Black Horse" Henry Lee. Conjured over the Atlantic by Lee's deception, Irving apparently decided to make the most of it, and, adjuring Brevoort to remind the fair Livingstons of him,[1] set off on a sight-seeing tour of Wales. On his return, however, he discovered the lamentable financial condition of P. & E. Irving and Company—indeed the lamentable condition of the whole Irving family. Washington Irving felt his fall greatly; he felt he had lost his caste.[2] Remembering his recent dreams, he could not return home a bankrupt or exist as the holder of a paltry government post. He had to stay in England to see Peter through the English bankruptcy courts; his gloom deepened when an old friend told him that he had heard Irving had died.[3] Irving did not return to New York until 1832, after he had been honored by his government with the secretaryship of the legation in London. He did not dwindle, as did Ichabod Crane on being driven out of Sleepy Hollow, into a schoolmaster, a justice of the ten-pound court, or a petty legislator. But he worked long hours and wrote many volumes before he satisfied himself that he could return.

Irving helped Peter with the affairs of the firm, often visited Birmingham, where his sister, Sarah Van Wart, lived, and deplored the political and economic system of England. In a rare, indiscreet letter to Brevoort, he described England's situation:

You have no idea of the distress and misery that prevails in this country: it is beyond the power of description . . . . here you have . . . the distress of the poor—not merely mental suffering—but the absolute miseries of nature—Hunger, nakedness, wretchedness of all kinds that the labouring people in this country are liable to. In the best of times they do but subsist, but in adverse times they starve.[4]

In his financial and mental distress, Irving turned to his pen for support. In America, Moses Thomas paid him to be his English agent, to send Thomas first copies of new books so Thomas could have a head start on other pirating booksellers, and also probably to conduct the *Analectic*'s "Notaria," which began appearing July, 1817.

In England, Irving probably contributed to various reviews; at least he was sufficiently well known in literary circles by August, 1817, to be invited to a dinner at Murray's—then the premier publishing house in England. He had earned enough to take a tour of Scotland that fall, a tour that combined both business and pleasure. He visited with Jeffery, editor of the *Edinburgh Review*, and with Constable and Blackwood, both of whom were publishing Edinburgh magazines, and both of whom asked him to write for them.[5] He also arranged with Constable to send the first sheets of *Rob Roy* to Thomas for American publication. But the high point of the tour always remained his visit to Walter Scott at Abbottsford. Scott welcomed him heartily, pressing him to stay days instead of the intended hours. From this visit, Irving received inspiration to write in his own way, to create something far above the hackwork he was doing.

In 1818, Irving continued sending books to Thomas, continued the "Notaria," and also probably started doing book reviews for the *Analectic*, as well as contributing to *Blackwood's*. This year may be the beginning of his association with the unknown "Tory review for which I write," mentioned later in a letter to John Lockhart, then editor of the *Quarterly Review*.[6] That fall his brother William wrote to him, advising him to turn over his present responsibilities to Peter, who would thus be able to support himself, and accept the position of undersecretary of the Navy.[7] This minor position Irving declined, but he excused his refusal by announcing his ability to "produce articles from time to time that will be sufficient for my present support, and form a stock of copyright property, that may be a little capital for me hereafter."[8] To do this, he must remain in England.

The "stock of copyright property" became *The Sketch Book*. It appeared first in America, in 1819, in parts, with either three or four essays to the part. It was so well received that Irving started preparing an English edition. The first volume was successful and, Irving's printer failing, Murray bought the book and continued publishing it. Only a little of its success derived from its being by a man from the wild woods of America. Except for Austen and Scott, there were few prose luminaries; anyone reading the periodical publications of the day can easily see how superior Irving's style is to that of the average contributor. For all its faults discovered by modern eyes, it was a welcome reprieve from the dullness of the publications in England in 1820.

Even with the English success of *The Sketch Book*, Irving did not feel secure; he had fallen too far not to feel that he might fall again. Thus, he promised William Blackwood that he would continue to contribute faithfully to his magazine.[9] But if he did this, it was from France where he sped as soon as he had reaped the financial rewards of *The Sketch Book*. He returned to England only rarely, usually to visit his sister or to see his books through the press. He felt he must consolidate his litarary success with another book. He used the Christmas sketches of *The Sketch Book* as the basis for his next, *Bracebridge Hall*. This was, the critics thought, not up to the level of *The Sketch Book*, but still very well done.

Irving, suffering from pains in his legs, sought spas in France and Germany, spending several months in Dresden where he became intimate with the Foster family, a substitute for the Birmingham Van Warts. While in Dresden Irving attended the court, was much taken with the young wife of a diplomat, Madame de Bergh, and revised *The Sketch Book* for the Dresden publisher Montucci. His love for the theater returned; he acted in private theatricals staged by the Fosters; he collaborated on dramatic scripts with Barham Livius. But soon Irving returned to Paris and his writing.

Although he was supposed to be working diligently on a German *Sketch Book*, Irving involved himself with a number of other literary projects. He collaborated with John Howard Payne on a number of plays, composing songs for them, revising them, editing them. He supervised a French translation of his work, and reedited *Salmagundi* and *Knickerbocker* for Galignani (a Parisian English-language publisher). Irving seems to have had printers' ink in his blood. In addition to revising his own works for Galignani, Irving composed pieces for Galignani's newspaper, and probably contributed to his magazine. He also agreed to edit for him British classics for continental use. While Irving, apparently, only edited the first four volumes (the works of Goldsmith), he was paid for doing ten. The series continued, generally under the editorship of J. W. Lake.

During a short trip to England in 1824, Irving saw his new work, *Tales of a Traveller*, through the press, then returned to France. *Tales of a Traveller* was not the anticipated German *Sketch Book*. Although it contained some of Irving's strongest writing since Knickerbocker's *History*, it was severely handled by the critics, who lambasted it, especially for its indecencies. Irving was shocked by the attacks on it. Compounding his despair at this time was the failure of a family banker and the poor results from a Bolivian copper mine in which he had invested many of the proceeds from *Tales of a Traveller*. No matter that he was a famous author, he was still poor; he still had to write to live.

II The Sketch Book

In 1820, when *The Sketch Book* first appeared in England, England, having conquered Napoleon, was a nation divided. The corn laws left many hungry; many, as Irving pointed out to Brevoort, were starving; recent inventions had put many out of work; a public gathering at Manchester had ended with the cavalry attacking and wounding up to four hundred people; habeas corpus had been suspended; sedition laws were rigidly enforced; local magistrates had the power to imprison anyone they thought had made a face at authority. Any movement by radicals, or even liberals, led to harsher repressive measures on the part of the government. *The Sketch Book*, chiefly through its images, reflects Irving's attitude toward such an England. To one coming to it straight from Knickerbocker's *History*, it is depressing, nothing but melancholy, sentimentality, death, and graves. But Irving wrote for the careful reader. And, especially in *The Sketch Book*, his truth lies in the whole of a part, rather than in one sketch or tale. I will, therefore, describe *The Sketch Book* as it first appeared in America, that is, in parts.

Geoffery Crayon's *Sketch Book* reverberates with images shared among sketches. Common themes include those of imprisonment, shipwreck, sterility, financial loss, and the role of the storyteller.

Interlaced throughout the entirety is the Jeffersonian ideal of the virtues of agrarianism. While Irving attributes moral feeling to the rural life, its temple is a plentifully stocked barn. Independence of thought is associated not with the nobility, nor with the peasantry, but with the substantial farmer. While, in some respects, *The Sketch Book* is a traveler's guide to England and the English character, it is also Irving's statement of determination to make a mark for himself in the English literary world.

The first part might be said to be an in-depth look at financial failure, although the beginning quotation suggests the stranger in a strange land. It deserves to be quoted, for this, from Lyly's *Euphues*, dominates much of the book: "the traveller that stragleth from his owne country is in a short time transformed into so monstrous a shape that he is faine to alter his mansion with his manners and to live where he can, not where he would." Again and again, we are reminded by Crayon that he is living where he can, "not where he would." But England offers great men, and here Crayon turns ironic: "I had read in the works of various philosophers, that all animals degenerated in America, and man among the number. . . . I will visit this land of wonders, thought I, and see the gigantic race from which I am degenerated." Irving plays upon this ironic image in several essays.

The prelude, "The Voyage," is dominated by images of blankness and death: "the vast space of waters, that separates the hemispheres is like a blank page in existence. . . . from the moment you lose sight of the land you have left, all is vacancy." The voyage is a gulf, "rendering distance palpable and return precarious." The vacancy is corrected by the artist, who transforms clouds into "some fairy realms." But reality intrudes even upon the artist; a drifting mast gives no indication of the ship's hapless crew, the captain tells of running down a smaller ship at night and being unable to help any survivors. Thus Crayon's voyage is one of terror (during a storm, "it seemed as if death were raging round this floating prison, seeking for his prey"), one of nonexistence, with no promise of a safe return.

The rest of the essays of the first part deal with financial failure and how to cope with it. The first, "Roscoe," describes the financial misfortunes of the Liverpool banker and biographer of the Medicis. Roscoe had failed, and his library had to be sold, and Crayon likens the scene of the sale to "pigmies rummaging the armoury of a giant, and contending for possession of weapons which they could not wield." Thus the fate of one of the giants Crayon had expected of England. While Roscoe survives his loss through philosophy, Leslie, the chief character of "The Wife," is able to cope with his ruin because of his wife's virtues. While "The Wife," when read by itself, is extremely sentimental, its sentimentality is somewhat palliated by its context.

It is in this context that Irving introduces "Rip Van Winkle," his third story of financial failure. The first failure resorted to philosophy; the second, to his wife; the third, significantly, to story telling. "Rip" is both Irving's acknowledgment of his New York readers and his promise to return to them. As to the tale itself, Irving borrowed its basics from a German folktale, the wandering into the mountains, the little people encountered, the loss of time. But it is not the plot that makes "Rip" live, it is the way that it is told. In its context, Rip's failure as a farmer becomes more significant; his little men are analogous to Roscoe's pigmies. On Rip's return, his village is no longer the quiet, sedate village it once was. Rip is fearful that, after so many years, no one knows him. But a few friends are still alive; his daughter-in-law cares for him; he gains a reputation in the neighborhood as a storyteller, and so his life becomes one of ease. His journey into the dark clefts, his sojourn with the little men, his death-seeming sleep (comparable to the "blank page of existence" of "The Voyage") turn out to be a fortunate essay. He is enabled to return, and to return to more comfortable circumstances than when he left. In "Rip Van Winkle," Irving combines the themes of the "stranger in a strange land" with that of the hoped-for success of the storyteller.

While all the essays of part 2 deal with England, Crayon constantly interjects the presence of America. The part is dominated by the beginning quotation from Milton: "methinks I see in my mind a noble and puissant nation rousing herself, like a strong man after sleep, and shaking her invincible locks." Crayon applies the quotation to America. In "English Writers on America," Irving criticizes the works the English have written about the United States. Although Americans resent these attacks, they should not: "the tissue of misrepresentations attempted to be woven round us are like cobwebs, woven round the limbs of an infant giant. Our country continually outgrows them." Irving warns English writers that, through their words, England "is instilling anger and resentment into the bosom of a youthful

nation, to grow with its growth and strengthen with its strength."
While throughout the essay England is pictured as a pigmy in
comparison to America, Crayon still values England as "the
fountain head from whence the literature of the language flows."

Having condemned English writers on America, in his next
essay, Crayon becomes an American writer on the English, declaring that "the stranger who would form a correct opinion of
the English character must not confine his observations to the
metropolis." It is only in the country that Irving finds Englishmen
at their best. There Irving discovers a "regular gradation from
the nobleman . . . down to the labouring peasantry; and while
it has thus banded the extremes of society together, has infused
in each intermediate rank a spirit of independence." This, however, is no longer true, "the larger estates having in late years of
distress, absorbed the smaller, and in some parts of the country
almost annihilated the sturdy race of small farmers." Where not
marred, however, "all these common features of English landscape evince a calm and settled security . . . that speak deeply
and touchingly for the moral character of the nation." Irving
ends the essay with a poem which closes with these lines:

> A world enjoy'd; that wants no witnesses
> But its own sharers, and approving heaven,
> That, like a flower deep hid in rocky cleft,
> Smiles, though 'tis looking only at the sky.

This seems pleasant. But the reader turns the page and comes
upon this quotation: "I never heard / Of any true affection but
'twas nipt / With care, that, like the caterpiller, eats / The leaves
of the spring's sweetest book, the rose." While this quotation
from Middleton is an appropriate headnote to its essay, "The
Broken Heart," the juxtaposition of the two poems is striking.
"The Broken Heart," too often reprinted alone, seems to appeal
nicely to the sentimental taste for young love, disappointment,
and death. But in context, it also serves to illustrate the cankers
even in rural England. Irving begins the story with general comments on how, if unhappy in love, women are destroyed: "as the
dove will clasp its wings to its side, and cover and conceal the
arrow that is preying on its vitals; so it is the nature of woman
to hide from the world the pangs of wounded affection." (This
seems an appropriate source for Henry James' title, *The Wings of*

the Dove.) To illustrate his general principle, Irving tells the story of a young Irishwoman who loved an Irish patriot who was convicted, by the English, of treason. He was executed; his love suffered not only his death, but exile from her home, for "she had incurred her father's displeasure by her unfortunate attachment." She "at length sunk into the grave, the victim of a broken heart." Again, Crayon closes with a quotation, this time from Thomas Moore, who asks that her grave be lit by sunbeams "From her own lov'd island of sorrow!" The "world enjoy'd" of the previous essay includes this "island of sorrow."

In "The Art of Book Making," which closes the second part, Irving weaves together many of his metaphors and themes to produce one of his best essays. While ostensibly describing the reading room of the British Museum, and how authors there manufacture books by borrowing from past authors, through his metaphors Irving is reminding us of all that has been said before. While in the British Museum, Crayon notices a distant door from which absorbed men come: "I determined to attempt the passage of that strait and to explore the unknown regions beyond." Having accomplished his voyage and entered this strange land, Crayon describes it as a room filled with a body of Magi, and is reminded of an Arabian tale of "a philosopher shut up in an enchanted library, in the bosom of a mountain . . . where he made the spirits of the place bring him books of all kinds of dark knowledge"—a situation not unlike Rip's mountain encounter.

The library itself he describes as "one of those sequestered pools of obsolete literature, to which modern authors repair, and draw buckets full of classic lore," reminding us of his description of England as the fountainhead of literature. While the ancient authors read there are giants, the modern ones are not: "thus it is in the clearing of our American woodlands; where we burn down a forest of stately pines, a progeny of dwarf oaks start up in their place." Crayon now begins to dream, but laughs during the dream. Marked by his laughter as a stranger, Crayon must retreat: "I soon found that the library was a kind of literary 'preserve,' subject to game laws, and that no one must presume to hunt there without special licence and permission. In a word, I stood convicted of being an arrant poacher." This metaphor, this comment on England's game laws, becomes important to *The Sketch Book.* He will bring up again, as he had with Rip,

Americans' freedom to go hunting or fishing. The real game laws are further attached to the metaphorical game laws by the "arrant poacher" image. Irving will later remind us that Shakespeare, too, was a common "arrant poacher" before the world proclaimed his success.

The bleakest section of *The Sketch Book* is part 3, for it abounds with images of imprisonment, death, and the present sterility of England. In "A Royal Poet," Irving deals with James I of Scotland, but does not emphasize his kingship, his ability as a soldier or a ruler, but with his imprisonment, after a voyage, in a strange land, in England. In describing the blessings of the imagination when the body is confined, Irving returns to his Magi image of the previous part: "it can create a world for itself, and with a necromantic power, can conjure up glorious shapes and forms, and brilliant visions, to make solitude populous, and irradiate the gloom of the dungeon." James was finally released and returned to Scotland, but only to find his kingdom "in great confusion." He sets things in order, but is murdered by the nobility. Irving views James "as the companion of his fellow man, the benefactor of the human heart, stooping from his high estate to sow the sweet flowers of poetry and song in the paths of common life." James, like Rip, is yet another released prisoner, returning home to a changed land, telling his tales.

In the next two sketches, Irving moves from the past to the present, from high to the low, but tells the same story. Crayon, in "The Country Church," describes a church where "on every side the eye was struck with some instance of aspiring mortality; some haughty memorial which human pride had erected over its kindred dust, in this temple of the most humble of all religions." In "The Widow and her Son," Crayon seeks the church as a place for meditation, but in vain, for "I felt myself continually thrown back upon the world by the frigidity and pomp of the poor worms around me." He observes the funeral of a poor pious widow's only son, a funeral conducted by a well-fed priest: "never did I hear the funeral service, that sublime and touching ceremony, turned into such a frigid mummery of words."

Crayon seeks to know more of the widow's story. She and her husband, "by various rural occupations and the assistance of a small garden, had supported themselves creditably and comfortably"; their son had been their pride and mainstay. But during a year of scarcity, the son went to work on a small river craft. There he was seized by one of his government's press gangs and carried off to serve his government at sea. The news of his impressment killed his infirm father. The son eventually returned, but, like Rip, is unrecognized, he is so "emaciated and ghastly pale." The mother, convinced of his identity, is overjoyed, but only briefly: "nature . . . was so exhausted in him, and if anything had been wanting to finish the work of fate, the desolation of his native cottage would have been sufficient." He dies, and the widow soon follows her son. Again we have the voyage, imprisonment, return to a ruined land, and death.

In the final sketch of the section, "The Boar's Head Tavern, East Cheap," Crayon is enabled to give in a tavern what he could not in the church, namely, his assistance and his blessing. Struck by the amount of enjoyment Falstaff has given the ages, he has his idea: " 'I will make a pilgrimage to East cheap . . . and see if the old Boar's head Tavern still exists.' " Once more, Crayon is off on his search for giants, passing, on his way, "the renowned Guildhall and its two stunted Giants." He arrives at Eastcheap, "that ancient region of wit and wassail, where the very names of the streets relished of good cheer," but much has changed; instead of the "mad cap royster" and the food-mongers' calls, now one hears the "accursed dinging of the dustman's bell."

The tavern exists no longer; it was bequeathed to the church and "the old Boar never held up his head under church government." Baulked in finding the tavern, Crayon then seeks a rumored picture of the tavern, and hunts up the church's sexton, finding him in "a corner of a small court, surrounded by lofty houses, where the inhabitants enjoy about as much of the face of heaven, as a community of frogs at the bottom of a well." The sexton cannot find the picture, but promises Crayon a look at the vestry vessels, kept at a nearby tavern, and the pilgrimage is on again.

Once inside the tavern Crayon is at last rewarded. The gloom of the surroundings is relieved by the interior scene of food and warmth. The inn is presided over by an appropriately named Dame Honeyball, who unearths the treasures, a tobacco box with its picture of the Boar's Head Tavern and a goblet which Crayon accepts as the very "parcel-gilt goblet" associated with Falstaff. With these poor reliques Crayon is content, and, on leaving, perceiving the hunger of the sexton, "my bowels yearned with sympathy, and, putting in his hand a small token of my gratitude and good will, I departed with a hearty benediction on him, Dame Honeyball and the parish club of Crooked Lane." On the one hand, his journey has been a failure, he has collected few materials; the Boar's Head Tavern has been converted to shops; in place of the food-hawker is the dust man. But one tavern still remains, still having the ancient qualities of plenty, and in it Crayon is enabled to give his token and his benediction, to give that which he was unable to give in the church.

Part 4 follows a similar pattern, beginning with Crayon being entombed, but ending with him joining humanity, again in a tavern. Paralleling this theme is a debate about what an author should write of: Crayon decides to debate in favor of the common heart. The debate begins in "The Mutability of Literature," in which Crayon is again seeking a place for meditation, again, in a church—Westminster Abbey—and is again frustrated, this time by the merriment of schoolboys. He is admitted into the library, "buried deep among the massive walls of the abbey." Thus buried in this "literary catacomb, where authors, like mummies, are piously entombed," Crayon muses upon the many authors who "buried themselves in the solitude of cells and cloisters; shut themselves up from the face of man, and the still more blessed face of nature," only to produce a soon-to-be-forgotten book. In his dreamworld, again, Crayon converses with a thick little quarto who asks after the current fame of "a poor half educated varlet, that knew little of Latin, and nothing of Greek, and had been obliged to run the country for deer stealing." He presumes Shakespeare, too, has sunk into oblivion. This Crayon denies, asserting that Shakespeare endures as a poet, and a poet "has the best chance for immortality. Others may write from the head, but he writes from the heart, and the heart will always understand him." In this essay we are presented with the paradox of Crayon fleeing merriment, being buried, while still asserting that it is only those who are closest to human life and nature who will be able to escape oblivion.

"Rural Funerals," though less well organized, deals with much the same topic. Crayon begins by noting the passing of the custom of placing flowers on graves, then proceeds to research the ancient poets to give their quotations on the subject. He describes the placing of the flowers as a poetical act. But he does not remain at the grave: "then weave thy chaplet of flowers . . . but take warning . . . and henceforth be more faithful and affectionate in the discharge of thy duties to the living." Thus Irving prescribes poetry springing from country life and human affection. After the act of poetry, one must rejoin the human family.

And this is what Crayon does in the next sketch, "The Inn Kitchen." The scene is a Flemish inn, the Pomme d'Or, or Golden Apple. Crayon has had a solitary supper, was "seated alone in one end of the great gloomy dining room," and, having nothing to do, asks the host for some reading matter. He receives a newspaper: "as I sat dozing over one of the latter, reading old news and stale criticisms, my ear was now and then struck with bursts of laughter." Instead of retreating, Crayon "explored" his way to the kitchen "to take a peep at the group that appeared to be so merry." And he sees the "church" of "the middle and inferior order of travellers." In this kitchen, the travelers and attendants are "seated around a great burnished stove, that might have been mistaken for an altar," scoured utensils reflect the light, a "broad side of a flitch of bacon" is evident, and a "strapping Flemish lass" is "presiding priestess of the temple." Here Crayon feels at home, and joins the tale-telling group around the stove. In this short piece, we have yet another presentation of Irving's previous themes. Crayon is again a stranger, again laughter intrudes upon thought and reading. This time he does not flee it, but enters the "temple of true liberty," filled with warmth, hospitality, buxom girls, and mirth.

Crayon concludes the part with a tale he asserts he heard at the inn. "The Spectre Bridegroom, A Traveller's Tale" can be read on many levels. Its primary one is a story of young lovers triumphing over parental jealousies and living (we assume) happily ever after. It is a tale told in Irving's New York manner. Although Irving locates the tale in upper Germany, we recognize some characters as old friends. The parent is Baron Von Landshort, whose tower still struggles, like the Baron, "to carry a high head, and look down upon the neighbouring country," reminding us of Olaffe van Courtland. The Baron has but one daughter, whose accomplishments are about as extensive as the heroine of *Salmagundi*'s "Uncle John." The Baron is enriched by a multitude of poor relations who take advantage of any event to assemble at the castle. The family is now gathered to meet the daughter's bridegroom, Count Von Altenburg, to whom she had been betrothed without ever seeing. But Altenburg, having met along the way a trooper, Herman Von Starkenfaust, of a family with long-standing enmity to the neighboring Landshorts, has been fatally wounded by robbers. He begs Starkenfaust to go to Landshort and explain the reason for his nonappearance: " 'Unless this is done . . . I shall not sleep quietly in my grave.' " Starkenfaust promises.

Irving shifts the scene to the castle, where the Baron awaits his guest in all impatience. Soon a stranger arrives, "a tall gallant cavalier, mounted on a black steed," who apologizes for his unseasonableness. His apologies are cut short by the Baron, who hurries him and all the guests in to the delayed dinner. As the evening wears on, however, the cavalier becomes more and more melancholy. All are affected; the boisterous merriment and conversation are replaced by tales of the supernatural, including a favorite told by the Baron of a goblin horseman who carried away a fair lady. At this, the guest rises, bids the company goodbye and, accompanied by the protesting Baron, goes to his waiting horse. He tells the Baron, "my engagement is with no bride—the worms! the worms expect me! I am a dead man . . . the grave is waiting for me—I must keep my appointment!' "

Needless to say, this throws the household into an uproar, a state intensified when the daughter and an aunt view the specter outside the daughter's window and even further, one day, when the daughter is missing, carried off by the specter. The Baron is horrified and is just setting off on a search when the couple returns. Starkenfaust explains the count's death and "how he had been sorely perplexed in what way to make a decent retreat, until the Baron's goblin stories had suggested his eccentric exit." The Baron, a fond parent, forgives the daughter, although "there was something, it must be acknowledged, that did not exactly accord with his notions of strict veracity, in the joke the knight had passed upon him."

"The Spectre Bridegroom" is a fine story, a humorous story containing many of *The Sketch Book*'s themes. The Count, in the mountains is, like Rip, robbed of wife and life. In order to win the only daughter, Starkenfaust has to die (or pretend to), and to take the place of one dead. He achieves his goal only by telling a tale, perpetrating a joke, by playing on the Baron's fondness for tales of the supernatural. Starkenfaust has won, but there are discords. At the feast, his head is framed by "a huge pair of antlers," and, further, the Count is uneasy in his grave.

The fifth part of *The Sketch Book* is the only one still reprinted as a section, usually under the title, *Old Christmas*. The title is appropriate, since Irving continually emphasizes that the bounty and plenty described are more familiar to the past than the present. In the past, "The poor from the gates were not chidden, / When this old cap was new." Nevertheless, Crayon sets out on yet another pilgrimage to observe rural holiday customs, for, "they recall the fond picturings of an ideal state of things, which I was wont to indulge in the May morning of life, when as yet I only knew the world through books, and believed it to be all that poets had painted it." He has chosen Christmas, because, then, "heart calleth unto heart, and we draw our pleasures from the deep wells of living kindness." It is "the season of regenerated feeling—the season for kindling not merely the fire of hospitality in the hall, but the genial flame of charity in the heart." Thus, as indicated in the previous section, Crayon's pilgrimage is now to the well of the heart, rather than to the fountainhead of literature. The month of May being unobtainable, he is seeking warmth.

But the images Irving uses at the close of this first essay, "Christmas," remind us that Crayon is still alone:

The scene of early love again rises green to memory beyond the sterile waste of years, and the idea of home, fraught with the fragrance of home dwelling joys, reanimates the drooping spirit—as the Arabian breeze will sometimes waft the freshness of the distant fields to the weary pilgrim of the desert.

The pilgrim, however, still has more desert to cross, as Crayon emphasizes in his next paragraph: "stranger and sojourner as I am in the land . . . yet I feel the influence of the season beaming into my soul from the happy looks of those around me. Surely happiness is reflective." Crayon can only enjoy this reflected happiness.

The remaining sketches of the part supply concrete details for the generalizations contained in "Christmas." "The Stage Coach," containing Crayon, holiday travelers, and presents of food, passes through the country, driven by a Falstaff-like coachman. In the coach with Crayon are three schoolboys, in high glee of anticipation for their holiday. They are met by a footman, their horse, and a dog. The coach stops for a moment to water the horses, then comes in sight of a country seat where Crayon can just distinguish a woman and two girls awaiting the boys: "I leaned out of the coach window, in hopes of witnessing the happy meeting, but a grove of trees shut it from my sight." Crayon is denied even this reflected happiness.

But Crayon, having met a continental traveling companion, Frank Bracebridge, at an inn, is invited to spend Christmas at Bracebridge Hall where he is promised "a hearty welcome in something of the old fashioned style." "Christmas Eve" opens with the journey to Bracebridge Hall, and with images of coldness, frigidity, sterility, and death. The porter's lodge "sheltered under dark fir trees," is "almost buried in shrubbery." The men walk through the park to the hall:

Our road wound slowly through a noble avenue of trees, through the naked branches of which the moon glittered as she rolled through the deep vault of a cloudless sky: the lawn beyond was sheeted with a slight covering of snow . . . and at a distance might be seen a thin transparent vapour, stealing up from the low grounds, and threatening gradually to shroud the landscape.

This tomblike atmosphere is broken by merriment drifting from the servants' hall, and completely dispelled when the two are finally admitted to the house. In the hall are gathered numerous members of the family, of all ages, although, "a profusion of wooden horses, penny trumpets, and tattered dolls, about the floor, showed traces of a troop of little fairy beings, who, having frolicked through a happy day, had been carried off to slumber through a peaceful night."

Crayon delights to see "the old Squire, seated in his hereditary elbow chair, by the hospitable fireside of his ancestors, and looking around him like the sun of a system, beaming warmth and gladness to every heart." Indeed, Crayon feels so much at home he allows himself to slip into gentle satire in describing the family. As the party breaks up, Crayon passes the dying embers of the yule log, and is "half tempted to steal from my room at midnight, and peep, whether the fairies might not be at their revels about the hearth."

In "Christmas Day," although "it seemed as if all the events of the preceeding evening had been a dream," Crayon is at last granted his sight or fairies. He hears a choir, opens his door, and sees "one of the most beautiful little fairy groups that a painter could imagine." The children remain but a moment, then scamper away. The family is summoned to prayers and the Squire's favorite hymn, which gives thanks for mirth and plenty. Then, after church, the service of which has given Irving ample material for his satirical pen, the Squire comments to Crayon, "I love . . . to see this day well kept by rich and poor; it is a great thing to have one day in the year at least, when you are sure of being welcome wherever you go, and of having, as it were, the world all thrown open to you." He goes on to praise the old style of keeping open house during the holidays. He tried it once, but "the country people, however, did not understand how to play their parts in the scene of hospitality: many uncouth circumstances occurred; the manor was overrun by all the vagrants of the country, and more beggars drawn into the neighbourhood than the parish officers could get rid of in a year." What a comment on the utter misery of the times.

The Christmas dinner soon follows, conducted as closely to the old style as possible, although the squire has to confess that the pie decorated with peacock feathers is really partridge. Still, "how easy it is for one benevolent being to diffuse pleasure around him, and how truly is a kind heart a fountain of gladness." The contagion is felt even by the parson, whom Crayon cannot help contrasting with the Squire: "the Squire had left the university to live lustily on his parental domains, in the vigorous enjoyment of prosperity and sunshine . . . whilst the poor parson, on the contrary, had dried and withered away, among dusty tomes, in the silence and shadows of his study." After the gentlemen had joined the ladies in the drawing room, Crayon, attracted by a peal of laughter, steals out to observe the children playing blind-man's bluff with Master Simon, but does not stay to participate, returning to hear the parson telling local superstitions. The Squire, while he loves the legends, "often lamented that he could not believe in them, for a superstitious person, he thought, must live in a kind of fairy land." At this point, the company hears laughter: "the door suddenly flew open, and a train came trooping into the room, that might almost have been mistaken for the breaking up of the court of Fairy." Master Simon, with the aid of the children, had gotten up a masque.

In this part, Crayon moves steadily away from the world as pictured in books ever closer to reality. The times may be evil, but there are benevolent persons who reflect light to others. Crayon is still not able to participate, as Master Simon can, in the real fairyland of the children, he is still prone to turn to tales of the dead, restless in their graves, but at least he is out of his prison, and now able to justify his art: "If . . . I can by any lucky chance, in these days of evil . . . if I can now and then penetrate through the gathering film of misanthropy, prompt a benevolent view of human nature, and make my reader more in good humour with his fellow beings and himself, surely, surely, I shall not then have written entirely in vain."

There are only three sketches in part 6: "John Bull," "The Pride of the Village," and "The Legend of Sleepy Hollow." In these, Irving, in addition to restating his major themes, describes the condition of England and contrasts it, by juxtaposition, with that of the United States. These three essays did not appear together in the English edition. The beginning quotation of "John Bull" emphasizes age: "an old song . . . / Of an old worshipful gentleman who had a great estate / that kept a brave old house at a bountiful rate," and age dominates the essay. It swarms with aged chargers, aged servants, aged owls, aged rats, and, of course, an ancient mansion. Although Irving declares he is but giving a sketch of the caricature of John Bull, it soon becomes clear that he is giving us a satiric description of the present English government, if not of the Prince Regent himself. Irving had not lost his talent for political satire.

Crayon describes John Bull's domestic establishment, which is enormously expensive. His house has a solid Saxon core, but has been added to over the ages so that it has become inconceivably rambling. Even the chapel is expensive, but the chaplain (the clergy) "always backs the old gentleman in his opinions, winks discreetly at his little peccadilloes, rebukes the children when refractory, and is of great use in exhorting the tenants to read their bibles, say their prayers, and above all, to pay their rents punctually, and without grumbling." Irving had no love for the English church. Some parts of John Bull's house are deserted, some are decayed, but John "will not hear even of abuses being reformed, because they are good old family abuses."

John's family is of different minds about the enormous expense of the establishment. His children, "as they have always been allowed to speak their minds freely, they do not fail to exercise the privilege most clamorously in the present posture of his affairs." The conservatives want to maintain the present expense, the moderates want John Bull to retrench, and seem to persuade him, but the radicals mar their argument by railing at the old man, declaring "that the whole family mansion shall be levelled with the ground." This provokes the old man to be more stubborn yet, and words between the two became so heated that the old man calls in his son Tom, a half-pay officer "to out sabre, and flourish it over the orator's head, if he dares to array himself against paternal authority." This is an obvious reference to the Manchester melee when government troops charged a radical meeting which was to have been addressed by "Orator" Hunt.

These dissensions have caused his neighbors to murmur and comment, " 'Mr. Bull's estate is a very fine one, and has been in the family a long while; but for all that, they have known many finer estates come to the hammer' "—an allusion to the threat still posed by the French Revolution. The effect on John Bull himself is striking; he has lost his corpulence and "has of late become as shrivelled and shrunk as a frost bitten apple." Crayon concludes that his estate is picturesque and should be retained, "as long as it can be rendered comfortably habitable," and recommends to him more prudence, so he can "renew the jovial scenes of ancient prosperity, and long enjoy, on his paternal lands, a green, an honorable, and a merry old age."

Having dealt with the pride of the nation, Irving next deals with "The Pride of the Village." By itself the standard tale of an innocent young girl, loved and left, who dies of a broken heart, its placement gives it more meaning. Irving begins it with a resurrection image, but ends it with winter, sterility, and the grave. Crayon is once more in a rural churchyard, stopping to muse, encouraged by the lovely sunset: "it seemed like the parting hour of a good christian . . . giving, in the serenity of his decline, an assurance that he will rise again in glory." A tolling bell breaks in on his thoughts and he observes the funeral of a young girl. The father seeks to comfort himself with religion, "but the mother only thought of her child as a flower of the field, cut down and withered in the midst of its sweetness." Crayon soon learns the story of this girl: an only child, "her father had once been an opulent farmer, but was reduced in circumstances." She is named Queen of May, and, as such, is seen by a young officer, who decides to make a village conquest. She is enamored, "it was the difference of intellect, of demeanor, of manners . . . that elevated him in her opinion." Gradually, the officer, too, falls in love, but, "his rank in life—the prejudices of titled connexions— his dependance upon a proud and unyielding father—all forbad him to think of matrimony." So, when he is ordered abroad, he asks her to join him without its benefit.

"When at last the nature of his proposals flashed upon her pure mind, the effect was withering." He marches away, she sinks gradually to death. Crayon revisits the church later: "it was a wintry evening; the trees were stripped of their foliage; the church yard looked naked and mournful, and the wind rustled coldly through the dry grass." Only the chaplet of flowers, withered now, still remains, emanating its poetry. John Bull has become "shrivelled and shrunk," the pride of the village is withered, the Queen of the May lies dead in a wintry church-yard.

It is in this context that Irving introduces "The Legend of Sleepy Hollow," and we turn gratefully toward the glorious autumn days and autumn harvests, to food, food, and more food, to buxom lasses and merriment and pranks. Although, on its more solemn side, "The Legend of Sleepy Hollow" is a reprise of "The Spectre Bridegroom," it is also a celebration of the bounty of the United States, and, because of its parallels, a contrast both to "John Bull" and "The Pride of the Village." And what parallels there are! Katrina Van Tassel belongs to "the pride and flower of the adjacent country," she is the only daughter of "a thriving, contented, liberal hearted farmer," whose "vast barn . . . might have served for a church." Ichabod Crane, like the officer, is a stranger to the neighborhood. As the English girl admires the English officer for his intellect, demeanor, and manners which are superior to those of the rustics around her, Ichabod also prides himself on his intellect (he is schoolmaster), demeanor (especially his dancing), and manners (particularly polished for his hostesses). As the officer awakened the girl "to a keen per-ception of the beautiful and grand," Ichabod teaches Katrina psalmody. The effect of the English officer is withering, Ichabod Crane is "the genius of famine." But what a different outcome. In the world of Sleepy Hollow, the only troops are sucking pigs, the only regiments are turkeys, the only squadrons are "snowy geese . . . convoying whole fleets of ducks." Crane is driven out of Sleepy Hollow, and one of the rustics "conducted the blooming Katrina in triumph to the altar."

But Irving also includes themes from his earlier works, especially regional satire. Ichabod Crane is pictured as the typical Yankee. He relies on singing psalms to ward off evil, he reads Cotton Mather, his nasal twang still resounds among the hills. Also returning from the earlier works are Irving's mockery of the stolidity of the Dutch as well as his praise of their cookery:

There was the doughty dough nut, the tenderer oly koek, and the crisp and crumbling cruller; sweet cakes and short cakes, ginger cakes and honey cakes, and the whole family of cakes. And then there were apple pies and peach pies and pumpkin pies; besides slices of ham and smoked beef; and moreover delectable dishes of preserved plums, and peaches, and pears, and quinces; not to mention broiled shad and roasted chickens.

Brom Bones is a caricature of the Southern backwoodsman. He, with his "great knowledge and skill in horsemanship," his readiness either for a fight or a frolic, his fur cap with its "flaunting fox's tail," and his "strong dash of waggish good humour" fits the part.

Irving varies some themes previously used in *The Sketch Book*, as can be seen by comparing "The Legend" with "The Spectre Bridegroom." The two stories are basically the same. Two men become enamored of the only daughter of a wealthy man. In order to win the girl, Starkenfaust/Brom rely on the effect of a superstitious tale. Both become specters. While Starkenfaust is a trooper, Brom pretends to be. Both have a strong predilection for merriment, both ride black horses and, of course, both get the girl by means of a prank. Further, both are from the same countryside as the girl.

The differences are enlightening. Altenberg is pathetic, Crane is richly comic. Altenberg is easily killed off and, although restless in his grave, appears no more in the story. Although Crane is thought to have died, there are reports in Sleepy Hollow that he is still alive, that he "had been admitted to the bar, turned politician, electioneered, written for the newspapers, and finally had been made a Justice of the Ten Pound Court." Irving's lenient treatment of Crane is consistent with Crayon's own move out of the grave. Yet another comparison is in order. Brom Bones-Crane are patterns of the Squire-parson. The Squire, living on his paternal lands is jovial and merry; the parson, shut up amid books and superstitions, is dry and withered. Crane, after spending an evening listening to superstitions, had to wend his way home "amidst the dim and ghastly glare of a snowy night . . . . How often was he appalled by some shrub covered with snow, which like a sheeted spectre beset his very path." Crayon moves away from the frigid, tomblike libraries; Crane, still a habitué of tales, is associated with these frigid images, which appear in the "Legend" only in connection with them.

"The Legend of Sleepy Hollow" is told by a narrator who is neither Crane, Crayon, nor Knickerbocker. It is this poor man who, at the beginning, describes Sleepy Hollow as a promising retreat "whither I might steal from the world and its distractions, and dream quietly away the remnant of a troubled life." Further, "though many years have elapsed since I trod the drowsy shades of Sleepy Hollow, yet I question whether I should not still find the same trees and the same families vegetating in its sheltered bosom." This suggestion of a return to an undevastated land is in strong contrast to the images of the early sketches, in which prisoners returned to ruined lands.

The last part is a microcosm of the entire *Sketch Book*. In it, metaphorically, Crayon begins with tomb and shipwreck but ends in the midst of life, with a joke. In "Westminster Abbey," as Crayon enters the Abbey, "it seemed like stepping back into the regions of antiquity, and losing myself among the shades of former ages." He enters through a low, subterranean-seeming vaulted passage and sees a verger, "seeming like a spectre." Once more, Crayon is entombed. He is musing over three abbots' effigies, "thus left like wrecks upon this distant shore of time," when the clock sounds, "telling the lapse of the hour, which like a billow has rolled us onward toward the grave." Having, by these images, reminded us of "The Voyage," Crayon moves into the Abbey, and wanders among its tombs. He is most impressed by the poets' corner, for their renown was "purchased . . . by the diligent dispensation of pleasure." In contrast, he observes that "not a royal monument but bears some proof how false and fugitive is the homage of mankind. Some are plundered; some mutilated; some covered with ribaldry and insult—all more or less outraged and dishonoured!" Crayon muses on Time, "ever silently turning over his pages . . . each age is a volume thrown aside to be speedily forgotten," thus reminding us not only of the mutability of life, but of the mutability of literature.

As a partial answer to "Westminster Abbey," Irving turns to the countryside and "The Angler." He begins the sketch by reminiscing on his fishing days in America, how he and his companions were inspired by Izaak Walton "and sallied into the country, as stark mad as was ever Don Quixote from reading books of chivalry." Crayon recalls being a bungler at the sport, but, "a lubberly country urchin came down from the hills with a rod made from a branch of a tree; a few yards of twine; and, as heaven shall help me! I believe a crooked pin for a hook, baited with a vile earth worm—and in half an hour caught more fish than we had nibbles throughout the day!" Once again, the attempt to see the world through books ends in failure.

But Irving offers all this as but memories inspired by his meeting a veteran angler on the banks of the Dee. The angler had a face which "bore the marks of former storms, but present fair weather." He is instructing two boys, one of whom had "the skulking look of an arrant poacher, and I'll warrant could find his way to any gentleman's fish pond in the neighbourhood in the darkest night." Crayon learns the angler's story. He had gone to America, there been ruined in trade, had been in the navy and had his leg shot off, "the only stroke of real good fortune he had ever experienced, for it got him a pension." With this, he returned to his native village, where he was, like Rip, "the oracle of the tap room; where he delighted the rustics with his songs, and, like Sinbad, astonished them with his stories of strange lands, and shipwrecks, and sea fights." His existence is serene, and Crayon comments, "how comforting it is to see . . . a poor fellow, like this, after being tempest tost through life, safely moored in a snug and quiet harbour in the evening of his days." The angler has picked out his grave site near where his mother and father lay buried, a grave that will be far more serene than those in Westminster Abbey.

Irving again affirms, in his next essay, "Stratford-on-Avon," the possibility of returning home peacefully to an undisturbed grave, even though one has left the village in dishonor. Crayon visits the church where Shakespeare lies buried. He admires his bust and regrets his early death: "for what fruit might not have been expected from the golden autumn of such a mind, sheltered as it was from the stormy vicissitudes of life, and flourishing in the sunshine of popular and royal favour." Crayon seems eager to believe that Shakespeare's epitaph has been effective, that although, once, the temptation was there, no one dared move his bones.

But of all Stratford, Crayon is most interested in the estate of the Lucys, the estate from which Shakespeare poached his deer, whose master imprisoned him, which provoked him to write a lampoon, which, in turn, provoked Sir Thomas to send for a lawyer "to put the severity of the laws in force against the rhyming deer stalker." Shakespeare left incontinently for London and "Stratford lost an indifferent wool comber and the world gained an immortal poet." Shakespeare, however, never forgot the injury, and "revenged himself in his writings; but in the sportive way of a good natured mind." Crayon pictures the scene of Shakespeare being brought before Sir Thomas:

Who whould have thought that this poor varlet, thus trembling before the brief authority of a country Squire, and the sport of rustic boors, was soon to become the delight of princes; the theme of all tongues and ages; the dictator to the human mind; and was to confer immortality on his oppressor by a caricature and a lampoon!

Crayon concludes by commenting on the appropriateness of retaining his grave at Stratford, for, "after all, . . . there is no love, no admiration, no applause, so sweet to the soul as that which springs up in his native place." In this one essay, Irving reintroduces several of his themes. He asks us, implicitly, to contrast the preservation of Shakespeare's grave with the depredations suffered by royal tombs. But he dwells for the most part on Shakespeare, the potential storyteller, imprisoned, having to leave his native village, but revenging himself on his oppressor by "a caricature and lampoon."

And, not surprisingly, the next essay, the last one of the American edition of *The Sketch Book*, is a caricature and lampoon, a notice to the undertaking societies that he was not ready for the grave yet, and a warning, expressed in his beginning quotation from Nashe, that "I have a whole booke of cases lying by me, which if I should sette foorth, some grave auntients . . .

would be out of charity with me." The sketch is entitled "Little
Britain," and ostensibly describes the concerns of that part of
London. The New York reader, however, unfamiliar with the
sections of London, would first think of Little Britain, New York,
birthplace of both Governor George Clinton and of Irving's
former oppressor, DeWitt Clinton. The sketch has all the bounce
and verve and merriment of Irving's New York productions.
Crayon received this account of Little Britain from an old inhabitant. But, as Crayon notes, the houses he describes are not
to be found in the district; they "have their gable ends to the
street; great bow windows, with diamond panes set in lead;
grotesque carvings; and low arched door ways," much like the
old Dutch houses.

While the narrator describes Little Britain as "the strong hold
of true John Bullism," its "sages and great men" belong to
Knickerbocker's world. First of these is the apothecary, who
"always [has] some dismal tale . . . to deal out to his customers,
with their doses." He excells: "no man can make so much out of
an eclipse, or even an unusually dark day; and he shook the tail
of the last comet over the heads of his customers and disciples
until they were nearly frightened out of their wits." This comet-
theorist is a familiar Knickerbocker figure. The apothecary has a
rival, a cheesemonger, whose "head is stored with invaluable
maxims which have borne the test of time and use for centuries."
He "has much to say on the subject of the national debt; which,
some how or other, he proves to be a great national bulwark
and blessing." He is a great traveler, and "is considered quite a
patron at the coach office of the Goose and Gridiron." His family
want him to voyage to Gravesend, but "he has great doubts of
those new gim-cracks the steam boats." Had not Irving located
this so securely in Little Britain, one would conclude, from the
goose, from the quotation from Hamilton, that this was a caricature of a New York Federalist.

In Little Britain, the apothecary and the cheesemonger head
rival parties, supported by rival burial societies. They are chal-
lenged by a third, which meets at a local inn bearing the sign
of the half moon and "a most seductive bunch of grapes." The inn
is kept by a "jolly publican of the name of Wagstaff," who prides
himself upon the fact that "Henry the Eighth, is one of his
nocturnal rambles, broke the head of one of his ancestors with

his famous walking staff." Thus, even Launcelot Langstaff is reincarnated in Little Britain. But the greatest man is the mayor of Little Britain. The people are all convinced of his power:

Under the protection of this mighty potentate, therefore, the good people of Little Britain sleep in peace. Temple Bar is an effectual barrier against all interior foes; and as to foreign invasion, the Lord Mayor has but to throw himself into the tower, call in the train bands, and put the standing army of Beef eaters under arms, and he may bid defiance to the world!

This last is a reminder of Knickerbocker's—and Clinton's—New York editors, who also "bid defiance to the world!"

But all is not politics in Little Britain; it also has its social dissensions, produced by the daughters of a retired butcher, the Lambs, and a widow and her daughters, the Trotters. Both ape French fashions, and both seek to be more extravagant than the other. One even attempts to direct patronage to a French dancing master—who decamps without paying his rent, and one is reminded of Aunt Charity's Frenchman. Because of these new fashions, the author fears "the total downfall of genuine John Bullism." Because he has been privy to both parties' "cabinet counsels and mutual backbitings," he fears, if the two ever compare notes, he is ruined. Therefore, he has determined to look "for some other nest in this great city . . . this found, I will, like a veteran rat, hasten away before I have an old house about my ears."

And so ends the American *Sketch Book*, with a rat threatening to leave "an old house" as if it were a sinking ship. Rat or not, Irving comes fully to life in this elaborate joke on both Great Britain and Little Britain, New York. Unlike Shakespeare, in this joke, this caricature, this lampoon, he did not succeed in immortalizing his oppressor, but not for want of trying. From the beginning blankness and threat of death of "The Voyage," and the succeeding images of entombment, frigidity, and sterility, from the beginning quotation that the traveler must "live where he can, not where he would," Irving moves steadily from frigidity to the warmth of the heart, from the sterility of books to the fairyland of children, from the grave to resurrection, from storms to a safe harbor, from living where he must to the rat's looking "for some other nest" and relocating. *The Sketch Book* is a unified chronicle of progress. It cannot be called a novel, but it is far more than a random collection of sketches. In it, Irving shows his artistry.

III Bracebridge Hall

Bracebridge Hall, while not as successful as *The Sketch Book*, may be Irving's most complex work. Irving sought to achieve greater unity by limiting himself to one place and set of characters, while still discussing diverse aspects of England. He describes England as the land of his fathers, his fatherland, but he sees it through republican eyes as a citizen of the United States, the "dear land that gave me birth," thus his motherland. Crayon describes himself as having, to some extent, caught "the contagion" of "old times, old books, old customs," and, throughout *Bracebridge Hall*, shows how this "contagion" or "infection" distorts reality.

In *Bracebridge Hall*, Irving sees England from two viewpoints. Although born in a new country, he was "educated from infancy in the literature of an old one," which gave him "historical and poetical associations, connected with places, and manners, and customs of Europe." Once in England, from this literature, he "pictured to myself a set of inhabitants and a mode of life for every habitation that I saw." *Bracebridge Hall* is Irving's creation of a mansion and a village, full of characters and events from his readings in English literature. But Irving is also a realist, and sees the present England and the past realistically. Williams deplores that, in Irving's journal, "at Tintern there was an excellent salmon for dinner, but no mention of Wordsworth." [10] But Irving was no romantic. He saw Tintern Abbey "buried in the bosom of a quiet valley, and shut up from the world, as though it had existed merely for itself." Conway Castle he sees as "a mere hollow yet threatening phantom of departed power." He sees in England "signs of national old age and empire's decay."

One English reviewer declared *Bracebridge Hall* worthless, for no such family as shown existed then in England, that "he can only have read of such persons in old books." [11] And so Irving failed, few readers perceiving his intention to take these "persons in old books," to set them in motion, and to sketch the

resulting confusion. This, despite his descriptions of the characters in terms of old books or old paintings. These characters (who
probably are also caricatures of living authors and critics) are
introduced in the first section, which forms a prologue like that of
the *Canterbury Tales*. In this first section there is little movement,
Crayon hinting only of possible future complications.

Crayon first introduces the Squire of Bracebridge Hall, whose
"bigoted devotion to old English manners and customs" agrees
well with Crayon's "unsated curiosity about the ancient and
genuine characteristics of my 'father land.'" Of the Hall's household, Master Simon is the Squire's "privy counsellor," who also
acts as father confessor. The hall's housekeeper is "the family
chronicler," and "has a stately air that would not disgrace a lady
that had figured at the court of Queen Elizabeth." She wears
such ancient garments that Crayon "sometimes looked from the
old housekeeper to the neighbouring portraits, to see whether I
could not recognize her antiquated brocade in the dress of some
one of those long-waisted dames that smile on me from the walls."
When younger, it is rumored, the Squire kissed her, whereupon
"she was observed to take to reading Pamela." She has an orphan
niece, Phoebe, who will be her heir.

"The Widow" (introduced by Chaucer's description of the
prioress) describes the Squire's sister, Lady Lillycraft. She is "a
fair fresh-looking elderly lady, dressed in an old-fashioned riding
habit, with a broad-brimmed white beaver hat, such as may be
seen in Sir Joshua Reynolds' paintings." Her home "must have
been built and furnished about the time of Sir Charles Grandison."
Like the prioress, "she is dainty in her living, and a little of an
epicure, living on white meats, and little ladylike dishes." She "is
always talking of love and connubial felicity." The occasion for
her visit to the hall is the forthcoming marriage of the Squire's
son and his ward, Julia. She, too, is old-fashioned, sings old songs,
wears old-fashioned dress, and "her hair was put up very much in
the style of Sir Peter Lely's portraits in the picture-gallery."

Crayon is more critical in presenting another portrait, that of
"An Old Soldier," General Harbottle. When the General bows to
Lady Lillycraft, "it is enough to remind one of those courtly
groups of ladies and gentlemen, in old prints of Windsor Terrace,
or Kensington Garden." The General passes his time visiting
country seats, loves to tell, in detail, of his army service, is a
huge feeder, and extremely loyal to the king. He is "apt to get a

little impatient at any talk about national ruin and agricultural distress":

"They talk of public distress," said the general this day to me, at dinner, as he smacked a glass of rich burgandy, and cast his eyes about the ample board; "they talk of public distress, but where do we find it, sir? I see none. I see no reason any one has to complain. Take my word for it, sir, this talk about public distress is all humbug!"

The general is a bachelor, of which Crayon asserts, "there is no character in the comedy of human life that is more difficult to play well."

The last major "pilgrim" of the prologue is "Ready Money Jack." In *The Sketch Book*, Irving gave us the modern-day, unfortunate John Bull. Here, in the character of Jack Tibbets, he gives us John Bull as he should be. He is, as Crayon describes him, "a kind of small potentate . . . for the empire over which he reigns has belonged to his family time out of mind." He works hard and "never allows a debt to stand unpaid." Ready Money Jack is a faithful picture of an English yeoman, "such as he is often described in books." Irving leaves it to the reader to juxtapose "John Bull" with "Ready Money Jack" and to realize that the world of books exists no more.

Irving's prologue ends, as Chaucer's does, with "Storytelling." The Squire one day calls on a nervous gentleman to give a tale. Thus is introduced "The Stout Gentleman," a mystery without a solution, a story whose effect depends not on what is told but the way in which it is told. It is also a tale which illustrates a storyteller in the act of peopling an inn-room with "an inhabitant and a mode of life," just as Crayon, in his introduction, says he did of England. The story is simple enough. The nervous gentleman is detained by a cold at an inn on a rainy Sunday. He hears the waiter at the bar: " 'The stout gentleman in No. 13, wants his breakfast. Tea and bread and butter, with ham and eggs, the eggs not to be too much done.' "

This intrigues the nervous gentleman and he begins to imagine what this unknown must be like. He collects additional evidence, and, with each new piece, revises his picture. But the nervous gentleman has to go to sleep without having caught a glimpse of No. 13, the mysterious stranger. Awakening late the next morning, he hears that No. 13 is about to leave. He rushes to his

window, but is in time to see only "a full view of the broad disk
of a pair of drab breeches." Although, in his preface to *Tales of
a Traveller,* Irving states that the author of *Waverly* (Sir Walter
Scott) recognized himself as the stout gentleman, in this tale, "the
great unknown" remained unknown; the nervous gentleman's
conjectures could never be confirmed, for the guest was gone.

In the next section, which begins with "Forest Trees" and concludes with "Hawking," Crayon begins setting his characters in
motion, only to discover they are poorly equipped to deal with
modern times. "Forest Trees" acts as a moral introduction. Crayon
compares the oak to "heroic and intellectual man," and an emblem of what "a true nobleman *should be:* a refuge for the weak,
a shelter for the oppressed, a defence for the defenceless, ward-
ing off from them the peltings of the storm, or the scorching rays
of arbitrary power." The nobleman who is not like this, "should
tempests arise, and he be laid prostrate by the storm, who would
mourn over his fall? . . . 'why cumbereth he the ground?'"
Irving, like Chaucer, draws on nature for his lesson on true
gentility.

Four sketches show us the results of the Hall's implementation
of old-fashioned customs and usages. The squire insists that his
sons and Julia be true equestrians. One result of this education
was, however, that his youngest son, at Oxford, not having
enough money for both horse and tutor, dismissed the tutor.
The General tries to impress Lady Lillycraft with his courtship
by reading *The Fairy Queen,* but he "being extremely apt to fall
asleep when he reads," makes little progress. Master Simon and
the parson try to educate captured hawks to pursue game with
the aid of "well-known treatises that were the manuals of ancient
sportsmen" and "some old tapestry in the house, whereon is
represented a party of cavaliers and stately dames, with doublets,
caps, and flaunting feathers, mounted on horse, with attendants
on foot, all in animated pursuit of the game." Their efforts are
somewhat hindered by Christy, the huntsman, who treats the
hawks according to his experience with gamecocks. But they
have great hopes for success with a recent gift to the Squire, a
Welsh falcon, "a descendant of some ancient line of Welsh
princes of the air, that have long lorded it over their kingdom
of clouds."

"Hawking" culminates the Hall's attempts to restore the past.
After breakfast, "the chivalry of the Hall prepared to take the

field," along with Julia and Lady Lillycraft who was "escorted by the general, who looked not unlike one of the doughty heroes in the old prints of the battle of Blenheim." The parson and Crayon lag behind, the latter, "that I might take in the whole picture." But the tapestry soon becomes unraveled. A flock of crows having risen, the rabble urge Christy to loose the falcon which, despite the Squire's protests, he does. The falcon pursues one crow, with whom Crayon sympathizes. The crow finally evades the falcon; the falcon does not return to Christy, and Julia suffers a sprained ankle and bruises. A carriage has to be fetched for her, and the party "returned slowly and pensively to the Hall."

Thus the wedding must be postponed, gratifying only Crayon, who is growing "more and more entertained" by his characters. Although it is probable that here Irving is writing satire (the crow reminds us of Robert Greene's warning to his noble friends about Shakespeare, "an upstart crow, beautified with our feathers") he is also demonstrating the impossibility of living by books, of attempting to recall the past. The rabble does not understand what falconry is about; the common crow escapes from the noble falcon.

The last section of the first volume begins with "St. Mark's Eve" and ends with "The Student of Salamanca." "St. Mark's Eve" begins with tales told by the parson, whose mind is "infected" by superstitions. He mentions a local superstition of the dead wandering after death, then offers some of the same sort from other lands. Alone in his chamber, Crayon ponders over these tales, and concludes that such beliefs are good, even though they triumph over reason and philosophy. He finds that such a belief takes away the bitter taste of death, for "it would take away, too, from that loneliness and destitution which we are apt to feel more and more as we get on in our pilgrimage through the wilderness of this world." He would welcome such visitants, but despairs of receiving any, for, at present, "our souls are shut in and limited by bounds and barriers . . . in vain would they seek to act independently of the body, and to mingle together in spiritual intercourse . . . the most intimate friendship, of what brief and scattered portions of time does it consist!" Thus our souls are fated to be widowed until they finally meet, "where soul will dwell with soul in blissful communion, and there will be neither death, nor absence, nor any thing else to interrupt our felicity." These pre-Emersonian-like musings are at once a personalization of the pastor's recital of superstitions and a spiritualization of *The Sketch Book*'s recurring themes of separation, imprisonment, and death.

Against this background of aeriel spirits and popular superstition, Irving presents his second story, "The Student of Salamanca." Ostensibly a typical sentimental, gothic tale set in Spain, if read according to emblems previously established by Irving it becomes a powerful, and somewhat horrible, story. Throughout "The Student" we meet variations on themes used earlier in *Bracebridge Hall* or *The Sketch Book*. The hero, Antonio, although from Salamanca, is studying in the strange city of Granada. In the library, he becomes intrigued by an old man, an avid reader, and asks him, " 'cannot you spare a moment to point out the road [to wisdom] to others?' " The philosopher will not, and "there was no replying to so complete a closing of the door of intimacy." At this point, Antonio is much like Crayon, shut out of the British Museum Reading Room. So shut out, he turns to other things, to the Moorish ruins, but, "many of the basins, where the fountains had once thrown up their sparkling showers, were dry and dusty," and we are reminded of the fountain as source of literature of *The Sketch Book*.

While so wandering, the student often encounters the philosopher of the library, and one day follows him home, outside the city, to an old ruin. The philosopher is admitted by a beauty, "like a brilliant flashing from its dark casket," so beautiful that Antonio returns with daylight, only to discover that the home "had the look of a prison rather than a dwelling-house." He sees the beauty and is further enamored. Antonio lingers as "a lover lingers about the bower of sleeping beauty."

Antonio continues his visits to the prison-house, and eventually gains entrance. He discovers the philosopher is an alchemist in search of the philosopher's stone, and, after having been admitted as his student (for a fee), learns his goals: "he looked forward to the time when he should be able to go about the earth relieving the indigent, comforting the distressed; and, by his unlimited means, devising and executing plans for the complete extirpation of poverty, and all its attendant sufferings and crimes."

One night Antonio observes a noble cavalier attempting to capture Inez. He foils the attempt, wounds the noble, but is wounded in return. He learns from Inez that her suitor's attentions have been distasteful to her, that he is Don Ambrosio, whom Antonio knows as "one of the most determined and dangerous libertines in all Grenada." Because of his wounds, Antonio now lodges at the ruin, about which "the fancy of the student had thrown so much romance . . . that every thing was clothed with charms." Somewhat recovered, he persuades the two to return with him to Valencia.

They agree to go and, now almost fully recovered, Antonio, in the gardens of the Generalife, opens his heart to Inez, and she reveals hers to him. But upon leaving Inez, "he found himself suddenly seized from behind by some one of Herculean strength . . . and he was hurried off with irresistable rapidity." Up to this point, Irving is repeating a pattern familiar to those readers of "Legend of Sleepy Hollow." Again there are two claimants for the hand of an only daughter. One is a poor scholar, a stranger to the region, the other is a wealthy native. The scholar, by an act of imagination, transforms the girl's home. At the point when he seems to be having some success with his wooing, he is hurried from the neighborhood by a Herculean figure. But now, we are in a different land, an ancient land. The girl's home, instead of being a place of bounty, as was Katrina's, is now a prison, and the father a poor philosopher. The girl is now like a jewel from a casket, instead of a blooming flower. Now the fountains are dry. The competitor, instead of being a local hero, is a noble libertine who seeks the heroine for his pleasure, instead of his wife. And the story continues, does not end with the removal of the poor scholar.

The story now follows the paths of Inez and her father. Men seize and imprison the father and, as familiars of the Inquisition, take him to a prison, "one of those hideous abodes which the bad passions of men conjure up in this fair world, to rival the fancied dens of demons and the accursed." Here, the alchemist is "buried, rather than confined." He is accused of practicing necromancy and having "raised familiar spirits by his incantations, and even compelled the dead to rise from their graves." At his final examination, the alchemist eloquently vindicates the goal of his art. But this talk of relieving the poor is condemned by his judges as being "rambling, visionary," and this "stranger and sojourner" is condemned to the auto-da-fé.

But now the story turns to Inez, and her fate. She, on the pretext that she is to meet her father, is taken to Granada, passing through a revel held by the nobility "to keep up some of the gallant customs of ancient chivalry." Arrived at her destination, Inez discovers, not her father, but Don Ambrosio, who attempts her gradual seduction. She escapes and hurries toward the auto-da-fé, where "seats were arranged for the great, the gay, the beautiful" at this "gloomy pageant of superstition." Inez sees her father, reaches him, and embraces him, but is separated from him: "the rabble murmured compassion; but such was the dread inspired by the inquisition, that no one attempted to interfere." Then Don Ambrosio appears before Inez, to reclaim her. Despite her protests, he succeeds, for, "his apparent rank commanded respect and belief." This part of "The Student of Salamanca" is a complete story in itself, and a rather horrible one. On the same evening the nobility are seeking, like the Squire, to reintroduce the ancient customs of chivalry, the poor visionary philosopher, who dreams of redressing the distress of the poor, is entombed in prison, while his daughter is taken to her noble seducer. Although Inez escapes, momentarily, to liberty, she cannot save her father, despite the support of the rabble, and is compelled, because of the deference for rank, to rejoin Don Ambrosio.

At this point, Irving inserts a dash, but continues the story. After the dash, Don Antonio reappears, rescues Inez, and her father. Inez and Antonio are married; and the father is given a laboratory in the garden and lived on "to what is called a good old age, that is to say, an age that is good for nothing." In the afterpiece to "The Student of Salamanca," we are told that the general had been sleeping through the last part of the story. The general thinks the story confused, but is glad " 'they burnt the old chap of the tower; I have no doubt he was a notorious imposter.' " While Irving takes the sting off the story by, almost miraculously, transforming the poor student into a wealthy noble with family connections enough to save both Inez and the father, he still states, although indirectly, that a good old age is "an age that is good for nothing," and he allows the general, at least, to hear the story as a tragedy.

Irving's criticism of the nobility and those who would live in the past is not lessened in volume 2. In the prefatory "English Country Gentlemen," he presents the highly privileged classes who neglect their duties to the people, those "high-feeding, and, as they fancy themselves, high-minded men" who talk of putting down the mob. Irving asserts that "there is no rank nor distinction that severs him from his fellow-subject." He finds that the country estates are mortgaged, with their owners leading extravagant court lives or practicing retrenchment on the Continent. Irving especially condemns the latter: "when the poor have to diminish their scanty morsel of bread; when they have to compound with the cravings of nature, and study with how little they can do, and not be starved; it is not then for the rich to fly, and diminish still further the resources of the poor." As for those that throng the court, "that moment they lose the real nobility of their natures, and become the mere leeches of the country." Irving concludes with yet another analogy illustrating the duties of the nobility: "they may be compared to the clouds, which, being drawn up by the sun, and elevated in the heavens, reflect and magnify his splendour; while they repay the earth, from which they derive their sustenance, by returning their treasures to its bosom in fertilizing showers." Irving is trying to persuade England's hereditary aristocracy to act as Jefferson's natural aristocracy.

In "English Gravity," Crayon introduces another caricature, Mr. Faddy, a tradesman "swelling into the aristocrat," who has come to the Squire for help in discouraging the forthcoming May Day revels. As soon as he leaves, the Squire, who fosters May Day, waxes indignant over Mr. Faddy's industrial England. Trade, according to the Squire, has not only ruined the looks of the countryside, but has taken away England's merriment. Crayon, while agreeing that England is graver, attributes the change "chiefly to the gradual increase of the liberty of the subject": "it is when men are shut out of the regions of manly thought by a despotic government . . . it is then that they turn to the safer occupations of taste and amusement; trifles rise to importance, and occupy the craving activity of intellect." Once more, Irving denies the lure of the past.

In the next two sketches, however, Crayon forgets the moral, and is once more willing to be deluded. Crayon admires the Gypsies that hang around the Squire's estate; he sees them as "among the last traces, in these matter-of-fact days, of the motley population of former times; and are whimsically associated in my mind with fairies and witches, Robin Good Fellow, Robin Hood, and the other fantastical personages of poetry." In "May Day Customs," the Squire promises Crayon a "shadow of May-day." Crayon recalls his first sight of an English May-pole, which, aided by his imagination, turned "all into a perfect Arcadia." He imagines how joyous May Day must have been in ancient London, and regrets that "little is heard of May-day at present, except from the lamentations of authors." But Crayon is eager to see its recreation.

"Village Worthies" begins a series of sketches that culminates with "May Day." This section includes "The Rookery," a fine sustained conceit describing the nobility. In "May-Day" Irving sets in motion his villagers as well as the gentry from the Hall with much the same result as in "Hawking," for the day ends in turmoil and confusion. Phoebe, hoping to make young Ready-Money Jack jealous, flirts with a servant, but Jack pays court to the Queen of May. "The chivalry of a neighbouring and rival village" arrives, with band and banner, but the games degenerate into a free-for-all when Phoebe seeks to aid Jack in his wrestling match. All are involved in the melee, the Squire is scandalized, and Crayon comments that "the reader, learned in these matters, will perceive that all this was but a faint shadow of the once gay and fanciful rites of May." And he doubts "whether these rural customs of the good old times were always so very loving and innocent as we are apt to fancy them, and whether the peasantry in those times were really so Arcadian as they have been fondly represented." And yet, Crayon concludes the sketch with a poem which still admires the dream:

> "Those days were never; airy dreams
> Sat for the picture, and the poet's hand,
> Imparting substance to an empty shade,
> Impos'd a gay delirium for a truth.
> Grant it; I still must envy them an age
> That favoured such a dream."

But even "such a dream" will be denied in Irving's next story.

"Annette Delarbre" has as its narrator Lady Lillycraft's parson, who heard the story in France. This lady's parson's tale condemns the "gay delirium" substituted for truth. As with *The Sketch Book*'s "The Pride of the Village," the narrator first sees the girl at church, this time with wandering wits. He asks for her story and learns that she is the only daughter of a prosperous farmer, "the pride and delight of her parents." In early childhood, she became attached to a neighbor, Eugene La Forgue, a widow's only son. After a lover's quarrel, Eugene sails away. In a storm, his return ship is dismasted and he is swept overboard and given up for lost. This news is too much for Annette: she falls ill, then recovers, but her mind "still remained unsettled with respect to her lover's fate." At times she dresses as if for a wedding, at times she seems to realize Eugene's shipwreck. The narrator, observing her enter the church to pray, wishes that heaven "may in time rear up this broken flower to be once more the pride and joy of the valley."

As in "The Pride of the Village," the narrator returns to the church later, and enquires of Annette. When news arrives that Eugene was alive, having been rescued by an outward bound Indiaman, his mother is told the news, but it is thought best not to tell Annette. Eugene returns, but is permitted only to see the beauty, sleeping. All await the return of one of her cheerful moods. At the approach of spring, Annette wreathes her bridal chaplet, and announces that Eugene will soon return. She is permitted sight of him, but "she did not sink under it, for her fancy had prepared her for his return." Her mind was still wandering, for "there was an absolute forgetfulness of all past sorrow." Her malady worsens, "her mind appeared to have subsided into a stagnant and almost deathlike calm." At length, she opens her eyes and realizes, " 'I've been ill, and I have been dreaming strangely.' " Her physician declares her mind restored: " 'she is sensible that she has been deranged; she is growing conscious of the past, and conscious of the present.' " And so the two are wed.

In addition to repeating previous patterns from *The Sketch Book*, Irving is also returning, through Annette's madness, to his *Bracebridge Hall* themes of the role of fancy and how one should view the past. The narrator first sees her delusion as " 'one of those mists kindly diffused by Providence over the regions of thought, when they become too fruitful of misery.' " Recovery would come, he predicts, " 'as she is enabled steadily and calmly to contemplate the sorrows at present hidden in mercy from her view.' " While in "May-Day" the dream is admired, in "Annette Delarbre" the delirium is merciful, but one cannot be restored to health until one is "conscious of the past, and conscious of the present."

But Crayon refuses to learn from the tales told. In "Travelling,"

Crayon tells of visiting "the Talbot," once the Tabard Inn, starting point for Chaucer's pilgrims. While waiting for his dinner,
Crayon spends his time "conjuring up recollections of the scenes
depicted in such lively colours by the poet, until . . . my fancy
peopled the place with the motley throng of Canterbury pilgrims." These spirits are dispelled, however, "by the less poetical,
but more substantial apparition of a smoking beef-steak." Once
more the conjurer/alchemist makes his appearance, but his
visions are routed by substantial food.

"The Culprit" is as disillusioning as "Hawking" and "May-
Day." In it, Star-light Tom, a Gypsy Crayon much admired, has
been caught poaching a sheep by Ready-Money Jack, who brings
him to the Squire, the magistrate, for sentencing. Although the
Squire favors the culprit for his skill at the old-fashioned sports
and games, and especially for his skill at archery, he nevertheless
has to condemn him. Tom, "like a hawk entrapped in a dove-
cote," is imprisoned in a loft, with a gamekeeper and Christy to
watch over him. The next morning, however, Tom (with the
conjectured aid of the Devil) has escaped, and, "what has particularly relieved the Squire is, that there is very little likelihood
of the culprit's being retaken, having gone off on one of the old
gentleman's best hunters." The Robin Hood of the present is a
poacher.

In "Lover's Troubles," Irving turns to consider his characters.
It is almost time for the wedding, but, "while . . . this leading
love affair is going on with a tranquillity quite inconsistent with
the rules of romance, I cannot say that the under-plots are
equally propitious." Here, Crayon again acknowledges that he is
watching characters act out their roles. But, before the stage
wedding, Irving gives us his tale, "Dolph Heyliger," which
also features a wedding. Crayon recites the tale to the hall, but
he has received the tale from Diedrich Knickerbocker, who has
received the main elements of the tale from John Josse Vandermoere, who received it, in turn, from Dolph Heyliger, himself.
In this work, Irving uses names symbolically: "Heyliger" means
"holy one"; the other important figure is Vander Heyden, and
"Heide" means "pagan," or "savage."

"Dolph Heyliger" has been regarded by critics as intrusive to
Bracebridge Hall, it being the only American tale. Williams
dismisses it contemptuously as "a Dutch tale of money at the
bottom of a well." [12] But "Dolph" fits Irving's scheme—he has

included a tale set in England, one in Spain, one in France, and now, one set in the United States. Moreover, in this story, as in the others, we again discover that Irving's local color should not blind us to what he is really saying. This is far more than a tale "of money at the bottom of a well": it is one of Irving's most complex allegorical works and, in terms of allegory, does not concern itself with money at all. In its placement, as well as its themes, it parallels "The Student of Salamanca." Now, Dolph Heyliger is the student who, by an act of imagination, has earned the right to return home as the prodigal son.

Vandermoere opens his story by introducing Dame Heyliger, a poor widow who has to keep a shop to maintain herself and her only son. Although poor and humble, she has a feeling of family pride in being descended from the Vanderspiegels. Her son, Dolph, is "full of fun and frolic," and continually plays pranks and gets into scrapes, so much so that the town is sure he was born to be hanged. The mother and her counselor, Peter de Groodt, are perplexed as to how to settle him when Peter, on returning from the funeral of a young apprentice of a German doctor, suggests that Dolph should take the dead boy's place.

And so Dolph first enters the doctor's house. He "felt struck with awe on entering into the presence of this learned man; and gazed about him with boyish wonder at the furniture of this chamber of knowledge; which appeared to him almost as the den of a magician." This doctor/magician/alchemist agrees to take Dolph "as disciple," and so Dolph moves from his mother's to the doctor's. Thus far Dolph follows the pattern set by Antonio in becoming the alchemist's disciple. But Dolph has no Inez; instead there is the crabbed housekeeper, Frau Ilsy.

As Dolph nears the end of his apprenticeship, as he nears the "M.D." his mother dreamed of for him, the doctor and the housekeeper become more and more irked by him. He has learned little medicine, cultivating instead other talents, such as shooting, riding, wrestling, swimming, and playing the fiddle. Then, too, the doctor's state of mind is made worse by rumors that his country house is haunted. Dolph, eager to escape his uncomfortable life, volunteers to "garrison the haunted house." He had been listening to the tales about it, but "he was fond of adventure, he loved the marvellous, and his imagination had become quite excited by these tales of wonder." Escorted by the doctor and Peter de Groodt, he goes that night, past the neighboring frog-filled swamp, to the old house, whose "splendour, however, was all at an end."

Left alone, Dolph is pondering his misdeeds when he hears footsteps enter his room, but sees no one. The second night, he sees the figure of "an elderly man, large and robust, clothed in the old Flemish fashion," but who says nothing. The third night, Dolph gathers enough nerve to ask the figure the reason for his visit, but the figure only rises and, indicating that Dolph is to follow him, goes out of the house, through the orchard, to a well, where he disappears. Dolph looks in the well, but sees only a reflection. He returns to his room and dreams about the figure, a voyage, a strange town, and a return voyage home "with a great bag of money!" On awakening, Dolph wanders about the fields, finds himself at the waterfront, where a sloop is preparing to sail for Albany, a voyage as momentous in those days "as a voyage to Europe is at present."

Startled there to recognize the captain from his dream, Dolph gets on board when the captain tells him to, and the sloop casts off. Dolph feels himself "under supernatural influence," remembers his mother with a pang, but then "the inspiring love of novelty and adventure came rushing in full tide through his bosom; he felt himself launched strangely and suddenly on the world, and under full way to explore the regions of wonder that lay . . . beyond those blue mountains that had bounded his horizon since childhood." Despite seeming "to be moving continuously in a delusion," Dolph makes up his mind to enjoy the voyage. Once more Irving has one of his characters willing to participate in a delusion, even while admitting it might be a "feverish fantasy."

As the sloop enters the Highlands and the region of echoes surrounding the Dunderberg, Dolph watches "a pile of bright, snowy clouds." But the clouds change, "their summits still bright and snowy, but the lower parts of an inky blackness." In the midst of the ensuing storm, a sudden gust of wind hits the ship, the boom swings round and knocks Dolph, "who was gazing unguardedly at the clouds," into the river. Dolph reaches shore with great difficulty, and attempts to penetrate inland, "but all was savage and trackless": "the rocks were piled upon each other, great trunks of trees lay scattered about." He tries to scale the heights, but is hindered by birds, and once by a snake which quickly coils, then glides away. Dolph "saw at a glance that he was in the vicinity of a nest of adders, that lay knotted, and writhing, and hissing in the chasm." At length he gains one height, only to find all wild and solitary. His foot dislodges a rock, which falls into the chasm below. Immediately a gun resounds, "and a ball came whistling over his head." With this, Dolph is "determined to penetrate no further into a country so beset with savage perils."

Dolph's dreams have turned into a nightmare in this savage land, these Highlands. It is not a coincidence that Dolph's smooth voyage is hindered by black clouds and by trees that encumber the ground, Irving's earlier emblems for the nobility. And, in this section, again and again Irving repeats that these Highlands are a "savage" land, complete with its nest of vipers. Finally Dolph sees a light, the only light in the savage land, and makes his way toward it. Nearing, Dolph is startled at seeing, "by the full glare falling on painted featues, and glittering on silver ornaments . . . an Indian." Again terrified in "so savage and lonely a place," he is about to retreat when his presence is discovered and he is welcomed to the fire by "a large stout man, somewhat advanced in life, but hale and hearty."

Thus we are introduced to Antony Vander Heyden, the only light in the savage wilderness, the commander of the Highland party, the stout gentleman. Not surprisingly, he bears a strong resemblance to Sir Walter Scott. In him, Dolph perceives a resemblance to "the old man of the Haunted House," despite his modern dress. Dolph, on being given his name, recalls that Vander Heyden is an almost legendary figure who "was a man of property, having had a father before him, from whom he inherited . . . whole barrels full of wampum, [and] he could indulge his humours without control." He likes "the Indian mode of life, which he considered true natural liberty and manly enjoyment," and, when at home, always had several Indians loitering about the house. He had perfect command over them, "though they were great nuisances to the regular people of his neighborhood." In "Gypsies," Irving had compared the Gypsy life to the Indian life, here, the Indians seem more like Gypsies. After supper, "there were many legendary tales told, also, about the river, and the settlements on its borders; in which valuable kind of lore the Heer Antony seemed deeply versed."

Vander Heyden believes "that these highlands were under the dominion of supernatural and mischievous beings." On hearing

Dolph's story of being knocked overboard, he identifies the
perpetrator as the captain of a storm ship, which legend he tells
Dolph, giving it from a manuscript of Mynheer Seleyne, "an
early poet of the New Nederlandts." Antony, shocked by Dolph's
dry course of study under the doctor, and feeling that one of his
abilities "could never fail to make his way," invites him to his
home while he looks about him. Dolph accepts, thinking that
Antony is connected with his dream. The party arrives at Albany,
Dolph admires "the neatness of this worthy burgh," but admires
more Antony's daughter, "a little, plump, blooming lass, his only
child, and the darling of his heart." Dolph promptly falls in love
with her.

That night Antony escorts Dolph to a bed chamber: he is
about to extinguish the candle, when he sees the figure of the
Haunted House, now in a portrait on the wall. He dreams that
the figure in the portrait "descended from the wall . . . that he
followed it, and found himself by the well, to which the old man
pointed, smiled on him, and disappeared." The next morning
Dolph is told by Antony that the portrait is one of his ancestors,
Killian Vander Spiegel, who was a miser, and who was rumored
to have buried his wealth. Dolph reflects on this, and concludes
that, through his mother, the old mansion is the land of his forefathers, that both he and Vander Heyden are descended from
the Vander Spiegels, and that he is to find the wealth of their
ancestor, marry Vander Heyden's daughter, "thus both branches
of the family will be again united." Inspired by this dream of
using the past to unite present disparate parties, Dolph determines to return to the well in the garden, despite the evident
disappointment of Heer Antony and his daughter.

On his arrival in New York, Dolph first seeks his mother's
house, but finds it "a heap of ruins." He joyfully finds his mother
still alive, living with Peter de Groodt. The next morning, Dolph
revisits the Haunted House and the well, having provided himself with a heavy fishing line. He fishes in the well, and pulls up
much trash, and, finally, a silver porringer (that relic of childhood), embossed with the Vander Spiegel arms, filled with broad
golden pieces. He repeats his angling until "he had hooked up
wealth enough to make him, in those moderate days, a rich
burgher for life." The rest, according to Vandermoere, is too
"tedious to detail"—how Heyliger hid the source of his wealth,
how he married Vander Heyden's daughter, how the two men

often roistered together. Dolph took great care of his mother, became a distinguished citizen, and died. His epitaph was written "by his friend Mynheer Justus Benson, an ancient and excellent poet of the province." Vandermoere swears to the truth of the tale, for he heard it from Dolph Heyliger himself, and Dolph Heyliger "was noted for being the ablest drawer of the long-bow [biggest storyteller] in the whole province."

"Dolph Heyliger" repeats many of the themes of *The Sketch Book* and *Bracebridge Hall.* Here we have the old patterns of the widow and her son, the only daughter of a prosperous landholder, the fountain (well) long disused, the alchemist, the clouds, the forest trees, the angler, unburied spirits, and the return of the prodigal son. We also have the wedding of two branches of the same family, united by Dolph's plumbing the well for the wealth of the past. Having succeeded in his enterprise, Dolph is able to return home, to be a success, and to have his epitaph written by Mynheer Justus Benson. As in *The Sketch Book*, this undertaking is premature. Mynheer Justus Benson is Mr. Justice Egbert Benson, who had written a critique of Irving's "The Wife." [13] Since Benson is described as a poet, but is a critic, it is all too probable that the other poet, Selyne, is another of Irving's critics. But Dolph disregards the critics, ignores his tuition at Dr. Knipperhausen's, leaves the Highlands to pursue his vision there gained, plumbs the well, and succeeds. Dolph does what Crayon does throughout *Bracebridge Hall,* that is, sets portraits to life and uses the past to view the present. Allegorically, Dolph does what Irving has done.

After "Dolph Heyliger," "The Wedding" seems only an obligatory tying up of the ends. Everything goes as supposed, Julia and the Captain are wed, Phoebe and Jack are reconciled, Lady Lillycraft wins old Jack over to their union, Hannah announces her intention to wed old Christy. The only pair that are not united is the General and Lady Lillycraft, which is not surprising, since her character is that of "the widow" and she cannot escape from it. After the wedding, Crayon makes his own departure.

In "The Author's Farewell," Crayon makes his good-byes to England. This farewell is not surprising, considering the omnipresent images of sterility and decadence. In his farewell, he asserts that he has not viewed England with a partial eye, that he has been " 'a stranger and a sojourner in the land,' " even though this land is his " 'father land.' " The English character, he observes, is "a character not to be hastily studied, for it always puts on a repulsive and ungracious aspect to a stranger." Despite this, Crayon congratulates himself that his *Sketch Book* essay, "English Writers on America," seems to have had an effect, which proves "what I have all along believed and asserted, that the two nations would grow together in esteem and amity, if meddling and malignant spirits would but throw by their mischievous pens." Crayon feels that "to the magnanimous spirits of both countries must we trust to carry such a natural alliance of affection into full effect," thus repeating his wedding metaphor. But, despite his pleasure with the new alliance, Crayon is ready to leave "the paternal soil," although he gives, in leaving, a final "filial" benediction: " 'Peace be within thy walls, oh England! and plenteousness within thy palaces; for my brethren and my companions' sake I will now say, Peace be within thee!' "

Few of Irving's readers understood *Bracebridge Hall*; few understood that his characters were previously created characters from the past. Most readers said, "no family such as this exists," not realizing that such a family did exist—in literature. The characters and scenes are idealized and were idealized when first created. Such characters cannot cope—and never could cope —with reality. *Bracebridge Hall* has "odd matter, strange and merrie, / Well sauc'd with lies and glared all with glee." It is, too, Crayon's retreat to the "gay delirium" of the past, because, like Annette, he cannot face the horrors of the present.

IV Tales of a Traveller

Irving is at his least gentle, most despairing in *Tales of a Traveller*, which contains some of his strongest work. Throughout the work are echoes of Robert Greene's title, "A Groatsworth of Wit, bought with a million of Repentance," and signs of Irving's frustration with being misunderstood. Again and again he has a narrator tell a tale, only to have his hearers ask for further details, details that are unnecessary to the truth of the tale. He tells us that these stories are lies, that the reader is being misdirected: "while the simple reader is listening with open mouth to a ghost or a love story, he may have a bolus of sound morality popped down his throat, and be never the wiser for the fraud." In a letter to Paulding, he says, "I consider a story merely as a frame on which to stretch my materials." [14] But, because of his skill at misdirection, most of his readers failed to perceive the satire and allegory underlying the stories—and this, in an age when allegories, fables, and *romans à clef* flourished. Some did; for the first time he was accused of being political. Whereas *Bracebridge Hall* closes with a wedding and the hope for a union, a closer bonding of the English and American cousins by recognition of their common heritage, many of these tales declare that such a union is impossible, that such a hope is the delirium of a madman. While *Tales of a Traveller* does end with a wedding, it is a wedding made possible only by a liberal king's decision to cut up his great estates for the benefit of the many.

Of the four sections of *Tales of a Traveller*, the first, "Tales of a Nervous Gentleman" is the strongest and most closely knit. The section is prefaced by this quotation from Fletcher:

> "I'll tell you more, there was a fish taken,
> A monstrous fish, with a sword by's side, a long sword,
> A pike in's neck, and a gun in's nose, a huge gun,
> And letters of mart in's mouth from the Duke of Florence.
> *Cleanthes.* This is a monstrous lie.
> *Tony.* I do confess it.
> Do you think I'd tell you truths?"

The stories in this first part are lies, but in them are concealed Irving's truths, conveyed through his themes and metaphors. The nervous gentleman sets the scene for the stories in "an ancient rook-haunted family mansion" where a hunting party has gathered. Forced to spend the night, the guests pass the time telling ghost stories, the first of which is "The Adventure of My Uncle." The plot has the uncle seeing a ghost in a French chateau and telling his host, a marquis, of his vision. The marquis does not believe his guest. But the plot is a lie, while the truth is in the way it is told.

The uncle is, like Irving/Crayon, " 'a great traveller, and fond of telling his adventures.' " He leaves "the miserable lodgment and miserable fare of a provincial inn" for a chateau "standing naked and alone in the midst of a desert of gravel walks and cold stone terraces . . . and fountains spouting cold water." His host tells stories of "the prowress of his ancestors" and displays a huge sword "as proof that there had been giants in his family." But the giants are no more, and the marquis was "but a small descendant

from such great warriors." The uncle is reconciled to his com-
fortless rooms where a breeze "came in as damp and chilly as if
from a dungeon" by the thought of "the great personages who
had once inhabited them." He awakens from sleep to see a lady,
dressed in ancient dress, before the fire. The next morning the
uncle sees a portrait of the lady and asks her identity. The
marquis finally reveals that the long-dead lady once spent the
night in the uncle's room and that a mysterious event transpired
there. The uncle tells of seeing the lady, but the marquis merely
says "Bah!" and walks away. The auditors of the hunting dinner
want to know more of the lady and her story, but there is no
more to tell, for the true story is the traveler's description of his
stay in the cold, ancient dungeonlike mansion, formerly inhabited
by giants (Irving's *Sketch Book* description of England) and
of his vision, which is not believed.

In "The Adventure of my Aunt," the aunt bears her jewels to
her bedroom, is preparing for bed when she sees, in her mirror,
an eye of a portrait move. She calls her servants, who take
down the portrait, and haul forth a "varlet, with a knife as long
as my arm . . . a marauding Tarquin, who had stolen into her
chamber to violate her purse." She punishes the interloper, and
marries "a roystering squire," which an auditor thinks is a pity;
she should have married the uncle of the previous story: "they
certainly would have been well matched." In place of marriage,
there is implication of distorted sexual union, of attempted rape.
In "The Bold Dragoon," Irving changes to broad burlesque, and
describes another interloper and another downfall.

"The Adventure of the German Student" more seriously denies
the possibility of marriage. Through too much study, the student's mind had become "diseased . . . he had an ideal world of
his own"; thus Irving continues the infection and contagion
metaphors of *Bracebridge Hall.* His friends hope to cure him by
sending him abroad, to Paris. But there he continues his studies
in the great libraries: "He was, in a manner, a literary goul,
feeding in the charnel-house of decayed literature." Too shy to
meet women, he dreams of them, and creates "a female face of
transcendent beauty . . . he became passionately enamoured of
this shadow of a dream." One night he meets the image of his
dream at the foot of a guillotine, takes her to his room—again a
dismal room in a mansion of former splendor—announces his
love, and suggests marriage by common consent. The lady agrees,

and they spend the night blissfully together. The next morning, the student returns from an errand to find the lady dead; a gendarme recognizes her as one who had been guillotined, undoes her neckband, and her head falls to the floor. The student goes to a madhouse. The ideal world does not correspond to the real, the study of past literature is a "disease," the vision of union is madness, for the sexual partner is already dead.

The rest of part 1 is concerned with a portrait viewed by the nervous gentleman in his bedchamber. Whether this portrait has a strange influence or not (whether it is a truth or a lie) is never made clear. In "The Adventure of the Mysterious Picture," the host bids his guests good night, warning them that one chamber is "peculiar." The nervous gentleman goes to his, and "could not but smile at the resemblance in style to those eventful apartments described in the tales of the supper table." The resemblance is strengthened when, after awakening from a nightmare, he focuses on a painting of a face, mistaking it for a real face at first. He fancies it has a "chilling, creeping influence," and looks elsewhere, but "caught a reflection of this accursed visage in the pane of glass," as the aunt had seen the painting reflected in the mirror. The rest of the room, too, grows more fearful: "there was a huge dark clothes-press of antique form . . . that began to grow oppressive to me," thus echoing "The Bold Dragoon." Although he concludes, like the German student, " 'it is my own diseased imagination that torments me,' " he still resolves to quit the room, and does: "the moment I found my self out of the neighbourhood of that strange picture, it seemed as if the charm were broken."

The next morning, the other guests mock him for his departure, but the host defends him, saying the picture did have a mysterious influence. He then explains it by recounting "The Adventure of the Mysterious Stranger" and its story, "The Young Italian." After hearing these stories, the guests desire to see the portrait, and all return suitably impressed. The nervous gentleman wonders at their unanimous reaction. The host agrees that such unanimity is remarkable, especially since none had seen the right portrait; the host had misdirected them. The picture they see is a lie—the guests believe it, since they have been influenced by their host's stories. But was the nervous gentleman's portrait also a lie, he believing in its influence because of the previous stories? Thus, "The Adventure of the Mysterious

Picture" is stylistically central to part 1, summing up, as it does, the previous tales and preparing the reader for the following ones.

"The Story of the Young Italian" in the final position of the section shares characteristics with previous stories so positioned, especially "The Student of Salamanca" and "Dolph Heyliger." "The Young Italian" parallels their themes, then goes beyond them; while they promise a marriage and a union, here the promised marriage comes to naught. The story describes a murder, while the themes and metaphors describe the tragedy of an author whose works are considered childish in his fatherland. The young Italian's father treats his younger son with indifference; he was "neglected, or noticed only to be crossed and contradicted." He is sent to a convent headed by an uncle "totally estranged from the world." There he is "immured," but becomes "expert with my pencil." In the convent, "the tomb of the living," he dreams of the outside world where "all the men appeared amiable, all the women lovely." Influenced by this dream, he leaves the convent, returning to his father, who "entertained no recollection of my person . . . I was doomed never to be properly known there." The father schemes to return him to the convent, he rebels, and embarks in a ship for the north. Up to this point, "The Young Italian" parallels "Dolph Heyliger" who leaves his ancestor's house after years of dry study with Dr. Knipperhausen.

As Dolph did, the young Italian finds a mentor in the north—this time a painter, who encourages him in his art. The young Italian "looked up to my master as to a benevolent genius that had opened to me a region of enchantment." The student falls in love with a girl, whom his imagination "elevated . . . into something almost more than mortal." After his master's death, a wealthy Count becomes his patron and he becomes friendly with the Count's only son, Filippo. The orphaned Bianca, the girl of his dreams, is sheltered by the Count, and the painter falls further in love. She causes "a delicious madness," and "a kind of idolatry," "then it was that the world around me was indeed a paradise." Like Dolph, he realizes his own poverty; he cannot drag Bianca to his level; and he feels as if he has abused the villa's hospitality, "as if I were a thief within its walls."

At this point he reads of his brother's death, and his father's appeal for him to return as the heir. He tells his story to Filippo, who engages to be the channel through which he and Bianca can correspond. Like Dolph, he returns to his fatherland and "felt like the prodigal son returned. I was a stranger in the house of my father." At this stage, Dolph concluded happily, but "The Young Italian" has a grimmer ending. His father, while still alive, is an intellectual and physical ruin, and the Italian can only write to Bianca through the medium of the young Count. He shows his father his pencil sketches of Bianca, "but he was too far sunk in intellect to take any more than a child-like notice of them"—an allegorically damning statement.

Finally, after his father's death, the young Italian returns to the north to claim Bianca, to forge the union. But Bianca, having been informed by the young Count that the Italian had died, had married the Count. She now shows "a whole history of a mind broken down by tyranny." He sees Filippo, stabs him to death, and then, "I fled forth from the garden like another Cain." He is haunted by the face of the corpse—to seek relief, he paints his picture. It is this portrait he leaves the host before he returns to Genoa to do penance. Again the union is denied, again the vision itself has been debased.

Poe said of originality, "to originate, is carefully, patiently, and understandingly to combine," [15] and few can surpass Irving's art of combining and recombining themes to produce apparently different stories. While the second section, "Buckthorne and his Friends," is not as intense as the first, it parallels the first, repeating its patterns and images. What was tragedy in the first now becames comedy, cartoon, and caricature. Perhaps in keeping with the tone, Irving gives "Buckthorne" a surprising, happy ending. The moral of the section, voiced by three characters, is that " 'the only happy author in this world is he who is below the care of reputation.' " The happy ending is possible only because Buckthorne abandons literature and poetry. Throughout the section, literature is termed a dream, a delusion, a seeming fairyland, but " 'the charm fades on a nearer approach, and the thorns and briers become visible.' "

"Buckthorne and his Friends" is a rambling, loosely organized comic and satiric look at theatrical and literary life in England. The section is presented by the traveler who is guided about London by Buckthorne. They go to "A Literary Dinner," visit "The Club of Queer Fellows," and hear the story of "The Poor Devil Author," a story which closely parallels Irving's early years in England. Buckthorne offers to tell the story of his life, but refuses to tell of his literary adventures: "let those who have never ventured into the republic of letters still look upon it as a fairy land."

His story, which appears as "Buckthorne: or, the Young Man of Great Expectations," is a comic rendition of "The Young Italian," with some new variations. The hero has a poetic temperament; his mother admires his poems, his father throws them out the window, his uncle (from whom he hopes to inherit) is contemptuous of them. He sends verses to Sacharissa, and is flogged for his pains. He runs away, joins a traveling theatrical troupe, falls in love with Columbine, and is flogged by Harlequin. Just then he is "kidnapped" back to his father's land and sent to a new school, then to Oxford, where he writes verses to a shopkeeper's daughter and sprains his ankle falling out of her window. After more misadventures, he hears his uncle has died, and travels to the ill-kept estate, only to find the heir is a lout, a previously unacknowledged son. His caricature is given in "The Booby Squire"—and a vicious caricature it is. More genial, and funnier, is the inserted "The Strolling Manager," detailing the vexations endured by the manager of a provincial theater.

The traveler is about to conclude this section, although regretting Buckthorne's decision not to tell of his literary life, for, "owing to the extreme fecundity of the press, and the thousand anecdotes, criticisms, and biographical sketches that are daily poured forth concerning public characters, it is extremely difficult to get at any truth concerning them." Once more we are told that the written word is a lie. Juxtaposed to this is Buckthorne's happy ending: the booby squire dies in a hunting accident and wills the estate to Buckthorne, who gives up literature, puts the estate in order, and marries Sacharissa. He writes to the traveler, inviting him to come to Doubting Castle and hear his story, " 'and a rattling history it shall be about authors and reviewers.' " The traveler promises this history to his readers, and gives it to them in the next section, "The Italian Banditti." Although all the tales are set in Italy, they contain allegories depicting the literary feuds of English and Scotch authors (travelers) and reviewers (bandits).

In the introductory "The Inn at Terracina," Irving describes the locale and principal characters of the section. He locates Terracina "on the frontiers of the Roman territory," in a mountainous region where vipers are plentiful, a region also plentifully infested with robbers. Arrived at the inn are a newly married Venetian couple (the lady believes implicitly in every tale she hears) and an Englishman (who disbelieves most of the tales). He is in a bad mood, perhaps "he was a little sore from having been fleeced at every stage of his journey," but agrees to dine with the Venetians. During dinner, the landlord, "like a true narrator of the terrible," gives the latest tales of the robbers, but the Englishman refuses to believe them, terming them "mere travellers' tales." More travelers arrive and they tell more tales. Of these, "The Adventure of the Little Antiquary" is probably an allegory, while "The Adventure of the Popkins Family" may only be a caricature of the English traveling on the Continent. "The Belated Travellers" depicts Thomas Moore as the Polish Count, his exile, and his defense of Spain with his *Rhymes on the Road, Fables for the Holy Alliance.*

The major story of this section is "The Painter's Adventure," which includes within it "The Story of the Bandit Chieftain" and the powerful "The Story of the Young Robber." The exterior story closely parallels that part of "Dolph Heyliger" that takes place in the Highlands, duplicating its events and imagery. The duplication begins with the afterpiece of the Popkins's story, as a Frenchman, the Englishman, and the Venetians stroll to the beach, where they see galley slaves, convicted robbers, rolling upon the sand. The Venetian compares them to " 'so many serpents writhing together,' " an image reminding us of Dolph's encounter with the nest of vipers. The Frenchman then volunteers the story of his encounter with the robbers.

This Frenchman is "an historical painter by profession" and, at the time of the story, was employed by a prince who lived not far from Rome. One evening the Frenchman encounters bandits, one of whom seizes him, thinking him the prince. The painter seeks to escape by attacking the bandit, but he is attacked in turn by another, and wounded. After he is borne away, the bandits discover their mistake. The chieftain "darted at me a ferocious look—swore I had deceived him, and caused him to miss his fortune." So far, there are four points of similarity between this and "Dolph": the encounter with the vipers, the hero threatening the life of one of the native party, the retaliation, and the chieftain's admission of being deceived (Vander Heyden thought Dolph a deer) and of missing his aim.

As in "Dolph," the next scene is the campfire of the hunting party-robbers. The painter describes the landscape as "savage," made still more savage by groups of banditti. The captain decides to make the most of his prize, and demands, as ransom for the painter, three thousand dollars. The artist finds the bandit chieftain, like Vander Heyden, "sociable and communicative": "I had my book of sketches in my hand; he requested to see it, and after having run his eye over it, expressed himself convinced of the truth of my assertion, that I was a painter." Whereas Vander Heyden had advised Dolph, now the painter advises the chieftain: "he had talents and qualities fitted for a nobler sphere of action . . . in a legitimate career, the same courage and endowments which now made him an object of terror would ensure him the applause and admiration of society." The chieftain agrees, but asserts that "it was the oppression of others, rather than my own crimes, which drove me to the mountains." He then tells the artist his story, "The Story of the Bandit Chieftain."

Then the artist probes the "ulcerated heart" of one of the robbers, and draws from him "The Story of the Young Robber," one of the grimmest of all of Irving's tales. The young man, "considered one of the smartest young fellows" of his village, falls in love with the daughter of a surveyor or land-baliff, she was "so different from the sun-burnt females to which I had been accustomed." Her father has no good opinion of him, however, and "brought home a suitor for her, a rich farmer, from a neighbouring town." He meets the bridegroom in the marketplace and, in a rage, kills him. He flees to the church for asylum, where the bandit chieftain "came to me in secret, and made such offers, that I agreed to enrol myself among his followers." Now a member of the band, the young robber continues to dream of the girl, Rosetta.

Later, when the band is again near his village, he catches sight of the girl in her father's vineyard. He shows himself, the girl shrieks, which brings the rest of the band upon them. The chieftain deems her a prize, to be held for ransom. The young robber urges his individual claim on the basis of his love, but this is denied by the captain, who reminds him that all prizes are parceled out by lot. He is, however, allowed to bear this "treasure" to the mountain retreat. He and the band are sent off on an errand; when they return, the chief has despoiled the girl. Then she is forced to write a ransom note demanding three hundred dollars: "it was with extreme difficulty and by guiding her hand that she was made to trace a few characters." Lots are cast and she is turned over to another of the band. The young robber feels he is in hell. His companions seem to him "like so many fiends exulting in the downfall of an angel." The father refuses to pay the ransom, thus, by the laws of the robber band, the girl must be killed. The young robber pleads to be her executioner: "I will do it as surely, but more tenderly than another." The chieftain grants him his wish: "I hastened to seize upon my prey. There was a forlorn kind of triumph at having at length become her exclusive possessor." While she is sleeping, he stabs her and she dies.

The truth contained in the story is somewhat less sensational than the story itself. The young robber depicts Thomas Young, a brilliant man who, among other works, had published studies on the heart (which the artist probes). He is more famous, however, for his work on the Rosetta Stone, vying with the Frenchman Champollion (the rich farmer from the neighboring village) as to which had first translated the demotic inscriptions on the stone. His first transcriptions of a few glyphs appeared in the *Encyclopedia Britannica* in 1818, the same year Young was given an honorary post paying three hundred pounds—not dollars. After having been attacked in the *Edinburgh Review*, he wrote for the *Quarterly Review* established by Scott—thus joining the chieftain's band.[16] But this tale of authors and reviewers is overwhelmed by the starkness of the tale itself, which is strongly comparable to "The German Student." Again, the idealized girl dies, the wedding is negated, the bride has been raped by others. This tale is light-years away from the genteel wedding of *Bracebridge Hall*.

Apparently, even the Englishman believed the Frenchman's stories, for the next day he hires an escort of soldiers to convoy him to Fondi. The Venetians ask that they be allowed to join him, and he assents. They forge ahead, however, as he is delayed. The escort and the Englishman catch up with the Venetians, only to discover their carriage overturned and surrounded by banditti. A general engagement ensues, a battle worthy of Peter Stuyvesant and Jan Risingh, except that here corpses litter the landscape. The Englishman, by himself, pursues the two robbers who have carried off the lady. One robber fires directly at him—and carries off his hat. The other fires—the shot passes between his side and arm. One draws a stilleto and closes with him on the edge of a precipice. The other rushes to his comrade's aid. At the last moment, the Englishman's servant arrives and shoots one bandit, while the Englishman dashes the remaining robber "headlong from the precipice." The Englishman then collects the insensible lady and restores her to her husband. When she recovers, she embraces the Englishman, calling him " 'my deliverer!—my angel!' " To this, the Englishman responds, appropriately, " 'this is all humbug.' " Again we are told, to our faces, that the story is a lie. The story is told in such detail, and with such verve, that we disbelieve the truth, and prefer the lie.

"The Money Diggers" is the last, and least, section. It has generally been regarded as being tacked on, since its stories are set in the United States. But the section is also inconsistent because it focuses on politics and economy, rather than on literature. In the introductory sketch, "Hell-Gate," Irving uses a New York place name to further underline his devil-angel metaphor, as well as to give a true place as the locale of the stories. For Knickerbocker, the narrator, Hell-Gate "was a place of great awe and perilous enterprise for me in my boyhood." It was, then, "a region of fable and romance," abounding with tales of pirates (instead of banditti) and buried money. In later years, Knickerbocker researched the truth of these stories: "in seeking to dig up one fact, it is incredible the number of fables which I unearthed." Our belief in pirates and their treasure extends to the stories; in them, we read of pirates as pirates and treasure as treasure, disregarding Knickerbocker's warning about fables.

"The Devil and Tom Walker," we are told, is a story of Kidd's buried money, and yet we never see either Kidd or the money—the truth lies elsewhere. While the strongest story of the section, occasionally Irving's allegory gets in the way of the story; his allusions, while probably consistent with themselves, produce inconsistencies. The protagonist of the story, Tom Walker, is one of Irving's most unlikeable. He is a "meagre miserly fellow," who dwells near Boston in a "forlorn-looking house, that stood alone" in a "land of famine." He has a wife as miserly as himself, and many are the conflicts between them "about what ought to have been common property." Any wayfarer "eyed the den of discord askance, and hurried on his way, rejoicing, if a bachelor, in his celibacy." While the wife is new, we have encountered the dilapidated mansion before, and, in the *Tales*, this aversion to marriage.

One day, Tom cuts through a swamp, supposed to be the devil's region. He sees a black man who introduces himself—he goes by many names, but, "in this neighbourhood I am known by the name of the black woodman." Tom continued the conversation, for "he had lived so long with a termagant wife, that he did not even fear the devil." The black woodman offers him treasure, but only on conditions, which Tom eventually accepts, and turns usurer.

Tom subsequently does very well, foreclosing mortgages, gaining land and more land. But then he grew fearful of the devil, turned devout Christian, became "a stern supervisor and censurer of his neighbours, and seemed to think every sin entered up to their account became a credit on his own side of the page." He built himself "a vast house out of ostentation, but left the greater part of it unfinished and unfurnished out of parsimony." One day, as he is at his counting house, the devil calls for him, in the midst of a thunderstorm, puts him on a great black horse, which rushes him back to the savage land: "shortly after a thunderbolt fell in that direction, which seemed to set the whole forest in a blaze." The narrator asserts of the story, "the truth of it is not to be doubted." If, in this story, Irving is giving us allegorical truths, it is one of the most vicious portraits he ever sketched.

The last story of *Tales of a Traveller*, "Wolfert Webber: or Golden Dreams," is a fable that ends with a wedding which is achieved only by the realization of certain conditions—conditions which had not been met when Irving was writing the tale. Thus, the tale itself is but a "golden dream." Unlike the earlier tales, here, at least, Irving does admit that such a dream is possible. "Wolfert" is introduced by Knickerbocker, again in the Hell-Gate region, but is told by John Josse Vandermoere. This tale is of a Dutch cabbage farmer who comes to realize that his land is more valuable than any pirate's hoard. But the metaphors tell a different story; they tell of a King who yearns mightily to enjoy the splendors of the past, but who is prevented from doing so by his fear of the example of the French Revolution. He desires to join the reactionary Holy Alliance in its repression of the revolutions in Spain's colonies, but is saved from this by his lawyer's convincing him that the way to wealth is to partition his estate

and make his tenants happy—thereby becoming the first gentleman in Europe.

Irving is consistent in his metaphors—in them lie his truth.
Wolfert Webber comes from a long line of cabbage-raising
"potentates": if their portraits had been taken, "they would have
presented a row of heads marvellously resembling, in shape and
magnitude, the vegetables over which they reigned"—a nice,
biting comment. A Dutch house was "the seat of government,"
and their "palace" became threatened by the progress of the
city: "still, however, they maintained their hereditary character
and hereditary possessions with all the tenacity of petty German
princes in the midst of the empire." Wolfert, "the last of the line"
(George IV had no direct heir), "swayed the sceptre of his
fathers, a kind of rural potentate in the midst of a metropolis."
Thus Wolfert "reigned and vegetated," although he, "like all
other sovereigns" had his troubles. His chief worry, however, was
inflation and its result: "while every one around him grew richer,
Wolfert grew poorer; and he could not, for the life of him, perceive how the evil was to be remedied." In his troubles, Wolfert
goes to an outlying inn where Ramm Rapelye was the "dictator,"
whose "word was decisive with his subjects." The inn furnishes
Wolfert with tales of buried treasure of the past. After hearing
these tales of past riches, Wolfert returns to his "little realm"
more unhappy than ever. He goes to sleep and dreams "that he
had discovered an immense treasure in the centre of his garden."
Dreaming this two times more, he decides the dream is true, and
so, at nights, he "went to work to rip up and dig about his
paternal acres from one end to the other." Soon, the garden,
"which had presented such a goodly and regular appearance . . .
was reduced to a scene of devastation."

Seeking companionship, Wolfert again visits the inn; many of
the old frequenters are there, "but one was missing, the great
Ramm Rapelye, who for many years had filled the leather-
bottomed chair of state." In his place was a stranger, "rather
under size," who ordered everybody about with "an authoritative
air." Wolfert is curious about this stranger, "who had thus
usurped absolute sway in this ancient domain." He is told that
the dictator had arrived with a great sea chest, always had
plenty of money, "regularly paid his bill every evening," and
"began to encroach upon the long established customs and

customers of the place, and to interfere, in a dictatorial manner . . . until in the end he usurped an absolute command over
the whole inn." Finally, "he took possession of the sacred elbow-
chair, which, time out of mind, had been the seat of sovereignty
of the illustrious Ramm Rapelye . . . from this time Ramm
Rapelye appeared no more at the inn; and his example was
followed by several of the most eminent customers." Wolfert is
amazed at this tale, "a wonderful instance of the revolutions of
mighty empires, to find the venerable Ramm Rapelye thus ousted
from the throne, and a rugged tarpawling dictating from his
elbow chair . . . filling this tranquil little realm with brawl and
bravado." Irving's metaphors tell the tale of the French Revolution, the deposing of the king, the ascendancy of Napoleon to
the dictatorship, and his domination of Europe.

During the reign of the dictator, Wolfert listens to more tales
of treasure. One, "The Adventure of the Black Fisherman," inspires Wolfert to seek treasure where Sam saw men in red caps
burying a body. His "infected fancy" turns the red caps into a
crew of pirates burying their gold (another instance of a story
being misunderstood). He seeks out Mud Sam, who agrees to
guide Wolfert to the cove by land. They find a ridge on which
Wolfert discovers three crosses, "nearly obliterated by the moss
that had grown over them." Even so, Sam does not know where
to dig, and they return home. As they go through the desolate
garden of the deserted house, they see a figure, wearing a cap
"of a most sanguinary red" approaching a vault. Wolfert, in
horror, recognizes him as the dictator.

Back home, Wolfert has great conflict of mind; he fears the
red cap, but wants the wealth of the three crosses. (The three
crosses are an emblem of the Holy Alliance, which pledged the
signatories to Christian behavior in foreign policy and reaffirmed
the divine right of kings. It was reactionary, and opposed the
revolutions in Spain's American colonies. George IV and England
did not join, but gave signs of doing so before the Monroe Doctrine.) Wolfert's wife and daughter, seeing this "returning touch
of insanity," consult a high German doctor, who, on hearing
Wolfert's confessions, is infected himself and offers to join
Wolfert. But to find the wealth of the three crosses, they must
first have a divining rod (the divine right): "which had the
wonderful property of pointing to the very spot on the surface

of the earth under which treasure lay hidden." The doctor agrees to fashion the rod and to accompany Wolfert to the location of the three crosses.

On the appointed night, Wolfert leaves home, much to the worry of his wife and daughter, who try to dissuade him, but "when once Wolfert was mounted on his hobby, it was no easy matter to get him out of the saddle." (This was literally true. George IV loved to ride, but grew so heavy he had to use a machine to get him in and out of the saddle.)[17] The "three worthies" land in the cove of the iron ring, and proceed to the region of the three crosses. The doctor uses his divining rod effectively, burns herbs, and utters Latin incantations (after George IV's English coronation, he went to Hanover and there was crowned Elector). Just as Sam strikes something, Wolfert looks up and thinks he sees the face of the inn-dictator. He drops the lantern, the fire is extinguished, the three panic, thinking they see "strange figures in red caps, gibbering and ramping around them." Wolfert makes for the waterfront, pursued by footsteps. He jumps from a height and falls unconscious.

Returned home, Wolfert, "sorely beaten down in mind," decides to die. He calls in his lawyer and starts to bequeath his domain when the lawyer declares that the domain is very valuable, or will be, when " 'laid out in streets, and cut up into snug building lots.' " At this, Wolfert, now in his red night cap, acquires vigor, decides to live, and becomes wealthy: "the ancient mansion of his forefathers was still kept up; but . . . it now stood boldly in the middle of a street." In *The Sketch Book*, Irving had recommended retention of John Bull's mansion, as long as it could be made comfortable. Here his plan is more drastic; the great estate must be cut up. Once Wolfert's estate is partitioned, Dirk Waldroun and Wolfert's daughter marry, and Wolfert inherits Ramm's chair at the inn. Now wealthy, "he was never known to tell a story without its being believed, nor to utter a joke without its being laughed at." *Tales of a Traveller* ends with this note of cynicism about tale-tellers and hearers. There is no afterword, or farewell, but with this last comment, Irving leaves writing fiction, only to return to it after the success of his history of Columbus. *Tales of a Traveller* shows Irving in a most grim mood.

CHAPTER 3

Later European Works

I *Historian and diplomat*

ON May 25, 1824, Irving wrote in his journal, "Anniversary of
my departure from America." [1] His mood was not lightened
by the reception accorded *Tales of a Traveller*. Although he was
not severely disturbed by the English criticism, he was distraught
over the hostile American criticism. Perhaps in reaction, on
February 5, 1825, he records that he had projected an American
work. But even before he learned of the hostile American criticism, he had changed his life style. On December 9, 1824, he
began an intense study of Spanish—both language and history—
that continued for the next nine months. He studied it through
the night, engaged a tutor, and spent the mornings at it. In this
period of study, he wrote little. He dedicated himself to Spanish.

On July 22, 1825, six months after he had begun this intensive
study of Spain, he met, in Paris, Alexander H. Everett, the United
States' minister to Spain. Apparently Everett talked vaguely of
attaching him to the legation, should he want to come to Spain.
But only after months of financial worry and economic retrenchment was Irving able to go. On February 4, 1826, he packed his
trunks and was off for Spain.

In Spain, Irving thought to make short work of translating a
work then appearing on Columbus. Having examined Martin
Fernández de Navarette's work, however, Irving decided that it
was too dry for the general public, being little more than a
collection of documents. He altered his intention, and settled
down to write a full-scale biography of the discoverer of America.
Irving spent three years in Spain working on his history of
Columbus—writing, revising, consulting Navarette, reading in
the library of American consul Obediah Rich and, briefly, in the
Archives of the Indies. The resulting *Columbus* was Irving's

first book to bear his own name on the title page. Thinking himself rid of *Columbus*, Irving turned to amassing material on the
conquest of Granada. In a few months spent in Granada, he tried
to unify the collected material, but was not entirely successful.
At the same time, he was working on an abridgment of *Columbus*
and had started to compose the tales for *The Alhambra*.

With the conclusion of *Columbus*, Irving was ready to go
home, as indicated by his year-end summary written December
31, 1828:

Thus ends the year—tranquilly. . . . the literary success of the Hist
of Columb has been greater than I anticipated and gives me hopes
that I have executed something which may have greater duration
than I anticipate for my works of mere imagination. . . . The only
future event from which I promise myself any extraordinary gratifi-
cation is the return to my native country, which I trust will now
soon take place.[2]

Irving has often been described as "lingering" in Europe, unable
to tear himself away from its pleasures. Yet he did not see his
stay in that light—he could not go home until certain conditions
had been met. One was a stable literary reputation, which he
thought he achieved with *Columbus*, the other was recognition
by his government. At the end of 1828, Irving trusted he would
soon return because Andrew Jackson, Burr's friend, had been
elected president and the Democrats were in power.

Irving was rewarded by a somewhat disappointing secretaryship of the legation in London. But, even though it meant more
years abroad, Irving accepted it. He performed his duties consci-
entiously, and, at the same time, completed *The Alhambra* and
The Companions of Columbus, changed publishers, and observed
the changing political scene. When Van Buren (also a former
Burrite) appeared in London as Jackson's nominee to the Court
of St. James, Irving greeted him wholeheartedly and, while re-
signing his position, toured England with him. Irving remained
to see debates on the Reform Act, which he had long thought
was badly needed, then sailed for America in May 1832. Finally,
after years of financial and literary worry, he was able to return
home, successful not only as a man of letters, but as a diplomat.
Finally, he had his caste again.

II Life of Columbus

In a letter to Paulding after the critical failure of *Tales of a Traveller,* Irving complains of American reviewers stabbing him in the back at the point when English reviewers were attacking him. Irving can understand the English attacks, for, "I have kept myself so aloof from all clanship in literature that I have no allies among the scribblers for the periodical press; and some of them have taken a pique against me for having treated them a little cavalierly in my writings." [3] It was the American response that most disturbed Irving. Irving's gloomy state of mind is reflected in his next work, *The Life and Voyages of Christopher Columbus* (1827). Whereas *Tales* was full of lies and fables, Irving now, in his preface, assures the reader of his "earnest desire to state the truth," declining to indulge "in mere speculations or general reflections, excepting such as rose naturally out of the subject." But the subject was a natural one for Irving to reflect on, at this disheartening point in his own career, and his sympathies for Columbus, especially in the first half, are greatest at those points where Columbus's career parallels his own.

Although Irving avoids allegory, one can see how he would be naturally sympathetic toward this citizen of a republic, who carried into a strange land his vision of uniting two worlds. Although Irving shows how Columbus's vision was delusive, that he persisted until his death in his belief he had found the route to Asia, he nevertheless applauds the discoverer's vision of unity. Irving sees that "the narrative of his troubled life is the link which connects the history of the old world with that of the new." In his *Columbus,* Irving is humorless, sober, cynical, melancholy, and weary, but he is still tenacious that there must be a link between the old and new worlds. He was not able to establish it by literature, now he tries it by history.

In describing Columbus's early life, Irving emphasizes the importance of the environment and the times. The environment, the maritime republic of Genoa, encouraged its youth to see the sea as "the high road to adventure and the region of romance." Thus Columbus went to sea and became familiar with it at an early age. The times were propitious also, for the press had disseminated the knowledge of the ancients. Irving comments, "there could never again be a dark age; nations might shut their eyes to the light, and sit in willful darkness, but they could not trample it out; it would still shine on, dispensed to happier parts of the world, by the diffusive powers of the press."

Thus Columbus could read the geographical speculations of the ancients, as well as the travels of Marco Polo. The Portuguese were seeking a route to India by creeping along the coast of Africa; Columbus reasoned it could be reached by sailing west. Having formed his theory, he viewed its accomplishment in a religious light: "the ends of the earth were to be brought together, and all nations and tongues and languages united under the banners of the Redeemer." As Irving records, many scoffed at this vision and the method of its accomplishment, but finally Granada's Moors were crushed, and Isabella pledged her jewels for Columbus's crusade. Irving holds this success in a moral light: "remember that eighteen years elapsed after the time that Columbus conceived his enterprise, before he was enabled to carry it into effect. . . . his example should encourage the enterprising never to despair."

Irving presents Columbus, having gained the means to confirm his theory, starting his voyage into a world of illusion and delusion. As the voyage extended, "the minds of the crew . . . had gradually become diseased. They were full of vague terrors and superstitious fancies." The crews scheme to turn back, for "any complaints made by Columbus would be of no weight; he was a foreigner without friends or influence." Fortunately, land is soon sighted, but even then there is delusion. Expecting to find the wealth of the Orient, the voyagers find only courteous Indians, offering them their food and valuables—and only a few traces of gold. But the Indians' tales of remote golden islands lure Columbus on, "no sooner . . . did one delusion fade away, than another succeeded." He left the Bahamas for Cuba, persuaded that it must be Marco Polo's wealthy Cipango: "the imagination of Columbus deceived him at every step . . . he wove every thing into a uniform web of false conclusions." The voyage, thus, was "a continual series of golden dreams, and all interpreted by the deluding volume of Marco Polo." Thus Irving continues to repeat his theme, that literature (this time, by Marco Polo) is a delusion.

However, led on by his delusion, Columbus discovers Hispaniola, whose Indians have gold, and give readily of it. There, after a shipwreck, which precludes further exploration, Columbus meets with great civility and hospitality from the natives, and concludes, " 'there is not in this world a better nation, nor a better land. They love their neighbors as themselves.' " Being charmed with the luxuriance, the hospitality, and the gold, some crew members ask to remain, to found a colony, and Columbus acquieses, laying down strict laws for the colony and its treatment of the Indians. Because of his discovery of the nature of the islanders, Columbus saw the shipwreck as divinely fortunate; Irving sees it as unfortunate, for it "shackled and limited all his after discoveries." This island was "to involve him in a thousand perplexities, and to becloud his declining years with humiliation and disappointment."

Thinking he had founded a lasting colony, Columbus returned to Spain, to universal acclaim, despite the fact that "no one was aware of the real importance of the discovery. No one had an idea that this was a totally distinct portion of the globe, separated by oceans from the ancient world." But now "the same obscure stranger, who but a short time before had been a common scoff and jest . . . derided by some as an adventurer, and pointed at by others as a mad man" became "the companion of princes," and fawned on by all. Irving, rather wistfully, wishes, "well would it be for the honor of human nature, could history, like romance, close with the consummation of the hero's wishes." But history cannot, and Irving continues, to show of "illustrious merit" that "its very effulgence draws forth the rancorous passions of low and grovelling minds, which too often have a temporary influence in obscuring it to the world." Thus Irving repeats, in history, another theme of *Tales*, that those only are happy, who are at the bottom of their profession.

Having been once successful, Columbus desires to consolidate his achievements, to establish his colony on a firm footing. Ferdinand and Isabella seek to aid him, and appoint Bishop Fonesca as treasurer for the enterprises. But Fonesca hinders rather than helps. In fact, in Irving's eyes, once Columbus is successful, he is doomed to misery, and Irving's tale of Columbus is henceforth a prolonged tale of bad men and bad passions beclouding the grand vision of the discoverer. Instead of looking upon Columbus's three further voyages in the light of expanding the world of knowledge about the unknown, Irving looks on them as disasters. After the first voyage, Irving's *Columbus* becomes a tale of mutiny, of horror, of genocide. Irving presents Columbus as a hero who is helpless, who cannot, despite his best intentions, combat evil in an evil world. He is a hero who is, in fact, indirectly responsible, because of his vision, for that evil.

The second voyage begins with illusion, for the returning first voyagers were "full of exaggeration; for in fact they had nothing but vague and confused notions concerning it, like the recollection of a dream." The shock of reality soon came. After an encounter with warlike Caribs at Guadalupe and the discovery of Puerto Rico, Columbus arrives at his colony to find it vanished. The men had not followed his orders, had not kept together, had not respected the Indians, had fought among themselves. Columbus establishes a new city, Isabella, but soon fevers rage, and the citizens, discovering reality, "their spirits flagged as their golden dreams melted away, and the gloom of despondency aided the ravages of disease." Soon there is mutiny against Columbus, and "the disadvantage of being a foreigner among the people he was to govern was clearly manifested." In order to establish the colony, Columbus even makes the nobles labor, which caused him much ill-will in Spain; he was seen as "trampling upon the rights and dignities of Spanish gentlemen, and insulting the honor of the nation."

But, according to Irving, the Spaniards were not the only sufferers of this second voyage. Columbus recommends to the sovereigns the enslavement of the warlike Caribs; Irving gladly reports that this recommendation is turned down. As Columbus departs from a visit to the interior plain, Irving looks back with "mingled pity and admiration"; "the dream of natural liberty . . . was as yet unbroken, but the fiat had gone forth; the white man had penetrated into the land . . . and the indolent paradise of the Indian was about to disappear forever." After Columbus's return from an exploratory voyage to Cuba, he returns to Hispaniola to find greater discontent. To propitiate the sovereigns, to prevent them from giving too great an ear to the complainers, he sends to Spain five hundred Indians to be sold as slaves, an action, in Irving's eyes, casting "so foul a stain" on Columbus's character. He subjugated the natives, and made them pay a tribute of gold: "in this way was the yoke of servitude fixed upon the island, and its thraldom effectually insured."

So Columbus returned to Spain, not in glory, but as a petitioner: "after having been so many years in persuading mankind that there was a new world to be discovered, he had almost equal trouble in proving to them the advantage of the discovery." His account of recently discovered mines on Hispaniola was met with incredulity, and there was a great delay thrown in his path by "politicians of petty sagacity and microscopic eye" in the fitting out of his return expedition. Irving sees Columbus, at this point, as yielding "repeated examples of the reverses to which those are subject who have once launched from the safe shores of obscurity on the fluctuating waves of popular opinion."

Finally allowed to depart, Columbus steered further to the south, and thus discovered the continental mainland of South America. He correctly deduced the continent, but still imagined it the coast of Asia, also deducing that in the interior of Paria must lie the Garden of Eden. While recording the value of these explorations, Irving seems more concerned with the fate of Hispaniola, the "favorite child" of Columbus's hopes. In his absence, there had been mutiny against his brother, the Indians had ceased to pay tribute or to cultivate the soil, and "the horrors of famine had succeeded to those of war." The Spaniards wished to leave this miserable land; the Indians were dying.

On his return to Hispaniola, Columbus is powerless against the mutineers, and must propitiate them with land and Indian slaves. He is just beginning to get the land productive again when Boabdilla, acting as agent of king and queen, arrives, arrests Columbus and his brother, and sends them to Spain in chains. On his arrival, there is great public outcry against this treatment of the great discoverer, and Isabella and Ferdinand denounce the act of Boabdilla, naming Ovando as governor of Hispaniola until the feeling against Columbus should die down. At the same time, they introduce into the island the first Negro slaves, an act, according to Irving, which was "a gross invasion of the rights and welfare of another race of human beings." And, he adds, "it is a fact worthy of observation, that Hispaniola, the place where this flagrant sin against nature and humanity was first introduced into the New World, has been the first to exhibit an awful retribution."

The rest of his *Columbus* focuses equally upon the plight of Columbus himself and the plight of the enthralled Indians of Hispaniola. Both are pitiable. The politic Ferdinand finally allowed Columbus to sail on his fourth voyage of discovery, this time in search of a strait which would unite his ocean with the

Indian Ocean, but forbade him to touch at Hispaniola. Columbus, reasoning that the strait must lie about Darien, discovers the realms of Costa Rica, and hears rumors of a civilized colony in Yucatan. Finally, he gives up the search for the strait: "he had been in pursuit of a mere chimera, but it was the chimera of a splendid imagination, and a penetrating judgment." He abandons his dream of unifying the oceans, and turns to finding mere gold to please his sovereigns. On his return, he is shipwrecked at Jamaica, and allowed to remain there, among mutinous men and hostile Indians, for nearly a year by Ovando, who then, finally, permitted him to land on Hispaniola.

Irving takes this opportunity to describe the decimation, if not genocide, of the Indians of Hispaniola. Ovando had brought out with him many adventurers after gold, who did not realize that mining was, "of all speculations the most brilliant, promising, and fallacious." The Indians were pushed harder and harder at their labors; and although Isabella had stipulated that they be paid, they were fed poorly, and rarely allowed to visit their families, who thus failed. The result was inevitable:

Many killed themselves in despair, and even mothers overcame the powerful instincts of nature, and destroyed the infants at their breasts, to spare them a life of wretchedness. Twelve years had not elapsed since the discovery of the island, and several hundred thousand of its native inhabitants had perished, miserable victims of the grasping avarice of the white men.

Irving details Ovando's massacre of the natives of Xeragua, admitting that he would have liked to withhold the details of such atrocities, but admits them, for "it is the imperious duty of the historian to place these matters upon record, that they may serve as warning beacons to future generations."

After Irving records Columbus's final return to Spain, and his final, futile endeavors to have his titles restored to him, he sums up his character. Columbus combined the practical and the poetical. His reason persuaded him that there was a world to the west, his poetry, while it continually deluded him (as it had many characters of the *Tales*) into believing the new world was the old, led him, nevertheless, to discover more and more new lands. But he died in ignorance of the real grandeur of his discoveries. A product of his times in his faith and credulity, Columbus, Irving finds, is guilty only of his enslavement of the Indians: "let it remain a blot on his illustrious name, and let others derive a lesson from him."

Thus Irving, who has always been a moralist, although previously disguising his morality, now becomes an overt moralist. Previously an amused observer of human frailty, now he is no longer amused. The satirist has turned cynic, the litterateur an historian, but Irving still believes that, by writing, he can still educate. He feels that, because of printing, there can never again be a dark age, that men can learn from the lessons of the past, and that one of these lessons is not to enslave. Irving, himself a mixture of the practical and the poetic, sympathized almost completely with Columbus. But he could not sympathize with slavery.

III *Agapida's* A Chronicle of the Conquest of Granada

In London, in 1829, appeared *A Chronicle of the Conquest of Granada,* printed "from the Mss. of Fray Antonio Agapida." But, on the title page, Murray added the words, "by Washington Irving," an action which infuriated Irving. He wrote Murray: "I put in the title page the name of Fray Antonio Agapida as author of the chronicle. You must have perceived that this was a nom de guerre to enable me to assume greater freedom & latitude in the execution of the work, and to mingle a tinge of romance and satire with the grave historical details." [4] Thus, Irving had intended to do with his *Chronicle* as he had done with his *History of New York,* which was taken from the manuscripts of Diedrich Knickerbocker. As Knickerbocker's *History* contains Dutch history and satire of contemporary New York, so Agapida's *Chronicle* contains Moorish history and satire of contemporary Spain, chiefly of its king, Ferdinand VII. Irving, in the midst of one of the most reactionary countries in Europe, who worked "always in the presence of a witness who received from Madrid the order not to lose sight for a second of the gifted traveler," [5] was certainly not amused by this betrayal by Murray. He left Spain three months later.

Agapida is no Knickerbocker. He is a stereotype of the ancient Spanish Catholic historian, unable to see beyond the boundaries of his faith. Despite Agapida's delight at the progress of the conquest of the Moors, the reader feels no satisfaction with it— Irving's feelings are for the Moors, despite his clear recognition of their faults. The chronicle moves from fertility to sterility, from laughter to tears, from the prosperity of a happy land to banishment, slavery, and death. Early in the chronicle, Irving makes it clear that the Moors are fighting for "property, for liberty, for life" (the good Lockean concept), whereas the Christians are fighting "for glory, for revenge, for the holy faith, and for the spoil of these wealthy infidels." As the end of the chronicle, Ferdinand and Isabella rule absolutely over a land, once glorious, the people of which have either been enslaved, imprisoned, or banished to Africa. In 1829, Ferdinand VII was absolute king of Spain, who, through his ministry of justice, had executed, imprisoned, banished, or sent to the African penal colony all liberals that could be hunted down.

Although, for his Author's Revised Edition, Irving converted this history-satire-romance into "true history," in this first edition we have the same sense of the inevitability of the defeat of the Moors, and, indeed, the same feeling that we wish Irving would hurry up and get to the end which we know is coming. While at the beginning, the raids and counterraids, the deeds of individuals are chivalric and glorious, as the conquest progresses, the cities are not captured by men but by machines, by great lombards; impregnable passes are overcome by road-builders. The last battle is hardly a battle; at Granada, Ferdinand prohibits individual sallies against the Moors, relying instead on laying waste all surrounding areas and waiting for famine to take its toll.

Interwoven with the faithful account of the conquest, as seen by Agapida from the view of Ferdinand and Isabella, is Irving's account of the Moorish kingdom. It is here that Irving injects his satire of contemporary Spain, simply by exploiting the parallels between Boabdil, the Moorish king, and Ferdinand VII. At the time the chronicle opens, Muley Aben Hassan is king of Granada, and has refused to pay the usual tribute to Ferdinand and Isabella. But Muley Aben Hassan's throne is none too stable. His first son is Boabdil, but now he is dominated by another wife, who is ambitious for her sons and has complete ascendency over her husband. She schemes to disinherit Boabdil, but he is spirited away, and thus saved. Paralleling this is Carlos IV, completely dominated by his queen and her favorite, Manuel Godoy, who was given the title, "Prince of the Peace." The heir, Ferdinand, headed a plot against Godoy, was charged with conspiracy against his father's throne, but was forgiven, and thus saved.

After the Moors' defeat by the Christians at Alhama, a faction of nobles decide to elevate Boabdil to the crown: "the Moors became separated into two hostile factions, headed by the father and the son, and several bloody encounters took place between them." Similarly, when the Spaniards found that Carlos IV had allowed the French passage through Spain to Portugal, the mob revolted, and Charles abdicated, giving the crown to Ferdinand. After a defeat of the Christians near Malaga, the Moors thought "that the days of their ancient glory were about to return"; as Boabdil sets out against the Christians, they hail him as their king. Unfortunately, Boabdil is taken prisoner, and delivered to Ferdinand and Isabella. The Moors soon learn that Boabdil "had surrendered himself captive to the Christians," and their feelings "underwent an instant change"—they reestablish Muley Aben Hassan.

According to Moorish chronicle, while Boabdil is a prisoner, he and his party offer his kingdom to Ferdinand, being content to serve him as a vassal. At the same time, Muley Aben Hassan offers also to enter into a confederacy with the Christian monarchs, offering a large ransom for his son (alive or dead) and release of Christian prisoners. Isabella does not favor the father's suit; Ferdinand agrees to Boabdil's, also stipulating safe passage and maintainance of Christian troops in Boabdil's land, in return for which the Christian monarchs agree to maintain Boabdil on the throne. According to Spanish history, Ferdinand VII went to Bayonne, France, where he surrendered his crown. His father, Carlos IV, accepted it, then tendered it to Napoleon, who then conferred it upon his brother Joseph, along with a new constitution. All this was approved by a council of nobles summoned to Bayonne in June 1808. Thus, in the chronicle, both kings of Granada offer their kingdom to the Christians; thus, in history, both kings of Spain offer their kingdom to the French.

But now the Moorish chronicle varies somewhat from Spanish history. Boabdil is released from captivity and approaches the capital, where his father is still enthroned, "by stealth, and in the night, prowling about its walls like an enemy seeking to destroy, rather than a monarch returning to his throne." At length he enters the city, rouses the lower orders, "large sums of money

were distributed among the populace," and "a doleful day succeeded." Granada was rent by civil war, and "many a warrior of
the highest blood of Granada was laid low by plebian hands, and
plebian weapons, in this civil brawl." According to Spanish history, however, Ferdinand VII's father, who had been somewhat
liberal, did not reign when he returned to Spain, but a spirit of
liberalism did, in the form of an elected Cortes and a constitution,
framed in 1812 at Cadiz. The Cortes gave, as terms for Ferdinand's return to Spain, that he should swear fealty to the constitution, which proclaimed Spain, not the monarch, sovereign,
and that he should recognize the Cortes. Ferdinand VII, supported by the church and the lower orders, entered Spain, went
first to his loyal cities, then announced his sovereignty, denying
that of the constitution. The eve before this declaration was
published in Madrid, the seat of the Cortes, "all prominent
Liberals present in the capital were arrested in their beds, and
haled off to prison amid the jeers of a frantic mob that yelled,
"Long live the absolute King! Long live the Inquisition! Down
with the freemasons!" [6] Consequently, twelve thousand liberals
were sentenced to banishment.

According to Moorish chronicle, amid the destructive inroads
of the Christian army, the brother of the old king, El Zagal, won
the hearts of the people by his sallies against the Christians.
The old king, Muley Aben Hassan, now was ill, and had no care
for the kingdom; he retired, and El Zagal virtually accepted his
sovereignty. The holy men address the populace; saying that
both kings were worthless, one old, the other "an apostate, a
traitor, a deserter from his throne, a fugitive among the enemies
of his nation." And they recommend the people accept as king
El Zagal, for, "he only is fit to sway a sceptre, who can wield a
sword . . . your general, the invincible Abdalla." And "the
multitude . . . were delighted with the idea of a third king
over Granada." The people, as Irving observes, "as usual . . .
attributed the misfortunes of the country exclusively to the faults
of their rulers: for the populace never imagine, that any part of
their miseries can originate with themselves." According to Spanish history, the army, in 1819, revolted, as they were encamped
waiting to be sent to South America to suppress the revolutions
in the colonies. Their hero was Don Rafael Riego, one who could
certainly "wield a sword." The Revolution spread, and Ferdinand

was obliged to acknowledge the constitution, and to summon the
Cortes.

In Moorish chronicle, no sooner did El Zagal have the ascendancy, than the old king died: "the corpse of old Muley Aben
Hassan was also brought to Granada; not in state, like the remains of a once powerful sovereign, but transported ignomini-
ously on a mule. It received no funeral honours." At the news of
the old king's death, the people translate him into a hero, and
begin to murmur against El Zagal for his treatment of the king's
remains. Irving comments, "as the public must always have some
leading person to like, as well as to hate, there began once more
to be an inquiry after Boabdil el Chico." With the growing popular mutterings, Ferdinand enabled Boabdil to establish "the
shadow of a court." In Spanish history, Carlos IV died, in Rome,
in 1819. Since the constitution and Cortes were again in force,
his funeral would not have been elaborate. As the Cortes became more liberal, there was a reaction within the country, and
within Europe, especially within the Holy Alliance, dedicated to
preserving the absolute sovereignity of Christian kings.

In Moorish chronicle, in the spring of 1486, Ferdinand and
Isabella prepare their next campaign, aided by others: "the fame
of this war had spread throughout Christendom: it was considered a kind of crusade; and catholic knights from all parts
hastened to signalize themselves in so holy a cause." The news of
this conclave stops the civil war in Granada, and the people
"forthwith resorted to their old expedient of new modelling their
government, or rather, of making and unmaking kings." They cannot decide between El Zagal and Boabdil, but finally agree to
divide the kingdom, to send Boabdil to Loxa, the threatened
point of attack. Boabdil "accepted one half of the kingdom as
an offer from the nation, not to be rejected by a prince, who
scarcely held possession of the ground he stood on. He asserted,
nevertheless, his absolute right to the whole." He goes to Loxa,
to defend it. But Boabdil is wounded, and Loxa falls. Boabdil,
"accustomed, as he had been, to be crowned and uncrowned; to
be ransomed, and treated as a matter of bargain, . . . had ac-
ceded of course to the capitulation." He becomes vassal of the
Christian king again.

In Spanish history, the events are similar. At the Conference
of Verona, in 1822, the Holy Alliance gave commission to crush

the Revolution in Spain; in January 1823, Russia, Prussia, and Austria ordered Spain to change her constitution. On January 25, Louis of France announced that "a hundred thousand soldiers under the Duke of Angouleme were about to march, invoking God and St. Louis." [7] At this news, warring Spanish factions united, and the Cortes eventually retired, with the king, to Cadiz. The French army was triumphant. It besieged the city of Cadiz, which finally fell, and on October 1, 1823, Ferdinand VII was absolute king once more, thanks to the Holy Alliance of Christian Kings.

Boabdil, now "looked upon as the enemy of his faith and of his country," reentered his capital. There ensued heavy fighting; his cause was doubtful, until Ferdinand sent Christian troops to establish his ascendancy. While Boabdil was "reviled as basely remaining passive while his country was invaded," El Zagal is also reviled; he "had sacrificed the army; he had disgraced the nation; he had betrayed the country." And so Boabdil was once more elevated by the people; "he ascended the throne as the rightful sovereign, who had been dispossessed of it by usurpation, and he ordered the heads of four of the principal nobles to be struck off, who had been most zealous in support of the usurper." In Spanish history, the Spanish army seemed to melt away in front of the French, offering little resistance. Upon reclaiming his absolute sovereignty, Ferdinand VII's first act was to condemn to death the members of the Regency established by the Cortes—they, however, escaped by the intervention of the French.

In Moorish chronicle, as Ferdinand and Isabella are slowly starving Malaga into submission, El Zagal again attempts a relief, but Boabdil sends a force to intercept it, which action causes popular murmurs against Boabdil. Aware of the insecurity of his throne, he sent to Ferdinand, asking for military aid. Ferdinand sent him three thousand men: "With this succour, Boabdil expelled from the city all those who were hostile to him, and in favour of his uncle. He felt secure in these troops, from their being distinct, in manners, language, and religion, from his subjects, and compromised with his pride, in thus exhibiting that most unnatural and humiliating of all regal spectacles, a monarch supported on his throne by foreign weapons, and by soldiers hostile to his people." In Spanish history, Ferdinand VII banished from the capital all members of the past administrations, and all who had enrolled in the national militia. The army was disbanded; French troops, paid by the Spanish, occupied Spain's fortresses.

The next year, Ferdinand moved against Baza, where El Zagal and his remaining followers lie. El Zagal's stand poses another threat to Boabdil, who, discovering a conspiracy, "had the heads of the leaders struck off . . . an act of severity, . . . which struck terror into the disaffected, and produced a kind of mute tranquility throughout the city." In Spanish history, Ferdinand VII, through his minister of justice, sought to exterminate the liberals: "they drove into exile all who were able to flee the country, they massacred many at their first onslaught, and they deliberately hunted down the rest." [8] Finally, the most Christian kings of France and Russia, through their ambassadors, protested the savagery, but Ferdinand VII persisted until June 13, 1825, when the courts-martial were closed.

In the Moorish chronicle, after the fall of Baza, El Zagal surrenders to Ferdinand and Isabella. On hearing this news, Boabdil rejoices, "he reigned without a rival, sole monarch of Granada." He would order public rejoicings, but is restrained by his adviser, saying, " 'the tempest has ceased . . . from one point of the heavens, but it may begin to rage from another.' " And it does. Ferdinand, now regarding Boabdil as a faithless ally, demands Granada surrender. Indeed, like Boabdil, Ferdinand VII, after suppression of the liberals, faced a tempest from another quarter. The Absolutist party rose, discontented because the king would not reintroduce the Inquisition; the Superior Junta of State, headed by Bishop Osma, formed the "Society of the Exterminating Angel," which carried devastation all over the country; finally the Superior Junta "addressed the King in threatening tones demanding further proofs of submission to the Church." [9] Ferdinand VII considered this rebellion, and again left his capital. He, however, returned to it in the fall of 1828, having broken the rebellion.

Fortune was not so kind with the Moorish Boabdil. Ferdinand and Isabella, having isolated Granada from all outside trade, laid waste its produce two years in a row, then prepared for the final siege. At length Granada capitulated, accepting with relief the terms of Ferdinand and Isabella, despite a warning: "Death is the least we have to fear: it is the plundering and sacking of our city, . . . cruel oppression, bigoted intolerance, whips and chains; the dungeon, the faggot, and the stake." Boabdil departs from Granada, takes his last look at it, weeping, and is censured by his mother: "'You do well . . . to weep like a woman, for what you failed to defend like a man!'" The gate by which Boabdil left the Alhambra is walled up, and "the Spanish sovereigns fixed their throne in the presence chamber of the palace, so long the seat of Moorish royalty."

Most modern commentators on Irving's *Chronicle of the Conquest of Granada* have read his revised, later edition, and thus have not recognized the "tinge of romance and satire" Irving gave to the first. Thus, we can excuse Williams's description of Irving's visit to Cadiz: "only a few years before Irving's visit, the French had marched through these streets; here, in 1823, the outrageous Ferdinand VII had been released; and now every citizen had memories of exile, of republican patriotism, and of the Cortes. But Washington Irving was thinking rather of the fifteenth century . . . not of nineteenth-century Spain." [10] In reality, Irving was thinking, and writing, of both.

IV   The Companions of Columbus

In 1829, once more in England, a happier Irving published *The Companions of Columbus*, the tone of which reflects the return of his good humor. While not as robust as Knickerbocker's *History*, *The Companions* may, nevertheless, be compared to it, for here Irving is again selecting from history. While generally chronological, this account of voyages of exploration following Columbus is by no means complete. Although, in the section dealing with Vasco Nuñez de Balboa, Pizarro is a major figure, Irving does not recount his further exploits, preferring to tell of the death of an astrologer. He gives the history of a shipwrecked scholar who was rescued by Cortez, but does not follow Cortez, nor, indeed, any of the exploratory voyages along Central America. Although Irving may have been saving these for later works, it may also be that they did not fit into this collection of characters (or caricatures). Irving touches each character with satire—good-humored satire, but satire nonetheless. The overt moralizing of *Columbus* is rare; the tone of the volume is that of one telling good stories, and enjoying himself in the telling. As Irving says in his preface, "the extraordinary actions and adventures of these men, while they rival the exploits recorded in chivalric romance, have the additional interest of verity." In *Columbus*, truth was all important to Irving; here, the tales come first, the fact that they are true is secondary.

The character of Alonzo de Ojeda dominates the first third of the book. He is labeled by Irving "the young adventurer." His rashness is restrained by the veteran pilot, Juan de la Cosa, "an oracle of the seas," "a kind of Nestor in all nautical affairs." Ojeda, small in stature, always carries with him a small painting of the Virgin to which he attributes "the remarkable circumstances, that he had never been wounded in any of the innumerable brawls and battles into which he was continually betrayed by his rash and fiery temperment." His first voyage to the Gulf of Paria in search of pearls is unsuccessful—although he was successful in attacking cannibals at the request of friendly Indians. His second voyage is more successful—he raids the Indians for furniture and provisions, and also captures Indian women, some of whom were ransomed, some given to his partners, some to the crew—"the rest, probably the old and ugly, were set at liberty." The wealth they do find causes dissensions, and Ojeda is imprisoned and sent to San Domingo for trial: "he finally emerged from the labyrinths of the law a triumphant client, but a ruined man."

Nothing daunted, Ojeda ventures again. Hearing that Ferdinand is looking for a governor of Costa Rica, Juan de la Cosa journeys to Spain to urge Ojeda's qualifications over those of another claimant, Diego de Nicuesa. Nicuesa's abilities are great; he was grand carver to the king's uncle, was skilled in tournament, could make his horse caracole to a viol, "was versed in the legendary ballads or romances of his country, and was renowned as a capital performer on the guitar!" Ferdinand resolves the dilemma by dividing the country between the two claimants, and giving Jamaica to them jointly. The two rivals prepare their expeditions in San Domingo, but soon there is trouble: "both possessed of swelling spirits, pent up in small but active bodies, could not remain long . . . without some collision." Nicuesa is a talker; Ojeda was "always ready to fight his way through any question of right or dignity which he could not clearly argue with the tongue." A duel is averted, however, by Juan de la Cosa, and both sail to their governments—and to disaster.

Of the early governors of this colony, the most fortunate is also the most comic. This is Martin Fernandez de Encisco, a

wealthy San Domingo lawyer, who is named "the Bachelor" by
Irving. Of "a restless and speculative character," Ojeda embues
him with a spirit of adventure, and promises him the office of
chief judge of the colony. He gathers supplies, then, when summoned by Ojeda, sails for the colony—with an absconding debtor,
Vasco Nuñez de Balboa, on board in a cask. Once at sea, the
stowaway emerges "like an apparition," to the indignation of the
Bachelor. Arrived at Cartahenga, he meets a brig carrying the
remnant of Ojeda's colony, commanded by Francisco Pizzaro.
Uncertain of Ojeda's fate, the Bachelor, hearing of great wealth
among the Indian sepulchres of Zenu, decides to disturb the
dead, but is met by hostile Indians seeking to deter him. The
Bachelor "retained sufficient of the spirit of his former calling,
not to enter into quarrel without taking care to have the law on
his side; he proceeded regularly, therefore, according to the legal
form recently enjoined by the crown." The Indians reply, denying
the right of the king to the land. The Bachelor, "having furnished
them with the law, now proceeded to the commentary," and attacked them successfully.

Content with the victory, the Bachelor gives up his grave-
robbing purpose, and proceeds to "the seat of government established by Ojeda in the Gulf of Uraba." Recognizing its hazardous
situation, Vasco Nuñez offers to conduct them to the river Darien
and a more likely place. But there, too, are hostile Indians. Before attacking, the Bachelor, "a discoverer at all points, pious,
daring, and rapacious," makes covenants with Our Lady of
Antigua and with his men: "never did warrior enter into battle
with more preliminary forms and covenants." He wins, takes
possession of the village "by unquestionable right of conquest,"
and issues his first edict—no private trafficking in gold. While
in accordance with royal edict, "it was little palatable to men
who had engaged in the enterprise in the hopes of enjoying free
trade, lawless liberty, and golden gains." Led by Vasco Nuñez
de Balboa, they rebel, and the "unfortunate Bachelor found the
chair of authority to which he had so fondly and anxiously
aspired, suddenly wrested from under him, before he had well
time to take his seat"—a truly burlesque description. Encisco
leaves for Spain, to complain—and to survive.

The account of Vasco Nuñez de Balboa is central to the book,
and is the most straightforward, although without the melancholy
of the *Columbus*. Irving presents Nuñez as an enterprising and

wise commander, one who was outstanding for his ability to get along with the Indians, who had the forethought to plant gardens and orchards, who won over the rabble, which, nevertheless, never forgot that "he had risen from among their ranks; he was in a manner of their own creation; and they had not become sufficiently accustomed to him as a governor, to forget that he was recently but a mere soldier of fortune, and an absconding debtor." Hearing of a great sea, he does not wait for reinforcements, seeks it, finds it, and claims it for the crown. Irving sees that this discovery strengthened his character: "he no longer felt himself a mere soldier of fortune . . . but a great commander conducting an immortal enterprise."

After such success, one would expect a defeat, and one comes. Vasco Nuñez prepares accounts of his discovery to send to Spain, but the ship is delayed. Encisco has the ear of the king, who sends Don Pedro Arias Davila as governor of the colony, to try Nuñez de Balboa; but, in a subsequent trial, Nuñez is acquitted. The governor remains suspicious of him, however, and finally summons him from the Pacific where he was seeking to embark in search of Peru, has him arrested by his friend Pizarro, tried for conspiracy to the king, and executed. Here Irving repeats his refrain: "his fate, like that of his renowned predecessor, Columbus, proves that it is sometimes dangerous even to deserve too greatly."

Having given us a true follower of Columbus, both in vision and fate, Irving now gives the stories of three men, neither companions, followers, nor in any way similar to Columbus. Irving must have included them solely because he liked the stories or because he found them offering analogies to contemporary characters. The first story deals with two members of the crew of Valdiva, sent to Hispaniola for supplies by Vasco Nuñez de Balboa. They are shipwrecked on the coast of Yucatan, and are captured by cannibals. Of all the crew, only these two survive, having been made slaves by a noncannibal chieftain. One of these, "a sturdy sailor," is traded to a neighboring chieftain, and "being a thorough son of the ocean," won the admiration of the cacique and of an Indian princess. The other, "a kind of clerical adventurer," Jeronimo de Aguilar, remembers the saintly vows of humility and chastity, and equally prospers—although subjected by his cacique to many temptations, including an overnight fishing expedition with a warm, buxom, tempting maiden.

After many years, the saint gets news of great ships off the coast, and a letter from Cortez, who has learned of their presence. Aguilar determines to escape, the sailor does not—he had been so tattooed and beringed in the custom of the country that "he made up his mind, therefore, to remain a great man among the savages, rather than run the risk of being shown as a man-monster at home." Aguilar becomes interpreter for Cortez, later mayor of Mexico City.

Then Irving devotes a slim chapter to the death of Micer Cordo, who had correctly predicted the year of Balboa's death. Cordo followed the explorers of the new world, but was "intent upon studying the secrets of its natural history, rather than searching after its treasures." Irving apparently thought highly of this scientist, whom he labels "the astrologer," for what would seem to be only matter for a note is awarded the status of a section.

The last section characterizes Ponce de Leon, a characterization reminiscent of that of Peter Stuyvesant. Irving consistently labels him "the old soldier," even though, historically, he was forty-eight years old when the account begins. Named by Ovando to command the province of Higuey, Juan Ponce "had all the impatience of quiet life and the passion for exploit of a veteran campaigner." He casts his eyes wistfully to Puerto Rico, which had never been explored. His aspirations for its governorship are apparently doomed when the king names Christoval Santomayer, and Diego Columbus names Juan Ceron. But the king changes his mind, names Ponce de Leon, who, "being a fiery, high-handed old soldier, his first step was to quarrel with Juan Ceron." Juan Ponce, "being firmly seated in his government," begins to settle colonists, and apportion Indians far labor. The Indians, by an empirical test, having concluded the Spaniards were not immortal, stage a successful insurrection, driving all the survivors to Ponce de Leon's fortress. But "Juan Ponce was a staunch and wary old soldier, and not easily daunted. He remained grimly ensconsed within his fortress" while sending for help. He is reinforced, kills the major chieftain, and has subjugated the island when the king changes his mind, naming Ceron as governor.

Ponce de Leon gives up the governorship without regrets. He then hears of a land of wealth to the north that possessed a river of youth, and also of an island called Bimini, in the Bahamas, that had a fountain of youth. Irving comments that "it may seem incredible . . . that a man of years and experience could yield any faith to a story which resembles the wild fiction of an Arabian tale; but the wonders and novelties breaking upon the world in that age of discovery, almost realized the illusions of fable," and that, further, Ponce de Leon had no trouble finding adventurers "ready to cruise with him in quest of this fairy-land." Thus, in Irving's terms, Ponce de Leon's voyage becomes one in search of a fountain and a fairyland.

Ponce de Leon sails first for the Bahamas, enquiring in vain for Bimini, and "as to the fountain of youth, he may have drank of every fountain, and river, and lake, in the archipelago, even to the salt pools of Turk's Island, without being a whit the younger." He steers for the northwest and, on Palm Sunday, discovers Florida. Returning by way of the Bahamas, he again fails to find Bimini, and finally returns to Puerto Rico, "infinitely poorer in purse, and wrinkled in brow, by this cruise after inexhaustible riches and perpetual youth." After a period of governing Puerto Rico "in a state of growling repose," he revisits Florida, but is there wounded, and dies in Cuba. Irving concludes, "it may be said . . . that he has at least attained the shadow of his desire, since, though disappointed in extending the natural term of his existence, his discovery had insured a lasting duration to his name." Like that of Columbus, his chimera led to a discovery greater than he knew.

Irving begins *The Companions of Columbus* with "the youthful adventurer," places the middle-aged Vasco Nuñez de Balboa at its center, and concludes with "the old soldier," thus giving the book a kind of unity. Despite this, the book remains a collection of sketches of characters. While he shows Ponce de Leon as subjugating and almost exterminating the aborigines of Puerto Rico, he does not deplore the action as he did in *Columbus*. For Irving, Ponce de Leon is "the old soldier" in search of a fountain and a fairyland, and as such he escapes history and enters literature. *The Companions of Columbus* lies in the mid-world of history and literature. One senses throughout that, as in Knicker-bocker's *History*, Irving is using history for his own purposes, for his own enjoyment. *Companions* is a transition between Irving's gloomy works written in Spain and his brilliant valedictory to Europe, *The Alhambra*.

V   The Alhambra

The Alhambra is the most unified of all Irving's books of tales and sketches. He so artfully mingles sketches of the present Alhambra with legends of the past that they blend together to form a dreamworld. While Irving really did stay in the Alhambra, for Crayon the ancient Granada becomes a symbol for all of Europe. In the book, truth mingles with fiction, the present merges with the past, and the Alhambra itself is, at one and the same time, a real palace and the symbolic "dilapidated mansion of former grandeur" in which so many of Irving's previous tales have been set. But the tone of this book is happy. The preface to the first English edition is dated May 1832, the month Irving finally sailed for home. Irving, having served his government, was going home, and *The Alhambra* reflects his joy. His allegories, while retelling many of the same stories, are now more cheerful. There are no more rapes or murders, although he does consign a few enemies to the bowels of the earth. If there are prisons, they are here escaped from, tombs fly open, the dead revive. The gloomy images and melancholy of *The Sketch Book* are reversed, love is now the theme.

By his great power of description, Irving so thoroughly convinces us of the reality of his visit to the Alhambra, that it is not until the fifth or sixth sketch that we realize that he has also conducted us back to his land of fable and allegory. In "The Journey," he presents us with a general account of the landscape (particularly noting that there are few birds—and yet his stories are full of birds) and mode of traveling in Spain. After several stops and stories along the way, the journey ends at Granada; the author is allowed a room in the Alhambra. He presents the ensuing sketches as "the result of my reveries and researches during that delicious thraldom," and, despite the "delicious," we are reminded of the previous imprisonment images.

Although, to Crayon, as he enters the Alhambra, "it seemed as if we were at once transported into other times and another realm, and were treading the scenes of Arabian story," he orients it securely in topography and history. From the Tower of Comares, he points out the landmarks. The Generalife is to the north, on higher grounds, to the west is Pinos, from where Columbus was summoned by the queen, to the south is the Vega and the site of the last view of Granada by Boabdil, the last

Moorish monarch. This leads Crayon to muse upon the fate of the Spanish Moors, who "formed an empire unrivalled for its prosperity by any of the Empires of Christendom." The Moors ruled Spain for as long a time as the time from William the Conqueror to the present, and little did they dream that their power would pass, as little "as the descendants of Rollo and William, and their veteran peers, may dream of being driven back to the shores of Normandy." But they did fail, and only the Alhambra remains, "an elegant memento of a brave, intelligent, and graceful people, who conquered, ruled, and passed away."

In "The Household" we encounter some of Irving's favorite characters. The housekeeper is an aunt, "a woman of strong and intelligent, though uncultivated mind," who has in her charge an orphan niece who will be (as in *Bracebridge Hall*) her heir. The niece is wooed by a cousin who hopes to wed her, waiting only for his doctor's diploma and to "purchase a dispensation from the Pope, on account of their consanguinity." Among the aunt's tale-telling circle is Mateo Ximenes, a "historiographic squire," who has "the locquacity and gossip of a village barber," who becomes Crayon's guide. The aunt's friends are "never vulgar," a sin Irving was often accused of.

Irving has not forgotten his experiences, and he presents them in "The Truant," a fable which repeats his old pattern. This time, the hero is the niece's pigeon, who inhabits a "tenement" with his mate, and there nourishes two eggs. One day the niece decides to give the male "a peep at the great world" and lets him loose: "for the first time in his life the astonished bird had to try the full vigour of his wings. . . . He seemed giddy with the excess of liberty, and with the boundless field of action suddenly opened to him." He does not return; the eggs perish. He is joined by "robber pigeons" who entice him to the Generalife. There he joins its birds, "the terror of all neighbouring pigeon fanciers." Fortunately, however, the truant returns, returns "like the prodigal son" to the feast. The niece takes care to clip his wings to prevent further flights. Crayon concludes, appropriately, "more than one valuable lesson might be drawn from the story of Dolores and her pigeon."

"The Author's Chamber" also repeats previous allegory—it is most similar in structure to the nervous gentleman's "Adventure of the Mysterious Picture." Crayon's first rooms in the Alhambra are in the modern part, not far from Tia Antonia's parlor, which "had boasted of some splendour in the time of the Moors, but a fire-place had been built in one corner, the smoke from which had discouloured the walls . . . and spread a sombre tint on the whole." He decides to move to more ancient chambers overlooking the garden of Lindaraxa. The garden still has flowers, the fountain still runs, but "the alabaster had lost its whiteness, and the basin beneath, overrun with weeds, had become the nestling-place of the lizard." Tia Antonia and the niece try to dissuade him with tales of robbers and foxes, but he is determined, and patches up the chamber.

The first night, left alone, Crayon is awed, and attributes the awe to "some thing . . . unreal and absurd . . . the long-buried impressions of the nursery were reviving, and asserting their power over my imagination . . . my chamber itself became infected." Like the nervous gentleman, he leaves the infected chamber, and wanders around the older part of the palace: "the rays of my lamp extended to but a limited distance around me; I walked as it were in a mere halo of light . . . the vaulted corridors were as caverns." He imagines all sorts of terrors, to which are added sounds of moans, howlings, and ravings. The next morning, again in his room, with the sun and its "truth-telling beams," "I could scarcely recall the shadows and fancies conjured up by the gloom of the preceeding night; or believe that the scenes around me, so naked and apparent, could have been clothed with such imaginary horrors." But the horrors are "not ideal"; the niece tells him that the howlings are real, made by a confined maniac. Once more we have the debate between truth and fiction, ideal and real, and the infection of tales heard in childhood.

In two sketches, Irving defends Boabdil and his actions, and, indirectly, his own treatment of him in his *Chronicle of the Conquest of Granada*. He rails against the popular misconceptions of Boabdil, attributing most of them to a fallacious history, "the whole of it . . . a mass of fiction, mingled with a few disfigured truths, which give it an air of veracity," a description similar to Clinton's of Kickerbocker's *History* ("the heterogenous and unnatural combination of fiction and history . . . perfectly disgusting to good taste").[11] Indeed, it strikes us that Irving is being too holy to be wholly sincere when he adds, "I confess there seems to me something almost criminal, in the wilful perversions of this work: great latitude is undoubtedly to be allowed to romantic fiction, but there are limits it must not pass, and the names of the distinguished dead . . . are no more to be calumniated than those of the illustrious living." Crayon visits the places associated with Boabdil and declares, "he may have been wavering and uncertain, but there is nothing of cruelty or unkindness in his aspect." He visits the dungeon where he was imprisoned by his father, the gate of his final exit, the site of his last view of his lost kingdom where he was upbraided by his mother for his loss. Obviously, now, Crayon feels at one with Boabdil: he resents the father who imprisoned him and the mother who criticized the gentle man at the moment of his worst defeat.

Crayon moves to "The Balcony" and back to the debate between romance and truth, illusion and reality. From the balcony, hung "like a cage" from the Hall of Ambassadors, Crayon observes a young girl, en route to enter a convent. Crayon imagines her to be reluctant, her father tyrannical, her lover despairing. But Mateo tells him the truth, "the heroine . . . was neither young nor handsome; she had no lover—she had entered the convent of her own free will . . . and was one of the most cheerful residents within its walls." Again Crayon romances, picturing a secret love affair between a man and a woman. Again Mateo tells him the truth: what he saw was merely a contrabandista husband receiving smuggling signals from his wife. In both cases, there is no romance, in both the women are not to be wooed.

Since the "historiographer" Mateo tells the next story, "The Adventure of the Mason," we may assume its truth, but it is Crayon's allegorical truth. Its pattern is similar to "Wolfert Webber." This time, the hero of the story is a poor mason with a numerous family. He is summoned one night by "a tall, meagre, cadaverous-looking priest," who "hoodwinks" him and leads him to an old house. In the center of the patio is "the dry basin of an old Moorish fountain, under which the priest requested him to form a small vault." He does so and, the second night, aids the priest in storing there jars of money. Time passes, the mason's family "grew up as gaunt and ragged as a crew of gypsies." Then, one day, he was "accosted by a rich old curmudgeon, who was noted for owning many houses, and being a griping landlord." He tells the mason of one of his houses, "'an old house fallen into decay, that costs me more money than it is worth to keep it in repair, for nobody will live in it; so I must contrive to patch it up and keep it together at as small expense as possible.' " On recognizing it as the house of the priest, the mason agrees to undertake the job: " 'I will engage to put it in repair, and to quiet the troubled spirit that disturbs it.' " The mason did as he promised: "by little and little he restored it to its former state . . . he increased rapidly in wealth, to the admiration of all his neighbours." What was a "golden dream" in Wolfert is now achieved, the dilapidated mansion is being put in order. In "Wolfert," the landlord and the "confessor" fail in their search for gold; here the landlord replaces the priest with a mason, and the mason uses the hidden wealth in the right way. It is probably not coincidental that this was written after King William, in 1830, replaced the Tories with the Whigs; that the beginning of the repairs, the Reform Act, came in 1832.

Nor is it just happenstance that Crayon, in the next sketch, consigns a holy father to the bowels of the earth. The sketch, "A Ramble Among the Hills," is a fine example of Irving's blending local color, scene description, symbol, allegory, and legend. The sketch describes sterility and fertility, death and hope, the end and a new beginning. The ramble leads Crayon and Mateo to the mountain of the sun, just at the hour of prayer. The setting sun just lights the summit of the Sierra Nevada, then "a star appeared over the snowy summit of the mountain, the only one yet visible in the heavens, and so pure, so large, so bright and beautiful, as to call forth ejaculations of delight from honest Mateo." Then, just below the star appear other lights, the bonfires of the gatherers of snow and ice who bring the pure refreshment to Granada. Turning from these lights, Crayon looks down the mountain, and perceives a succession of lights coming up. Soon they pass him; it is a funeral train, bearing a corpse. This sight "put me in mind of the old story of a procession of demons bearing the body of a sinner up the crater of Stromboli."

Irving then translates what he has seen into a story from Mateo about a gatherer of snow. The snow gatherer, on his way down the mountain one night, fell asleep. When he awoke, Granada was as it was in the time of the Moors, the crosses were crescents. He sees, coming up the mountain, a great silent Moorish army, leading the Grand Inquisitor, "famous for his hatred of Moors, and, indeed, of all kinds of Infidels, Jews and Heretics, and used to hunt them out with fire and scourge." The snow gatherer asks for his blessing, but receives a buffet instead. When he regains consciousness, all his snow has melted. He goes to Granada and tells his story, but is only laughed at. A year later, however, the Grand Inquisitor dies, and Mateo adds, " 'I have often heard my grandfather, the tailor, say that there was more meant by that hobgoblin army bearing off the resemblance of the priest, than folks dared to surmise.' " Crayon asks Mateo whether he thought the Inquisitor was borne to a Moorish purgatory, but Mateo cannot say. But we are left with the idea that the oppressor, the priest, has come to a well-deserved end—and that the tale of the water carrier had its truth.

Irving associates his next story, the "Legend of the Arabian Astrologer," not with the Alhambra, but with the "house of the weathercock" in the city of Granada. The weather vane, a bronze soldier, was intended by an Alcalde, Aben Habuz, "as a perpetual memorial to the Moslem inhabitants that, surrounded as they were by foes, their safety depended upon being always on their guard, and ready for the field," a good Burrite sentiment. But Irving also tells a more marvellous legend concerning the weather vane in which the Alcalde is transformed into a king, the house into a palace, and Granada into a kingdom. While the story contains many folktale motifs, it also contains political history, a history that has occurred in many kingdoms. Of the kingdoms of Irving's own time, its history closely parallels that of Russia under Alexander I and Nicholas I. And we remember that Irving was accompanied to the Alhambra by the Russian diplomat Prince Dolgorouki.

The last tale of the first volume, "Legend of the Three Beautiful Princesses," retells Irving's own history and imprisonment, but so zestfully and joyfully that we can almost hear him carol as he writes it. He is having all sorts of fun, especially with the number three. Once there was a king, Mohamed the Left-Handed, who was three times driven from his throne, and three times got it back again. He falls in love with a captured Spanish beauty. The Christian princess gives in, conforms outwardly to her husband's religion, and produces three daughters at a birth.

Astrologers warn the king to trust no one but himself to guard them when they reach marriageable age. As a precaution, the king has them reared in a remote beautiful palace on the coast, watched over by the discreet Kadiga. The three princesses grow beautiful: "their names were Zayda, Zorayda, and Zorahayda;

and such was their order of seniority, for there had been precisely three minutes between their births." The three, as they have different names, have different characteristics. Zayda, like Knickerbocker, "was curious and inquisitive, and fond of getting at the bottom of things." The second "had a great feeling for beauty . . . delighting to regard her own image in a mirror or fountain." And Zorahayda, like Crayon, is gentle, loves the flute, musing, and reveries, and "the least uproar of the elements . . . filled her with dismay; and a clap of thunder was enough to throw her into a swoon."

One day, the three see a galley bearing three noble Spanish prisoners, and the discreet Kadiga tells them tales of Spain, their mother's land. Zayda "drew from the duenna the most animated pictures of the scenes of her youthful days and native land," tales of love, of jousts, of feasting. Kadiga, realizing the three have matured, sends for the king, who arrives and sees them for the first time in three years. He escorts them to Granada, their father's land, but on the way they see again the three Spanish cavaliers, who each fall immediately in love with a different princess. Arrived at the Alhambra, the king imprisons his daughters in a luxuriously appointed tower, but the three princesses are unhappy; they look "like three blighted rose-buds, drooping from one stalk." Kadiga soon makes them happier by arranging that Hussein Baba should employ the three Spanish cavaliers in a ravine below the tower. This is done, and a musical courtship is carried on until, one day, the cavaliers are ransomed and appear no more. The third morning after their departure, Kadiga brings news to the princesses that the cavaliers have arranged their elopement, and she is to go too, with Hussein Baba.

The princesses debate leaving, but Zayda declares, " 'our father has never placed any confidence in us . . . but has . . . treated us as captives.' " Further, " 'is not the land we fly to, the native land of our mother, where we shall live in freedom . . . the Christian faith was the original faith of our mother . . . I am ready to embrace it.' " Zorayda agrees, only the gentle Zorahayda hesitates. When the time for flight arrives, she hesitates even more, looking back at her chamber: "she had lived in it, to be sure, like a bird in a cage; but within it she was secure: who could tell what dangers might beset her, should she flutter forth into the wide world!" The other two successfully reach Spain. It was thought that Zorahayda "secretly repented of having remained behind." She died at an early age and was buried in a vault in the tower: "her untimely fate has given rise to more than one traditionary fable." And indeed it did, and we have read those fables in Crayon's other works. But we do not mourn Zorahayda's entombment as we did Crayon's in *The Sketch Book*; the tone is too joyful for that. Somehow, we assume, Zorahayda will be set free.

Irving presents the tales of the second volume as having been heard during a grand celebration of the saint day of a Spanish count who had elected to spend the hot summer months at the Alhambra. But they are his own fables and allegories. The first, "Legend of Prince Ahmed Al Kemel, or The Pilgrim of Love," purports to be an Arabian legend, and it certainly has the trappings of the *One Thousand and One Nights*. But its pattern conforms too exactly to those of Irving's previous tales for it not to be another allegory. The prince, like the Young Italian, is imprisoned by his father to keep him from learning about love. He is imprisoned in the Generalife, and tutored by a philosopher in all the dry sciences. As the prince grows older, he grows bored with his studies. To entertain him, the tutor teaches him the language of the birds. Confined to his high tower, the prince meets a hawk, "a pirate of the air . . . whose talk was all about rapine and courage and desperate exploits," an owl, "grievously given to metaphysics," a bat, who "derided things of which he had taken but an imperfect view, and seemed to take delight in nothing," and a swallow, "a mere smatter, who did but skim over the surface of things."

The prince knows only this society of high-flying birds until one spring day he hears song birds, far below his tower, singing of love. He asks his feathered literary acquaintances of love, but all are contemptuous of it or know nothing of it. Then one day a dove, pursued by a hawk, flies into his chamber and tells the prince of love. The prince releases the dove, but, a few days later, it flies back to the prince and describes for him a princess, also imprisoned, who should be his mate. The prince, enraptured with this vision of beauty, addresses a letter to her, signing it, "A Pilgrim of Love," and sends it off by the dove. The dove finally returns with a miniature of the princess, and the prince, inspired by her beauty, determines to escape his prison to seek his love. In his search he is guided by the metaphysical antiquarian owl and by an unusual parrot.

The owl, the parrot, and the prince arrive at Toledo, the home of the princess, on the eve of her seventeenth birthday. They discover that there is to be a tournament; the champion to win the princess. The prince regrets his learning has gone for nought; he knows nothing of jousting. But the owl reveals to him a magical Moorish steed and lance, and thus equipped he enters the lists— only to discover that he cannot compete since he is a Moor. But the horse carries him against the others anyway, the lance overthrows every champion, even the king himself. The spell nearing its end, the horse rushes the grieving prince away: "never should he dare to show his face at Toledo after inflicting such disgrace upon its chivalry, and such an outrage on its king."

He sends the owl and the parrot out to reconnoiter; they report that the life of the princess is despaired of, she only weeps over the prince's letter. Encouraged by this, the prince tries again. Disguised as a singing shepherd, he is allowed to entertain the princess. Singing verses from his letter, he reanimates her: "never was triumph of music more complete." The shepherd prince asks as his reward only a silken carpet. He spreads it out, the princess joins him on it, and they are wafted away to the Alhambra. The two live happily, the owl serving as prime minister, the parrot as master of ceremonies. This is a far happier ending than that of "The Young Italian," whose pattern this repeats from the early passionless education and imprisonment by the father to the painting of the beauty, the separation from her, the striking out at her champion, and the hero's consequent despair that he can never attain her. But "The Pilgrim of Love" progresses beyond the despair to the triumph of the wedding, although it took a little magic to accomplish it.

The "Legend of the Moor's Legacy" also ends happily ever after, even though it concerns a poor water carrier named Peregil. Although poor, Peregil, with the aid of a Moorish incantation, a candle, and a Moor, find riches in the Alhambra. Their wealth is discovered, however, by a neighboring barber, "a sort of scandalous chronicle for the quid-nuncs of Granada," who sees Peregil's wife, bedecked with jewels, in a mirror. He reports this to the alcalde, who, with the alguizil and barber, demand more of the treasure. This the Moor and Peregil fetch for them from the vault, but refuse to go back after still more. The three officials enter the vault, whereupon the Moor blows out the candle, entombing them: "whenever there shall be a lack in Spain of pimping barbers, sharking alguazils, and corrupt alcaldes, they may be sought after; but if they have to wait until such time for their deliverance, there is danger of their enchantment enduring until doomsday." To safely enjoy their wealth, the Moor and Peregil leave the Alhambra and Granada.

Another tale of departure from the Alhambra, another successful love story, is "The Legend of the Rose of the Alhambra." Its heroine is Jacinta, imprisoned in the tower of the princesses by an aunt, who fears the wiles of men. A page of Elizabeth's court, however, meets her in the aunt's absence, and the two fall in love. The court moves on, however, and the page is heard of no more. As Jacinta bewails her love by a fountain, its waters begin to bubble, and Zorahayda rises to view. She tells her story: "I was a convert in my heart, but I lacked courage equal to my faith, and lingered till too late." For this hesitancy, "I remain enchanted in this tower until some pure Christian will deign to break the magic spell." Jacinta baptizes her, Zorahayda "smiled with ineffable benignity . . . and melted from sight," leaving only her silver lute. Thus the last of the roses is freed; the gentle Zorahayda gets to leave her imprisonment in the Alhambra.

Jacinta, too, is freed, for in her hands, Zorahayda's silver lute possesses magical powers, and she is hailed throughout Andalusia as "the Rose of the Alhambra." Meanwhile, at the court of Philip and Elizabeth, the king, after a long imaginary illness, "fairly, in idea, gave up the ghost, and considered himself absolutely dead." This would have suited the whole court, but the king went further, he wanted himself buried. Here, the court hesitated, not wanting to commit regicide. The queen summons Jacinta to play for the "dead" monarch. She does, and "poured forth one of the legendary ballads treating of the ancient glories of the Alhambra and the achievements of the Moors." At this, the king, like Wolfert, rejects death: "the demon of melancholy was cast forth; and, as it were, a dead man brought to life." Irving then gratifies his literal reader with the wedding of Jacinta and the page, but the real ending is here, with the reviving of king and kingdom, and the end of melancholy.

Here Irving is prophetic. *The Alhambra* was published in May 1832. In September 1832, Ferdinand VII, believing his end near, revoked the succession of his daughter Isabella. The Carlists, reactionary supporters of his brother Don Carlos, took over the country. "The Queen, abandoned at her husband's bedside, had given up the struggle; the king was supposed to be dead; only confirmation of the news was awaited for the proclamation of his brother." At this point, the queen's sister Carlotta arrived, forced her way to the king's bedside, gave new courage to the queen, and tore up the revocation. "Then to the astonishment of all, Ferdinand rallied," [12] assumed his powers by the first of the new year, and became more moderate.

Irving varies his tone in the next two stories, which both concern Governor Manco of the Alhambra. Both stories probably contain allegories of the literary world. "Governor Manco and the Soldier" repeats the pattern of *Bracebridge Hall*'s story of the imprisonment of Starlight Tom. This time, it is "an old soldier" who escapes with the governor's maid, and jewels and horse.

The last tale is the "Legend of the Two Discreet Statues" and it, again, involves a departure from the Alhambra by a hero, bearing treasure, and a consequent wedding. In it, Irving again consigns a priest, if not to hell, at least to a hellish ride. This time the hero is a gardener, a poor merry man named Lope Sanchez. Lope has a domineering wife and but one daughter, Sanchica. By freeing a Gothic princess from a spell, Sanchica is enabled to find treasure. Lope and Sanchica remove the treasure, and now Lope's troubles begin: "for the first time in his life the dread of robbers entered into his mind . . . [he] became the most miserable animal in the Alhambra." His friends, noting his changed demeanor, begin to pity him, then desert him. Worse, his wife tells her confessor of the discovery. Fray Simon demands the myrtle wreath as a votive offering, then some of the Moorish gold for candlesticks, then more treasure for a saint. Lope concludes that "unless he got out of the reach of this holy friar, he should have to make peace offerings to every saint in the Kalendar." He determines, therefore, to leave the Alhambra.

Fray Simon suspects Lope's purpose, and awaits for him to pass with his loaded donkey. As the animal passes, he leaps on behind, only to discover himself aboard the Belludo, the nightmare horse of legend. The horse rides him a terrible ride all night, and knocks him off, battered and bruised, in the morn. Fray Simon gives out "that he had been waylaid and maltreated by robbers," but consoles himself with the gains from Lope he had already made. But they, like Tom Walker's wealth after his ride, have vanished. Years later, a friend from the Alhambra sees Lope in a distant city. Lope claimed "that a rich brother had died in America and left him heir to a copper mine," but the gossips of the Alhambra never believed this, preferring the legend of the two discreet statutes. Once more a treasure finder leaves the Alhambra to enjoy the wealth.

As Irving concluded *Tales of a Traveller* with a "sound bolus of morality," a lesson on political economy disguised as the tale of "Wolfert Webber," so Irving ends *The Alhambra* with another lesson in political economy, this time disguised as historical accounts of the founder and finisher of the Alhambra. He first presents a Moorish tradition, that the founder of the Alhambra was versed in alchemy, and thus acquired the gold for its erection, but, he says, "a brief view of his reign will show the real secret of his wealth." And the real secret is that the founder was an enlightened ruler, with an enlightened administrative program —one which sounds more like New York under Clinton than Granada under an ancient Moorish king. In foreign relations, the king entered into an alliance with Ferdinand, thus obtaining an interval of peace, during which time he "improved the present interval of tranquillity by fortifying his dominions and replenishing his arsenals, and by promoting those useful arts which give wealth and real power to an empire." Despite his great accomplishments, "he was simple in his person and moderate in his enjoyments. His dress was not merely void of splendour, but so plain as not to distinguish him from his subjects." He spent much time in his garden, improving varieties of plants and reading histories. He "retained his faculties and vigour to an advanced age," and died in his seventy-ninth year. Despite his vast undertakings, his treasury was always full, but he was no alchemist: "those who have attended to his domestic policy, as here set forth, will easily understand the natural magic and simple alchemy which made his ample treasury to overflow."

With this solid Jeffersonian foundation, Yusef Abul Hagig, a "high-minded prince," completed the Alhambra. He "was of a lively genius, and accounted the best poet of his time." In peace, he "devoted himself to the instruction of his people, and the improvement of their morals and manners." To this end, he, like John Quincy Adams, "established schools in all the villages, with simple and uniform systems of education." He completed architectural works and commenced others. The nobles of Granada imitated his fine taste, and the city became beautiful. Thus, the fine arts flourished under Yusuf, and Irving's ideal nation is complete. His vision emphasizes the people; the people themselves provide the wealth of the nation. With this vision, with this faith, Irving returned to the United States, to his motherland, to enjoy, once more, his mother's religion. Through the stories of *The Alhambra*, some joyous, some mocking, some with elements of pathos, but none bitter, we realize how intensely Irving felt his separation from home, how much his departure from Europe meant. To quote the description of Zorahayda: he left "with a smile of ineffable benignity."

CHAPTER 4

Return to America

I *Irving at Home*

WASHINGTON Irving returned to the city of New York almost as a stranger, so greatly had the city grown. But he soon found his family and old friends—the storyteller had returned to an undevastated land. He relaxed and enjoyed this society; English visitors were amazed that the sleepy Irving of English gatherings was now so convivial. At a public dinner he spoke well, declaring, "I come from gloomier climes to one of brilliant sunshine and inspiring purity. I come from countries lowering with doubt and danger, where the rich man trembles, and the poor man frowns—where all repine at the present and dread the future. I come from these, to a country where all is life and animation . . . where every one speaks of the past with triumph, the present with delight, the future with growing and confident anticipation." [1] To those who would ask how long he would remain, he answered, "as long as I live." And, except for the period of his ministry to Spain, he kept his promise. Like his founder of the Alhambra, he retired to a country seat, busying himself with agricultural improvements; like the finisher of the Alhambra he sought, through his works, to educate and cultivate his fellow citizens. Now he covered the "sound bolus of morality" (which he had formerly conveyed by his tales) with a coating of history or biography. As in earlier works, he rarely pointed his morals, content to leave it to the reader to derive the correct lesson.

Before he wrote, however, he educated himself about the United States as it had become. First he journeyed to Washington and was introduced to Andrew Jackson. Then, in the course of a year, he visited, as nearly as can be ascertained, all but five of the states then in the union, as well as the future states of Arkan-

sas, Oklahoma, and West Virginia. He went to Boston and New
Hampshire's White Mountains with Martin Van Buren, candidate
that year for vice-president. Later in the year he met Henry
Ellsworth, Jackson's commissioner to determine the new location
of the Cherokee tribes (a relocation Irving later deplored). Ellsworth offered Irving the secretaryship of the commission, and
thus began Irving's tour on the prairies. Following this tour,
Irving returned through the lower southern states to South
Carolina, arriving in time to dine with Governor Hamilton on
the day of the passage of the nullification ordinance—and promised to return with the first federal troops. He returned then to
Washington, met again with Jackson, and lingered there to hear
the Senate debates, thus furthering his education in contemporary
affairs.

Irving's first published works on his return looked backward
and forward. *The Crayon Miscellany*, combining the volumes of
A Tour on the Prairies, Abbotsford and Newstead Abbey, and
Legends of the Conquest of Spain, did both, the first two looking
backward, the third, a grim look into the future by means of the
past. He consolidated the affections of those who longed for an
American writing on American themes with *Astoria*, admittedly a
history of the past, but also a present document establishing the
future claims of the United States to the lands drained by the
Columbia. Soon followed *The Adventures of Captain Bonneville*
—again a recognition of the future in its preservation of the
customs, dress, and physical appearance of tribes Irving was
certain would soon disappear. In this work, most especially, we
see the concerns of the eighteenth-century enlightened man.
Certain parts of *Bonneville*, indeed, are comparable to Jefferson's
Notes on the State of Virginia.

And so Irving once more made a part of a much larger United
States than the one he had left—and lived comfortably in it. Although disappointed in imminent riches from land speculations,
he retained sufficient funds to buy property near Sleepy Hollow
and there to erect a simple country retreat, which became a snug
cottage, then a large comfortable home. Irving's letters to his
nieces and nephews concerning Sunnyside are delightful: his
pride in his pig Fanny, his pleasure that his geese had driven off
a neighboring squadron, his concern to build an ice pond deeper
in the woods—all reflect the contented man. Although, in a letter
to nephew Pierre, he comments mockingly that "I beat all the

gentleman farmers in my neighborhood, for I can manage to raise my vegetables and fruits at very little more than twice the market price," [2] when he left for Spain, he carefully directed brother Ebenezer's attention to "books about gardening, farming, poultry, &c, by which to direct yourself." [3]

Through the economic fluctuations of the years, Irving felt driven to write to protect Sunnyside—and to enlarge it. In 1838 he was inspired to write of the conquest of Mexico, but discovering that William H. Prescott was employed on it, gave up the subject (perhaps he never admired Cortez). In a later revealing letter to Pierre, he regrets the sacrifice and details how he would have proceeded with the work. (Pierre, in printing the letter in his biography, notes that it was "marked (Private); but, now that both are gone, I have felt at liberty to give this interesting portion of its contents." [4] Irving biographers must regret that so few of such "private" letters have survived.) Now having no large project, Irving shortly thereafter agreed to contribute to the *Knickerbocker* magazine, then edited by Louis Gaylord Clark. Although Pierre and others have depicted this contracted writing as being drudgery for Irving, it probably was not. As shown before, Irving was always drawn to the periodical press, and had contributed to it most of his life. Certainly Clark's portrayal of the association shows Irving dropping into the editorial offices, sharing the "in" news of the day, and thoroughly enjoying himself. The *Knickerbocker* had a wide circulation, and Irving took advantage of it to inculcate his lessons to the public.

It was the economic distresses—and the radical *loco foco* solutions to them—that led Irving to abandon Van Buren in his reelection efforts, despite Van Buren's offer to him of the secretaryship of the Navy. Those who had read his works attentively could have predicted such a move; he had always written against free availability of credit and wild speculation; his hero had been Ready-Money Jack, who paid as he went. While Van Buren proposed a subtreasury scheme and Treasury notes, Irving wanted a national bank "properly restrained and guarded," partially to "curb the power of Mr. Biddle, who is now getting a complete financial sway." [5] Irving was rewarded for his shift of allegiance by his appointment as minister to Spain. Although a reward, it was a munificent one, and demonstrates also the shrewd assessment of Irving's political abilities by the presidents of his time: Jackson had used him as advisor, Van Buren offered him a cabinet post, Tyler made him minister. None of these positions were due him because he was a famous writer.

Irving went to Spain by way of England. There, he was invited to stay in Westminster Abbey. In a letter, he recalls his description of it in *The Sketch Book* and compares this stay to his stay in the Alhambra, adding, "am I always to have my dreams turn into realities?" [6] After a short visit to friends in France, he proceeded to the troubled capital of Madrid. Irving took several leaves of absence from his post—the most important one coming at the end of 1845 and extending to the spring of 1846. During this leave, he was called to London by American Minister Louis McLane, to aid in the treaty negotiations concerning the northwest territory. Irving knew the English negotiators, and knew intimately the Oregon question and what would be acceptable to his countrymen. In a letter after he left London, before the treaty was concluded, he insists on the importance of the forty-ninth parallel to the Americans; the United States must possess both banks of the Columbia. The forty-ninth parallel was achieved; Irving's earlier call for the restoration of Astoria was accomplished.

His tour of duty over, Irving immediately returned to Sunnyside. From there, in the following years, he made occasional excursions—to Baltimore, to Pennsylvania, to Saratoga Springs, to Virginia. His home was Sunnyside, when he visited the city he would stay with friends, or, once, in a hotel—the new Irving House, where he was childishly delighted that his name gave him magnificent accommodations. Although now in his declining years, he kept hard at work, revising his works for Putnam's new edition and adding to them his works on Goldsmith, Mahomet and his successors, and *Wolfert's Roost*. There was one more work to be done, a work Irving had contemplated doing probably as early as 1817, the biography of Washington. He was able to complete the last of its five volumes before his health gave way.

Washington Irving died on November 28, 1859, and was buried, next to his mother, in the Sleepy Hollow cemetery. He had taken care to remove the remains of his family there from New York City, commenting, "I look forward with serene satisfaction to being gathered at last to a family gathering place, where my dust may mingle with the dust of those most dear to me." [7] Thus, the hope of the storyteller of "Sleepy Hollow" was realized; the wish of "The Angler" was satisfied; like Shakespeare,

Irving found a quiet grave near his home; once more his dreams had become reality.

II The Crayon Miscellany

In a letter to his brother Peter, Irving announced the plan of *The Crayon Miscellany*, a series of volumes rather than tales: "in this way I mean to clear off all the manuscripts I have on hand, and to throw off casual lucubrations concerning home scenes, &c." [8] This casualness is deceptive; just as Irving had previously been willing to retell any old tale, as long as it suited the purpose and unity of a volume, so the contents of this collection, however old their origins might be, suited Irving's current purposes. Again and again we are reminded of his assertion that it is not the tale but the way it is told that counts. In these volumes we again have Irving's favorite themes: the hunting party, the meeting with Scott, Crayon in the act of peopling places with literary inhabitants, and political allegory.

Of the three volumes, the first, *A Tour on the Prairies*, has proved most enduring. Chief of the reasons for its continued popularity is the artistry and detail of the sketches contained in it. We read and cannot doubt the fidelity of the pictures. The first view of the ranger camp, the picture of Irving fording the stream in the buffalo-hide boat, the bee hunt, the buffalo hunt, the turmoil of the camp when threatened by fire and Indians—Irving's pictorial power is at its strongest. In these sketches, Irving fixes in time the conditions of the frontier.

But the volume is more than a series of sketches, it is also a unified narrative of the journey, filled with character and incident. It is true that nothing momentous happens, not a life is lost, not a hostile Indian is met. But there are characters that are developed through their words and actions. We come to know the ranger captain and old Ryan, a "real old Leatherstocking," the commissioner, the Virtuoso (Charles J. Latrobe) and the Count de Pourtales, and, especially, Tonish and Beatte (the Indian), guides for the commissioner's party. Irving recaptures the emotions of the moment, anticipating nothing: the glee and freshness of spirits of all on first setting out to the Indian hunting grounds, the excitement over the prodigality of game and honey, the growing caution further into the hunting grounds, when orders are given that none may hunt without prior permission, renewal of excitement during the buffalo hunt, and the chase after wild horses. Then we feel with the troop no more excitement on seeing more buffalo, but begin to feel the increase of autumn, the lack of streams, the sterility of the country. The long trek back becomes painful, food is short, the horses give out. And we feel with the men the relief and joy of the return to the frontier farmhouse: "here was a stable, and barn and granaries teeming with abundance; while legions of grunting swine, gobbling turkeys, cackling hens, and strutting roosters, swarmed about the farm-yard." Here also was the mistress of the house, a Negress, wife of a white man, ladling out boiled beef and turnips, bread and butter— "Head of Apicius, what a banquet!"

A Tour on the Prairies is yet still more than sketches and narrative, for it contains allusions to Irving's European themes and experiences. Irving directly refers to these in his preface to the American edition. He tells of his first "bright anticipations," the ensuing "reverse of fortune," the baffled hopes, the thorny path, the "dreary dreams" of returning a stranger to "scenes of his youth gone to ruin and decay." He touches on the accusation of being alienated from his native country: "I should as soon think of vindicating myself from the charge of a want of love to the mother that bore me!" [9] He details his return, his first glimpse from the ship of the " 'blue line of my native land'," and the happy catastrophe of his return to friends and prosperity. *A Tour on the Prairies* repeats this pattern.

The volume also includes motifs and metaphors from his earlier works. The first view of the ranger camp presents "a wild bandit or Robin Hood scene," and the Creek Indians are compared to Gypsies. Soon after encountering this camp and meeting the captain of the band and old Ryan—"the veteran huntsman," "the Nestor of the camp"—occurs the felling of the bee tree, which Irving describes in terms of a bankruptcy. During the glory of the hunt, the rangers are described as banditti. Like Dolph in company with Vander Heyden's hunting party, Irving shoots off a gun in the middle of a stream, "the report echoed along the woody shores." Dolph had shot at an eagle, who dropped a tail feather; in the *Tour*, soon after, we have an Indian tale of an eagle dropping a tail feather. Dolph had great difficulty with the vines; Irving is nearly unhorsed by a grape vine. The captain of the Italian banditti had forbidden all private captures; the captain of the rangers forbids private hunting.

At first, Irving feels he is entering into a "region of adventure" and builds "castles in the clouds," but soon, in the Cross Timbers, the way becomes thorny and arid, "the channels of the streams being dry, and the country being destitute of fountain heads." After this point, we have the dream of union told by Beatte, "the Indian" (in *Bracebridge Hall*, Irving says he was regarded as "a kind of demi-savage, with a feather in his hand, instead of on his head"). Beatte's heart, we are told, "yearned toward his mother's nation," and his tale is prefaced, as was Dolph's, with an anecdote of a skull being unearthed. The tale itself concerns an Indian brave engaged to a beautiful Osage named, not surprisingly, "The Flower of the Prairies." He must make a journey, and on his return to the encampment sees only his future bride, weeping. She conducts him to the new encampment but will not enter it. The brave does, and learns that his beloved had died some days previously. Again the union is denied. Now the journey in the hunting grounds becomes tedious, for "the delirium of the chase had passed away." On the return, Irving watches one night the stars, "like watching them from the deck of a ship at sea." That night, "my dreams partook of the happy tone of my waking reveries." Finally comes the chapter titled "A Look-out for land," and the weary traveler arrives successfully at the abundance of the farm house, owned jointly by black and white. Thus, in metaphor, allusion, and allegory, Irving repeats his European journey and return.

In "Dolph Heyliger," after Dolph encounters the hunting party, he is invited by Vander Heyden to his home. In *The Crayon Miscellany*, after the journey to the hunting grounds comes "Abbottsford," Irving's account of his stay with Walter Scott. To an audience enamored with Scott, the account, picturing Scott's daily life and conversations, was well received; to an Irving biographer, knowing how important this meeting was, the account is frustrating. All is Scott; in the whole, Irving's conversation consists of two or three sentences. In "Abbottsford," Irving is deliberately selective, keeping the light on Scott, leaving himself in the shadow. Again Irving is sketching: we picture Scott limping down the avenue with his dogs to first welcome Irving; Scott at dinner with the family, the dogs, and the cat; then Scott surrounded by the quarry workers, all eager to have a word with the sheriff. We see him sharing his plaid with Irving during a rainy walk, examining attentively a Roman artifact, walking ahead,

WASHINGTON IRVING

repeating fragments of a ballad—always astir, always referring to local lore, anecdote, and poetry.

While these pictures of Scott are loosely ordered by the chronology of the successive days of the visit, the work is further unified by Irving's deepening appreciation of Scott's use of local lore and local scenes. At first the theme is treated lightly; on a visit to Melrose Abbey, Irving gently mocks the circumstance that "the fictions of Scott had become facts with honest Johnny Bower," the guide to the Abbey. But soon Irving, too, is caught up in the poetical associations of the neighborhood: "every turn brought to mind some household air—some almost forgotten song of the nursery, by which I had been lulled to sleep in my childhood." He sees the same effect on Scott, "his mind was fraught with the traditionary fictions connected with every object around him, and he would breathe it forth as he went." As Irving is guided about the region by Scott, Irving more and more finds associations with the land and the inhabitants and Scott's own writings. Finally he concludes, "incidents and feelings that had appeared in his writings, were apt to be mingled up in his conversation, for they had been taken from what he had witnessed and felt in real life, and were connected with those scenes among which he lived, and moved, and had his being." It is, perhaps, this last discovery, that the fictions of Scott were fact, that had such an influence on Irving, that colored his own writing thereafter, that caused him to honor Scott, to look forward to a new work by him "as a traveller in a waste looks to a green spot at a distance, where he feels assured of solace and refreshment."

The second part of this second volume of *The Crayon Miscellany*, "Newstead Abbey," is more elaborately orchestrated than the first. "Abbottsford" relies for its effect on the good humor and happiness of Scott at a time before his cottage had swollen to a baronial pile. There is no such character at Newstead Abbey, there are only relics associated with Lord Byron. The effect of "Newstead Abbey" is disquieting; it exists in a more complex world, with horrors lurking around and within it. While "Abbottsford" would be the basis for an excellent documentary on Scott, "Newstead Abbey" offers materials for a surrealistic movie.

Irving prefaces "Newstead Abbey" with an historical note detailing the establishment of the Abbey, its passage into the family of the Byrons during the reign of Henry VIII, and the misdeeds of the poet's predecessor and granduncle, "the wicked Byron."

Thus from the beginning, Newstead is the product of history, in contrast to Abbotsford, just becoming history. Throughout this section we are made to feel the weight of the past upon the present—Irving, in first proceeding to the salon to meet its present owners, is intensely aware of the former monks and the former knights who once inhabited the Abbey.

Except for the beginning historical note, "Newstead Abbey," as "Abbotsford," is accretive—we become more and more familiar with the estate and the surrounding Sherwood Forest as Irving himself does. As at Abbotsford, Irving sees the Abbey and the region through literature. As Irving treads each chamber, each woodland, he associates it with appropriate quotations from Byron's poetry, or from legends of Robin Hood. But a minor key resounds amid this poetic worship, the motif of mental derangement. Byron's predecessor was a misanthrope whom the countryside thought slightly mad. And the poet's conduct while at Newstead also is eccentric; he dug up a monk's coffin, and kept it inside; he kept two monks' skulls in his own chamber. He was said to have believed the superstitions connected with the Abbey, a belief described by Irving as an "innate infirmity."

While Colonel Wildman, the present owner of the Abbey, is trying to restore its dilapidated condition, Annesley Hall, the home of the poet's first love, Mary Ann Chaworth, is not so fortunate. On a visit to it in search of more scenes associated with Byron's poetry, Irving finds the garden gone to ruin, ceilings fallen in, and the whole house barricaded: its owner's Norttingham house had been sacked by the mob. Again the motif of madness enters; Mary Ann Chaworth had, after marriage, gone mad. Despite this ominous motif, Irving persists in attempting to recall the poetical past: "I felt I could . . . spin reveries and dream dreams, until all became an ideal world."

Irving extends his poetical tour to those scenes associated with the days of Robin Hood. He views the Parliament Oak, and imagines the courtly scenes of the time of King John, a "phantasmagoria" that soon vanishes, "I awoke to all that remained of this once stirring scene of human pomp and power—a mouldering oak, and a tradition." He rides to a grove of most ancient trees, and pictures Robin Hood and his band, but again the vision is short, stopped by the sound of an ax: a "noble agriculturist; a modern utilitarian, who had no feeling for poetry or forest scenery" is clearing the forest. This puts Crayon's "cobweb fan-

cies" to flight, and he is out of sorts until he hears the evening
bells of Mansfield, and discovers Friar Tuck's Fountain Dale—
there is still poetry in the world.

Irving concludes "Newstead Abbey" with the story of "The
Little White Lady," a story which brings together the themes of
madness and of peopling the countryside from the literary past.
The Little White Lady is a poor woman who has become deaf
and dumb and whom the country people believe "to be under the
influence of mental hallucination." She haunts Newstead Abbey,
having an idolotry of the genius of Lord Byron. At Newstead she
is content, she has an ideal world around her, she exists "as in a
dream." Entrapped in this monomania, and fearful of absolute
poverty, she determines to go to London in an attempt to better
her fortune. She leaves with Mrs. Wildman her poetry written on
Byron and Newstead, and a letter, depicting her grief at leaving
and her dread of what she fears is her increasing insanity. Mrs.
Wildman sends her assurance that she can remain at Newstead,
but the Little White Lady had already gone to Nottingham,
where she was run over and killed by a cart.

Abbotsford and Newstead Abbey begins with Scott, his mind
filled with the poetical associations of the countryside, and ends
with the monomania of the Little White Lady, her mind filled
with the poetical associations of Byron. We move from Melrose
Abbey to Newstead Abbey, from Scott's varnished monk's skull
to Byron's two monks' skulls. But Scott is not a monomaniac; he
participates in all the society around him, and "looked upon poor
human nature with an indulgent eye." The health of Abbotsford
becomes disease at Newstead as Irving repeats his themes of
Bracebridge Hall and *Tales of a Traveller*

The minor key on which the second volume ends becomes
dominant in the last volume of *The Crayon Miscellany, Legends
of the Conquest of Spain.* While both Scott and Southey wrote of
Roderick, the last Gothic King of Spain, Irving focuses on Count
Julian, who betrayed both Roderick and his own country. In this
volume, Irving makes no pretense to historical accuracy, declaring that he is merely recording legends. But these are carefully
selected legends, depicting a country divided against itself, and
consequently overrun and conquered. This was the least well
received of the three volumes, and Irving never reprinted it
during his lifetime.

The volume consists of three legends: "The Legend of Don

Roderick," "The Legend of the Subjugation of Spain," and "The Legend of Count Julian and His Family." Although the events they chronicle are in chronological order, the three legends are distinct, the second being told from the view of the Moslems. The first legend begins with the reign of Witzia, an elected sovereign, one who was also commander in chief of the armies and who held in his hands the disposal of patronage. He is noted for issuing a doctrine to the pope: "'we will suffer no foreign ecclesiastic, with triple crown . . . to domineer over our dominions.'" Witzia, during his reign, disarmed his subjects and enfeebled the land's fortifications. He is succeeded by Roderick (Irving has some doubts on whether Roderick was truly elected or not), grandson of a former sovereign, who followed Witzia's policy of turning swords into ploughshares. He is courted by Count Julian, "a man of an active but irregular genius, and a grasping ambition; he had a love for power and grandeur, in which he was joined by his haughty countess."

Count Julian had been military advisor to Witzia, but so persuades Roderick of his altered allegiance, that Roderick gives him further honors. In pledge of his faith, Count Julian leaves his daughter, Florinda, in the care of Roderick's queen, Exilona. Roderick, debauched by voluptuousness, seduces her. The Count, on hearing from Florinda of the loss of her chastity, urged on by his haughty wife, swears a dreadful revenge: to punish not only his sovereign, but to betray his own country, to deliver it into the hands of the same enemy he had just defeated in battle. Disguising his purpose, he visits the Spanish capital, received the honors paid to him for his victory, and easily persuades Roderick to send the best troops of the country to the province he governs and to the far frontier, "so that the kingdom was left almost wholly without defense against any sudden irruption from the south." He conducts his family to his hereditary dominions, where he rallies his adherents. Having convinced the Arabs of the practicality of an invasion, he sets in motion the consequent defeat of Spain. The legend ends with a malediction on Count Julian.

While this legend is overlaid and embossed with oriental and gothic fantasy, its bare bones are parallel to events of the United States. Monroe issued his doctrine, primarily to the Triple Alliance. He was succeeded by John Quincy Adams, son of a former president. John C. Calhoun, who had been secretary of war under Monroe, was vice-president under Adams and during Jackson's first term. Calhoun and Jackson split on the question of a lady's chastity, that of Peggy Eaton, new wife of Jackson's favorite advisor and cabinet member. Floride Calhoun, to protect her daughters, refused to visit Mrs. Eaton; she returned to South Carolina with her family so she would not have to meet Mrs. Eaton. Calhoun, angered by the Tariff of Abominations, had conceived the doctrine of nullification, which was put into effect by South Carolina in 1832. When Calhoun returned to Washington to take his Senate seat, many of his colleagues ignored him; many considered him a rebel and a traitor.

The second section, "Legend of the Subjugation of Spain," centers on the invaders. Muza ben Nosier, director of the Arabs' war efforts in Western Africa, on Count Julian's invitation sends Taric el Tuerto to invade Spain. Taric's success is rapid and overwhelming; Muza becomes jealous and orders him to halt his career, to wait until he, as his superior, arrives with reinforcements. Taric, disappointed, proceeds to obey, but is dissuaded by the treacherous advice of Count Julian: "over run the provinces, seize upon the cities, make yourself master of the capital, and your conquest is complete." Taric listens, and proceeds with his conquest. On his arrival in Spain, Muza censures Taric for insubordination and has him arrested, only to free him later on orders from his sovereign. The two, together, complete the subjection of Spain.

After the conquest is complete, Muza and Taric, or rather their partisans, strive to win the approbation of the sovereign and to injure the other. The caliph orders the two to appear before him at Damascus. Muza gathers together a great spoil, to appear in glory at Damascus. Taric, having given all his booty to his troops or to Muza, is unencumbered, and arrives at the capital first. The multitude honors Taric as conqueror of the West: "they were charmed with his gaunt and martial air, his hard, sun burnt features, and his scathed eye." When Muza arrives, he abrogates all honor to himself as commander in chief, making no mention of Taric. This incenses the sovereign, who honors Taric and deprives Muza of his spoil. The successor to the caliph is more vengeful to Muza, listening with willing ear to accusations that Muza had embezzled, stripping him of his offices and contriving the death of his sons.

Again, there are historical parallels to this legend, parallels again involving Calhoun, but from an earlier date than the first.

When Calhoun was secretary of war, Jackson was directed to put down an Indian uprising in south Georgia. Poised on its border with Florida, then owned by Spain, he sent to ask of Monroe if he could invade. He thought he received private affirmation from the president; Calhoun's orders had been " 'Adopt the necessary measures to terminate the conflict.' " [10] And so Jackson invaded Florida, like Taric, making short work of capturing city after city, accomplishing the whole in fifty-nine days. Neither the British, the Spanish, nor the American Cabinet were pleased by the invasion. Calhoun, according to Adams, " 'seems personally offended . . . that Jackson has set at naught the instructions of the Department.' " [11] Calhoun asked that Jackson be made the object of an official inquiry; later rumor had it he demanded his court-martial. But, unlike Taric, Jackson was never imprisoned by his rival. Both Calhoun and Jackson appealed to the sovereign people in the following election; the people, like the Damascus multitude, preferring Jackson (although Adams was elected by the House of Representatives). And, like Muza, Calhoun was accused of having embezzled funds while he was secretary of war.

As Muza's sins were visited on his sons, so are Count Julian's in the last, very brief, legend. After the conquest, Count Julian continues his successful alliance with the Moslems, but is not happy. His daughter, Florinda, when she sees the devastation brought on Spain in her name, commits suicide. His wife takes his only son to the stronghold of Ceuta, but is there overcome by a force of the new ruler of Spain, who fears that Count Julian, having once betrayed, will betray again. The son, although hidden by his mother in the vault of his sister's tomb, is found, led to a high tower, told to reach out his arms to Spain, and is pushed to his death on the rocks below. The Countess's death is even more horrible; captive Christians are forced to stone her to death. Count Julian's own death is obscure, but said also to be horrible. His name is forever hated in Spain, and Irving concludes, "such ever be the lot of him who betrays his country." Obviously, there are no historical parallels for this third legend, but we cannot doubt the sincerity of Irving's last wish. Few, today, see Calhoun as a traitor, but many then and now saw that his nullification doctrine led directly to secession. It is clear that Irving, in 1835, anticipated a civil war.

III   Astoria *and* Bonneville

With *Astoria* (1836), Irving returned to true history and to
a truly American theme. *Astoria* is the account of the various
adventures, by sea and land, involved in John Jacob Astor's establishment of the Pacific Fur Company and its post at the mouth of
the Columbia River. In Irving's time the book was hailed as being
almost as good as a romance; today it is regarded as being a
remarkably accurate history and, in some parts, as the only source
remaining of the events it records. The book consists, basically,
of four narratives, unified by references to the overall scheme of
Astor. The first is that of the ship *Tonquin*, which carried the
men and supplies to found the post on the Columbia. The second
is of the overland expedition of Wilson P. Hunt and his band of
trappers. The third details the return trip overland of Robert
Stuart and his party with dispatches for Astor. The fourth tells of
the fates of various supply ships and the fall of Astoria. Although
the narratives are distinct, the whole is unified by the nature
of the attempt itself.

The *Tonquin* put to sea from New York on September 8, 1810,
and arrived at the Columbia on March 22, 1811. Of all the narratives, the tone of this is lightest, at times it is almost mocking.
Irving brings the ship's passengers to life: the three Canadian
partners, very aware of their dignity, quarreling with each other
over the best way to construct the fort; the young clerks, scribbling away in their journals and teasing the captain by speaking
Scots; the French voyageurs, seasick, offering up their tributes to
the windward, to the great disgust of the captain. And then there
is Captain Thorn—one of Irving's best seriocomic portraits. Accustomed to naval discipline (he was on leave from the U.S. Navy),
he resents the voyageurs, quarrels with the partners, fears the
clerks are fomenting a mutiny, and will not let anyone touch the
cargo. The voyage is full of major and minor spats, which continue even as the *Tonquin* lands that part of the cargo destined
for Astoria. Having landed the Astorians and their supplies, the
Tonquin sailed north to trade along the coast. At her first harbor,
her captain and crew are surprised and massacred by Indians. In
revenge, the ship's clerk blew her up, along with over one hundred Indians. Despite this catastrophe, this first narrative is entertaining, chiefly because Irving is indulgent toward all the
parties—showing how natural it was for each to act as he did,

and also how natural it was that each action should offend the other party.

The narrative of the journey overland, led by the fourth partner, Wilson P. Hunt, a citizen of the United States, is of a different sort, for here Irving is more concerned with landscape than with character. Hunt's journey began in July 1810, in Montreal, where he received his trading goods and attempted to recruit French voyageurs. From thence he proceeded by river to Mackinaw, then to St. Louis. Here he recruited hunters and made his way up the Missouri to northern South Dakota, where he purchased horses, then crossed the Rocky Mountains. Encountering bitter weather and little food, he cached his goods on the Snake River plain and, dividing his men, sought the best way to the Columbia. At length he arrived at Astoria on February 15, 1812.

This narrative is the longest and most detailed; it gives the daily incidents, extensive description of the lands, characteristics of the various Indian tribes, and accounts given by previous travelers in the same region. Unlike the first narrative, in which Irving regards the characters from a distance, this is more immediate; the reader goes with Hunt, is perplexed when he is, encounters treachery as he does. In this, Irving is again sympathetic to the Indians: he anticipates and pities their gradual reduction, he deplores the transfer from the East to the West of whole tribes, he foresees them turning into marauding, predatory bands. He also pleads for the retention of Indian place names, which would "remain mementos of the primitive lords of the soil, of whom in a little while scarce any traces will be left."

The third narrative is briefer, and deals with a return trip, overland, by Robert Stuart and six others, bearing dispatches to Astor concerning the state of the post. They leave Astoria on June 29, 1812, and arrive at St. Louis on April 30, 1813. The return trip is not as severe as the outgoing one had been; the band encounters the Rockies at a better time of year and finds easier routes, although there are still hesitancies and uncertainties. They find the headwaters of the Platte and descend it to the Missouri and thence to St. Louis. From there they send to Astor the news of the safe arrival at Astoria of Hunt and his party and of the safe arrival of the supply ship *Beaver.*

Meanwhile, war had broken out with England, and the final section details the effects of that war. The North West Fur Company persuaded the English of the strength and importance of

the port on the Columbia, and the harm it would do its trade.
That company fitted out an armed frigate, and the English sent
the *Phoebe* and three other ships to accompany it. Astor armed
the *Enterprize*, to sail for Astoria with the U.S.S. *Adams*. But the
men of the *Adams* were needed for Lake Ontario; the New York
harbor was blockaded, thus, no help for Astoria could come from
New York. With these details as background, Irving gives us the
narrative of Hunt's travels by sea, a narrative which borders on
the marvellous and which is told with something of the same detachment and humor as the first of the *Tonquin*. According to
Irving, Hunt boarded the supply ship *Beaver*, which proceeded
north up the coast to New Archangel, where it delivered supplies
to the Russian garrison, and where Hunt was compelled to match
drinks with the Russian governor in order to bargain with him. In
return for the supplies, the *Beaver* received seal skins, and was to
return to Astoria, but her captain, fearful of the Columbia's winter
currents, sailed instead to Hawaii, where he landed Hunt, and
proceeded to Canton, to sell the furs.

In Hawaii, Hunt first heard of the outbreak of the war, and
chartered the *Albatross* to take him and supplies to the Columbia.
Hunt having successfully arrived there, the three Canadian partners suggested that he should reembark in the ship to seek a ship
to carry the collected furs to market and to return the Hawaiians
they had earlier conscripted to their home. And so Hunt re-
embarked on the *Albatross*, went in it to the Marquesas, where he
met with Commodore Porter, who promised to engage, if he
could, with the British fleet sent to reduce Astoria. Hunt then
went to Hawaii, there met the captain of an Astor supply ship
which had been wrecked, and purchased the *Pedlar*. Then he proceeded in it to Astoria, intending to remove Astor's property
therein to the Russian Alaskan settlements (such had been his
instructions carried by the shipwrecked ship), but discovered, on
his arrival at the Columbia, that the remaining three partners
had already sold out to the North West Company on October 16,
1813, that on November 30, 1813, a British sloop of war, the
Racoon, had come to seize the fort and its contents, but had been
chagrined to find them already in British/Canadian hands. Hunt,
and the *Pedlar*, arriving on February 28, 1814, took away with
them the bills of sale and two of the clerks.

Irving subsumes a few details to this last narrative—the return of Astoria to *status ante bellum*, Captain James Biddle's

formal reclamation of it after the war, and subsequent treaties with England, allowing natives of both countries to settle in the region afer the war. *Astoria* ends with Irving's call for the re-acquisition and control of the Columbia in order to give the United States a port on the Pacific and to open up the fertile regions of Oregon to settlers. Thus, *Astoria* is propaganda, setting forth to the nations the rights of the United States to the Columbia River basin. It is also propaganda aimed at the citizens of the United States, showing that, although there were hostile Indian tribes, they could be awed, avoided, or propitiated, that the route across the Rockies was not impossible, and giving them, in word and by maps, the best route to Oregon.

Astoria is both history and propaganda. Eminent historians have attested to the truth of what Irving wrote; the literary style of *Astoria* and its contemporary popularity attest to the power of its propaganda. And yet, while *Astoria* is a monumental work with which every student of American history should be familiar, the whole has about it an air of misdirection, in fact, the whole enterprise has an air of misdirection. Our attention, the attention of the North West Company, the attention of the English is constantly directed to the new post on the Columbia. Yet this soleness of direction should itself invite questions. Astor, the head of the very successful American Fur Company, with numerous loyal company men, selected three clerks of the rival North West Company, with relatives high in the echelons of that Company, as partners in his new Pacific Fur Company. Their immediate action, Irving tells us, upon hearing of Astor's full plans, is to report to the English Consul in New York. Having thus clearly disclosed his intentions of stealing a march on the North West Company and, consequently, the English, Astor sent off the *Tonquin*, and sent Hunt to Montreal, to further advertise the expedition by receiving his supplies there, and there recruiting voyageurs.

What is the result of all this effort by both land and by sea? We share the chagrin of the commander of the British sloop of war, who came to batter down the walls of this important fort (which, at its height, may have contained fifty men). There was nothing to capture but a wooden palisade and some bundles of furs, which had already been sold to the Canadians (the majority of the goods Hunt had brought overland had either been stolen by the Indians or taken back East by Stuart). There was little for the English to capture—no profits accrued to the crown.

That Astor sincerely believed in the advantage to the United States of possessing the Columbia is undoubted. That this was his most compelling motive in this enterprize is questionable. Very early in his narrative, Irving tells us that part of Astor's plan was to supply regularly the Russian settlements in Alaska, thus soothing a Russian complaint against erratic American ships who armed the natives with guns. Irving also tells us that, at that time, Russia was almost the only friendly power (although Irving leads us to believe that Astor's movements had the sanction of Jefferson, they were undertaken during Madison's presidency, at a time when wars with both England and France were feared). Irving also tells us, very late in the book, that an Astor agent (conducted to Europe in a U.S. ship) concluded an agreement with the Russian Fur Company—with the consent of the Russian government—to act in concord against a mutual enemy. With Astor on the Columbia, and the Russians extending their sway down from Alaska, this treaty might have excluded the Canadians from the Pacific. The treaty with the Russians was also important because New Archangel, the capital of the Russian Alaskan colony, was a major Pacific port, much visited by American ships, which were excluded from the California ports.

With this in mind, we review the cruise of the *Tonquin* and her captain's care that none of the partners inspect her cargo. After landing the Astorians's supplies, the *Tonquin* still contained enough munitions on board so that the ship's clerk was able to produce a spectacular explosion that not only demolished the ship, but killed one hundred Indians and maimed countless others. Would the ammunition for her ten guns alone be enough to produce this explosion? Or was the *Tonquin* carrying ammunition to the Russian colonies? The second Astor ship, the *Beaver*, touched briefly at Astoria, taking on board Hunt, then successfully landed her stores at New Archangel, where Hunt remained over a month, negotiating with the Russian governor. This governor, we are told, had great influence along the Pacific coast; New Archangel was a fort of one hundred guns and "the common rendezvous of the American vessels trading along the coast." We further see the importance of this fort when we hear of Astor's orders, sent out by the shipwrecked *Lark*, that, in case of danger, the property of Astoria is to be removed there.

Thus, we suspect, the post on the Columbia was never intended to be more than a frontier outpost for the main base of operations at the already established and fortified port of New Archangel. While all eyes were focused on the Columbia, Astor—and the United States—had secured a safe harbor where American ships could resupply—and possibly rearm—further to the north, at New Archangel. Astor's vision included the Columbia, Alaska —and Hawaii; he hoped, Irving says, to gain possession of one of the islands to supply his China ships. Astor lived to see the United States gain possession of the Columbia, but neither he nor Irving lived to see the admission of the forty-ninth and fiftieth states.

Did Astor misdirect Irving also? It is doubtful. Irving's tone in the first and fourth narratives betrays him. His picture of the Russian governor, comic as it is, obscures the fact that Irving neglects to tell us what Hunt and the governor were bargaining about, just as his comic characterizations of the passengers and captain obscure the cargo of the *Tonquin*. Although this is just the kind of misdirection Irving loved, in 1836 he wanted the readers' full attention focused on Oregon and the West. The treaty with England was due to be reviewed in two years and he, like Astor and Jackson, saw the need of the Pacific coast. He foresaw the waves of emigration reaching to the Rockies, "and they will become impatient of any barrier or impediment in the way of what they consider a grand outlet of our empire."

Irving's next work, *The Adventures of Captain Bonneville* (1837), savors even more strongly of misdirection. He tells us, in his preface, that he met Captain Benjamin Bonneville at Astor's, when he was working on *Astoria*, and later met him when Bonneville was trying to fashion the account of his adventures in the Rocky Mountains into a book. The book not finding a ready publisher, Irving bought it, added to it, and issued it as *The Rocky Mountains: Or, Scenes, Incidents and Adventures in the Far West* (its present title was given it by Irving's English publisher). The first title is accurately descriptive; his brother Peter mentions this soon-to-be-published work in these terms: "It is a picture of a singular class of people midway between the savage state and civilization, who will soon cease to exist, and be only known in such records, which will form a department of great interest in the history of our country." [12]

Irving, who in *Astoria* had called for the preservation of Indian names and customs before all vanished, here presents us with these details, unified by Bonneville's wanderings. The book is thus not merely the rewriting of Bonneville's book; it may be that less than half is derived from it (although this may never be ascertained, for both Bonneville's and Irving's manuscripts have disappeared). Irving collected additional details from another explorer, Nathaniel Wyeth, from fur trappers and traders, and from sea captains. The book is valuable as a fixed picture of the tribes of the West in 1832–1835. Here are recorded the names of the tribes, their dwellings, their armament, their enemies, their annual movements, their games, their artifacts, their food, their loves.

One anecdote, concerning a Nez Percé Indian, seems Irving's own. The Indian was the "prodigal son in his native village" and was soon expelled. He then went "to the society of the border Indians, and had led a careless, haphazard, vagabond life." He was an expert hunter, and Captain Bonneville fitted him out in fine style. So arrayed, he decides to revisit his people, and does so in great glee. But he returns, naked and forlorn, explaining his poor cousins had admired his array, had asked for this and that: "in fine, what with the poor devil's inherent heedlessness, and the real generosity of his disposition, his needy cousins had succeeded in stripping him." Unfortunately for the literary quality of the work, there are too many scenes and incidents; the informal anecdotes of Indian life are too few to make *Bonneville* the romance *Astoria* was.

But this does not entirely explain why *Bonneville* is the worst book Irving ever wrote. In this book Irving loses the trust of the reader. The suspension of belief does not come when Irving details the Indian life, nor when he quotes directly from Bonneville, but when he tells of the motives for Bonneville's movements. Irving's misdirection is here so blatant (admittedly the work was hurriedly written) that we must either disgustedly declare, as Alan Sandy implies in his perceptive introduction to the Twayne edition of *Bonneville*, that Irving pandered his pen to the government and wrote what it wanted written,[13] or admiringly claim, that even despite the misdirection, Irving recorded all the details of the expedition, so that its true nature could be reconstructed in the future. The major illusion of the book is that the Bonneville expedition was a fur-trapping expedition. Historians have long since concluded that the expedition was sent by the government to collect intelligence of the British and Mexican movements in the West. The government, however, disguised it as a fur-trapping expedition, and Irving records the disguise—although, it must be noted, he never records Bonneville or his immediate party actually trapping furs. Irving's work is thus our major source for this intelligence expedition. It has been found to be extremely accurate geographically, it is probably accurate in dating and, except for one major omission, in recording the movements of Bonneville's men. Even omitting all the camouflage of fur trapping, the book is still a remarkable document of the Western military campaigns of 1832–1833, 1833–1834, and 1834–1835.

In May 1832, on leave from the army and ostensibly as the head of a private fur company, Captain Bonneville left Independence, Missouri, for the great rendezvous of trappers and suppliers, to be held that year at Pierre's Hole in western Wyoming. With his two lieutenants, J. R. Walker and M. S. Cerré, who were both familiar with the western Mexican settlements, and with 120 mounted men and twenty wagons, he struck due west into Kansas, then northwest to strike the Platte at Grand Island, thus avoiding any settlements along the Missouri and at the mouth of the Platte. He failed to make use of the steamboats which, we were told in the appendix to *Astoria*, were then in use on the Missouri and Yellowstone rivers. The wagon train detoured around Chimney Rock, then followed the North Platte and the Sweetwater to the Green (Colorado) River, where was built Fort Bonneville. There Captain Bonneville cached part of the wagons' contents *and the wagons*, thus hiding any evidence of a wagon train. Here he met Lucian Fontenelle of the American Fur Company, who gave him guides and may have also given him trapping supplies. Here also Bonneville detached twenty men to winter on the Bear River, from which, via the Great Salt Lake, a trapping expedition had, in 1826, penetrated to California.[14]

Only after the trapping rendezvous at Pierre's Hole had broken up did Bonneville proceed thence on his way to winter quarters on the Salmon River. Meanwhile, Captain Nathaniel Wyeth, guided by a brigade of trappers, had proceeded from Pierre's Hole to the British Fort Vancouver, well established on the Columbia, arriving there in late October. In late September, Bonneville detached his lieutenant, M. S. Cerré, and twenty men to hunt with the Nez Percés; in late November he detached his other lieutenant, J. R. Walker, with fifty men, to winter on the

Snake. Bonneville himself wintered near the headwaters of the
Salmon. Whether Walker's detachment did remain on the Snake
is unknown, but Cerré's detachment probably went to California;
he had returned to Bonneville by February 19, 1833. Thus, as
the nullification controversy was coming to a crisis, and when
fears of secession, civil war, and invasion were at their height,
Jackson had men at the most important northern fort on the
Columbia, men in California, ranging between Monterey and
San Francisco, and Bonneville, strategically in the middle, with
a fort already built near the head of the only previously un-
fortified major river to the heartland, the Platte. (And Irving
was with a company of Rangers scouting between the Red and
Arkansas Rivers.)

All the detachments—Walker's, Wyeth's, Cerré's—and the
regular yearly rendezvous of the trappers came together in early
July 1833, on the Green River. Here Bonneville may have received new orders via the trappers' supply train. From here he
sent Cerré East, to report in person, and sent with him his own
report to Major General McComb. Wyeth also returned with
Cerré. Bonneville also sent back furs: that the various detachments did trap is evidenced by an article in *Silliman's Journal*
for January 1834 (which Irving published in the "Appendix" to
Astoria):

Another company of one hundred and fifty persons from New York,
formed in 1831, and headed by Captain Bonneville of the United
States army, has pushed its enterprizes into tracts before but little
known, and has brought considerable quantities of furs from the
region between the Rocky Mountains and the coasts of Monterey and
Upper California, on the Buenaventura and Timpanogos rivers.[15]

This paragraph is also evidence that one of the Bonneville de-
tachments did go to California in 1832–1833; that it was probably
Cerré's is deduced from the fact that he was chosen to bear
Bonneville's letter to Major General McComb.

Now, at his original caches on the Green River, Bonneville
outfitted his lieutenant, Walker, and forty men, from their contents. The wagons were probably not reassembled (Bonneville,
revisiting the caches the following winter, found one had been
broken open, but that it had contained only scrap iron—probably
all that remained of the wagons). Walker and his men went, via

the Bear River and Great Salt Lake, to Monterey, then the capital of California. There, presumably, he delivered his goods, and returned the following spring (1834), empty handed, to Bonneville, then on the Pont Neuf. That winter (1833–1834) Bonneville had left his main force on the Pont Neuf, and, with a few men, had visited the lower Columbia, although not venturing to Fort Vancouver. He visited chiefly among the Nez Percés and returned to the spring rendezvous on the Pont Neuf. There he met Walker, returning from California, Wyeth, on his way to the Columbia with a detachment of sixty men, Cerré, returning from the East with supplies, and Montero, with a new detachment of men. After the rendezvous, all dispersed. Bonneville sent Walker and some of the men who had been to California back East with Cerré; Wyeth detached some of his men to establish a fort on the Pont Neuf, then continued to the Columbia; Montero proceeded to the Crow country, around the Black Hills; and Bonneville returned to the Blue Mountains of Oregon. Montero and Bonneville were to rendezvous on the headwarters of the Arkansas the following spring, but Montero not completing his mission, the two met in the Wind River Mountains instead. From here, Montero returned to his post, and Bonneville returned East by the Sweetwater and North Platte.

Thus, despite the illusions and misdirections of Irving's book, we can still detect the major movements of the various detachments. Irving's account of Bonneville's own movements, and his descriptions of the Indians are probably recorded with great fidelity. But Irving is most at fault in his treatment of the expeditions to California. He omits all mention of the first and slanders the second by implying that its men disobeyed orders by going there, and, once there, that they did nothing but make merry. What Walker carried to California we may never know; we do know that Jackson tried to buy California from Mexico and we know that, two years after the Walker expedition, the Californians rebelled against Mexico.[16] Despite our disbelief of Irving's truth-telling, despite the tediousness of parts of the narrative, *Bonneville* remains fascinating for its mystery.

IV   *The Literary Biographies:* Davidson *and* Goldsmith

Irving's next work, the *Biography of the Late Margaret Miller Davidson* (1841), has a curious resemblance to *Bonneville*. This biography of a young poetess who died at sixteen was chiefly drawn from notes furnished by the mother. Like Bonneville's book, these notes have since disappeared. Unlike *Bonneville*, however, in which Irving's quotations from Bonneville are infrequent, in the *Biography* quotations from the mother are both frequent and extensive. While Irving bought Bonneville's book and kept the copyright in his own name, he secured the copyright of the *Biography* to the mother and gave her the proceeds of its sale.

The *Biography* is a curious document, revealing the mother as well as the daughter. Margaret's sister, Lucretia, also a poetess, had died when Margaret was two—her works were published posthumously. As the child begins to speak, we see the invalid mother urging her on to poetry, talking to her of Lucretia and her works. On Margaret's composing her first poem, much is made of it, thus further directing her to that field, and Irving adds, "for good or for evil." Indeed, Irving, who in so many of his works describes the poetical feeling as productive of nothing but illusion, warned the mother against "fostering her poetic vein . . . [instead] enlarge that common sense which is the only safe foundation for all intellectual superstructure." And, as with the Little White Lady, we find that while, at first, Margaret "seemed to live in a world of her own creation, surrounded by the images of her own fancy," later "these moments of intense poetical exaltation sometimes approached to delirium."

While Irving's comments are occasionally sentimental, the quotations from the mother invariably are. At one point Irving feels compelled to remind the reader that "though these memoirs, which are furnished principally from the recollections of an afflicted mother, may too often represent this gifted little being as a feeble invalid struggling with mortality, yet in truth her life, though brief, was a bright and happy one." And he counters the mother's sentimentality with letters from Margaret, full of playfulness—and common sense. Her letters, more than her poetry, compel our admiration. But it was her poetry and her mother's letters to Catharine Sedgwick detailing her death that were most hailed by contemporary reviewers. Today, the *Biography of the Late Margaret Miller Davidson* remains as a cultural document of Victorian sensibility and of the education and daily pursuits of a young American girl.

In his *Oliver Goldsmith: A Biography* (1849), Irving shows

us anew how very well he can write when he is happy, and happy with his subject. He had previously written at least two biographical prefaces to editions of Goldsmith's works; now, inspired by a recent scholarly biography, he composed his longer work. Some have dismissed it as a typical Victorian biography; but few Victorian biographies are so well unified, so well written, so enjoyable as this. Irving is not compiling a factual tome of dates and honors and works and letters of a famous author, such as Lockhart's *Life of Scott*, or Pierre M. Irving's own biography of Irving, or any of the "Life and Letters" that then predominated. What Irving does is to introduce us to the man, to make us acquainted with him, revealing his strengths and weaknesses, so that, when we close the book, we feel that we not only know poor Goldsmith, but we like him.

The fascination the life of Goldsmith held for Irving seems to have been that it "lets us into the secret of his gifted pages. We there discover them to be little more than transcripts of his own heart and picturings of his fortunes." This theme Irving emphasizes again and again. Of a Goldsmith manuscript that was never published, Irving comments, "like the author's other writings it might have abounded with pictures of life and touches of nature drawn from his own observation and experience and mellowed by his own humane and tolerant spirit." And, throughout the volume, in detailing the misadventures of Goldsmith, Irving shows them transmuted into his literary works.

The life of Goldsmith may also have interested Irving because of other similarities to his own earlier career. In reading the first part of Irving's *Goldsmith*, we feel almost as if we are reading another version of "Buckthorne and His Friends." As in that section of *Tales of a Traveller*, we have the poetic youth, impatient of logic, and his fond mother, who persuades the father to devote the son "to poverty and the muse." We have an episode of orchard poaching, which is likened to Shakespeare's deer stealing, we have a disastrous stay at a university, and finally, we have the hero hackwriting in London, just as did the Poor-Devil Author who inherited Goldsmith's chambers. One of the most vicious lines in this otherwise genial work concerns the publisher Newberry, who lived by the writings of such poor-devil authors: "He coined the brains of his authors in the times of their exigency and made them pay dear for the plank put out to keep them from drowning. It is not likely his death caused much lamentation among the scribbling tribe; we may express decent respect for the memory of the just, but we shed tears only at the grave of the generous."

While some circumstances of Irving's early English career and that of Goldsmith's are similar (both poor, both bachelors, both in a foreign land, both hackwriters, both enamored of the theater), the two had quite different characters. Yet Irving sympathizes completely with poor Goldsmith—he questions the received picture of Goldsmith, as presented by Boswell and others, that Goldsmith was a vain man, an idiot in conversation who, although (barely) a gentleman, had a distinct taste for low life. Irving controverts this picture in several ways: he discredits Boswell by quoting Johnson's and other contemporaries' ridicule of him; he shows, in each negative Boswellian passage, how easily another interpretation could be placed upon the recorded conversation. As to the general charges of vanity and a taste for low life, Irving does not simply record them, or deny them, but looks beyond them, seeking the causes of these faults. Irving ascribes Goldsmith's love for elegant clothes to Goldsmith's compensating for his ugliness—early ridicule of his person had been deeply felt. As for Goldsmith's preference for low life over high society, Irving claims that Goldsmith, like his friend Hogarth, "was guided not by a taste for what was low, but for what was comic and characteristic." And we are reminded of the same preferences of the Poor-Devil Author, and his less elegant claim that low life "manured his brain."

But for all its insights into Goldsmith's character, Irving's biography is now virtually unread—Goldsmith's scholars turn to more scholarly works. It stands, however, as a fine example of Irving's style; in this work, Irving seems to have borrowed something from both Johnson and Goldsmith, and gems glitter upon the pages. Again and again we encounter sentences so concise, so witty, so balanced, we can but relish them; his concluding remarks stand as an example for any biographer. "Poor Goldsmith"—Irving makes us admire him.

V   Mahomet *and* Mahomet's Successors

Irving took notes on the life of Mahomet when in Madrid during the winter of 1827, possibly in conjunction with his researches for *The Conquest of Granada*. In 1831, he offered for Murray's

perusal part of a work entitled "The Legendary Life of Mahomet," in which Murray was uninterested. In Spain as diplomat,
Irving read further of Mahomet, and finally, in December, 1849,
published *Mahomet*, a compact volume of digested materials
suited for popular reading. Although Irving includes legends
which had grown up around Mahomet, he distinguishes them
from biographical fact. He presents Mahomet as an intelligent
man who sincerely believed he was God's last prophet, sent to
reform the idolatrous and to return them to the pure faith of
Abraham and Ishmael.

Irving sees Mahomet's life as falling into three divisions: pre-
prophetic, prophetic and persecuted, and prophetic and perse-
cuting. He presents the young Mahomet as unlettered but
intelligent, with a retentive memory and an inquiring spirit. He
learned early the doctrines of the Nestorian Christians as well
as the creed of the Jews and saw that they were preferable to
the debased religions of the Arabs. Having married a wealthy
widow, he had time for religious meditation. At forty, he had the
vision in which the angel Gabriel showed him the Koran, and,
although Mahomet was unable to read, he "felt his understanding
illumined with celestial light." Thus he received the decrees of
God, the only miracle of his faith. At first the faith was practiced
privately, but four years after the vision, he received the inspiration directing him to publish it, and the years of persecution
began.

Irving comments that "the sect, as usual, increased under
persecution," and, in the same chapter, records that after the
death of his wife Mahomet "henceforth indulged in a plurality
of wives." While Irving does point out that polygamy was accepted among the Arabs, he uses Mahomet's various troubles
with his wives to add humor and humanity to his character. It is
in this period of his career that Irving is most compassionate to
Mahomet. He shows him being stoned as he attempted to preach
in Tayef, then driven from the city "and even pursued for some
distance beyond the walls by an insulting rabble of slaves and
children." He became an outlaw in Mecca: "still he persevered
. . . we find him, after having sacrificed ease, fortune, and
friends, prepared to give up home and country also, rather than
his religious creed."

And so the Hegira, Mahomet's welcome in Medina, his success
at gaining converts, and then the moment when, in Irving's eyes,

he shows his moral weakness—the promulgation of the doctrine of the sword: "his human nature was not capable of maintaining the sublime forbearance he had hitherto inculcated." Having now the means of retaliation, he used them—first upon his own unbelieving kinsmen, then against all Arabian unbelievers. He continued until he had united the tribes of Arabia under one faith, had taken Mecca, and had cleansed the Kaaba of all idols. He was now ready to lead forth his armies to propagate the faith in foreign lands, made an incursion into Syria, and was ready to send another army there when he died.

Irving's *Mahomet* does not conclude with the death of the prophet, but with a curious chapter entitled "Person and character of Mahomet, and speculations on his prophetic career." In it, Irving emphasizes Mahomet's personal moderation—except for perfumes and women—his justice, and his charity. He asks, "was he the unprincipled imposter that he has been represented? Were all his visions and revelations deliberate falsehoods, and was his whole system a tissue of deceit?" Irving answers "no" to both questions. He excludes all later legends of miracles and attributes many of the incoherencies of the Koran to the fact that it was dictated to different scribes at different times, and only gathered after his death. To the charge that Mahomet was an impious and stupendous impostor, Irving answers that Mahomet had no worldly motive for such an imposture during the first part of his prophetic career: "In proportion as he made known his doctrines and proclaimed his revelations, they subjected him to ridicule, scorn, obloquy, and finally to an inveterate persecution; which ruined the fortunes of himself and his friends; compelled some of his family and followers to take refuge in a foreign land; obliged him to hide from sight in his native city, and finally drove him forth a fugitive to seek an uncertain home elsewhere." It is after the Hegira that Irving sees him infected by "worldly passions and worldly schemes." Even so, "his military triumphs awakened no pride nor vainglory, as they would have done had they been effected for selfish purposes." Even then he had a "perfect abnegation of self," gave his riches to the poor, and, at his death "he still breathed the same religious devotion, and the same belief in his apostolic mission." Thus, while Irving does not believe in Mahomet as prophet, he believes in Mahomet's belief that he was the prophet of God. Contemporary ecclesiastics did not appreciate Irving's temperate position.

But why, in 1849, did Irving bother with the defense of this latter day prophet of God? The usual answer is that Irving was attempting to get all his literary "lumber" published before he died. Another answer might be that Irving thought this story of the formation of the Moslem nation, destined to be so powerful, whose people lived simply and frugally, would be a valuable lesson for the United States. Yet we must not neglect a third possibility, that Irving perceived the great number of parallels between the founding of the Islamic faith and that of the Mormon faith. While there would not have been a great need, in the United States, in 1849, for a defense of Mahomet and his followers, one of Joseph Smith and his followers was needed.

Mahomet's Successors is an entirely different book; it was published five months after *Mahomet*, has a separate preface, and is a chronicle of the Moslem empire rather than a biography. In addition, as E. N. Feltskog [17] has shown, *Mahomet's Successors* did not have the years of research behind it; Irving seems to have researched it as he went along. Feltskog, consequently, deems it literary hackwork. The tone, too, of *Mahomet's Successors* is different from Irving's two previous works. In *Goldsmith*, his tone is happy; in *Mahomet*, neutral; in the last half of the *Successors* it is despairing. That Irving was writing this volume in the years when the South, fearful that the admission of California as a free state would upset the balance of power, was again suggesting secession, at a time when Calhoun was proposing a dual executive, each having veto power, at a time when civil war once more seemed imminent, has never been considered in the studies of this book.

Irving notes in his preface that the events of this book cover the period from 632 to 710, less than four score and ten years, and that in those years Moslem arms conquered lands stretching from sea to sea. Although Irving never denigrates the Moslems as believers in a false prophet, he does belittle them for their later disunion and degeneracy from the absteminous habits of the founders. This is neither a tragedy of the fall of the Roman Empire, nor a romantic exaltation of the Arabs. It is a work that claims that all empires are apt to fall, either from old age, effeminancy, or war—civil or external.

The volume falls into two almost equal parts: the first covers eleven years and the caliphates of Abu Bekar and Omar and the taking of Syria, Palestine, Egypt, and parts of Persia; the second

covers the civil wars, the double Caliphates, and finally the
reunification of the Moslems and their further victories. The first
half is the better written and organized; here the contrasts between the hardy, abstemious Arabs and the voluptuous, degenerate Greeks and Persians are most striking. Abu Bekar and Omar
clung single-mindedly to the teachings and aims of the prophet,
and their armies were eminently successful: "It is singular to see
the fate of the once mighty and magnificent empires of the
Orient, Syria, Chaldea, Babylonia, and the dominions of the
Medes and Persians, thus debated and decided in the mosque of
Medina, by a handful of gray-headed Arabs, who but a few years
previously had been homeless fugitives." But this simplicity and
this unity were not to last; indeed, tokens of disunity were evident on the death of Mahomet, who had not named a successor.
While the people agreed on an elected Caliphate, Medina and
Mecca vied to do the electing. A compromise was suggested,
"that each party should furnish a ruler and the government have
two heads." Omar rejected this on military grounds, and Abu
Bekar, "remonstrated against a measure calculated to weaken
the empire in its very infancy."

But after Omar, during the reign of Othman, the single-
mindedness of the founding fathers of the faith gave way: "other
objects beside the mere advancement of Islamism distract the
attention of its leading professors; and the struggle for worldly
wealth and worldly sway, for the advancement of private ends,
and the aggrandizement of particular tribes and families, destroy
the unity of the empire, and beset the Caliphat with intrigue,
treason, and bloodshed." Othman was accused by the people of
having displaced men of worth and given their places to his
favorites, and of lavishing public funds on Merwan, his secretary
of state, who had "an undue ascendency over him." Othman is
slain, and the charges and countercharges following his death
divide the empire. Ali defeated two other candidates for the
caliphate at the battle of Karibah, "an obstinate and bloody
conflict, for Moslem was arrayed against Moslem, and nothing
is so merciless and unyielding as civil war." Ali established his
caliphate at Cufa; an opposing caliphate is established at Damascus by Moawyah. The empire remained divided and in disunion
until 694 when Abd'almalec reunified it and further extended its
dominions. The volume ends with the caliphate of Abd'almalec's

son, Waled, whom Irving pictures as a voluptuary who left governing to his emirs and conquests to his generals.

Feltskog has commented on the deficiencies of the book: its double organization by caliphates and by territory, its lack of authorial involvement in its characters, its "conception of Islam corrupt and imbecile in heart and head while full of vigorous and triumphant life in all its extremities," and its very abrupt concluding chapter, in which, according to Feltskog, Irving sought "to reconcile the fundamental contradictions of his narrative and his theme." [18] All of these charges are true: the book does not have the polish and good humor of other Irving works; his distance from all characters in the last half of the book is great; but he does, in the last half, focus on the disunion, the falling away from the original faith, the increasing desire for luxury and plunder rather than on the triumphs of arms and the acquisition of new territory. And this is exactly the focus that Irving wanted. In his preface he tells us that the work is "not to be consulted as an authority," and in the text he refers to the "lessons furnished by history." *Mahomet's Successors* is a tale of the founding of an empire, its rapid expansion across a continent, its disunion and civil wars, all taking place in less than ninety years. Irving thought that the history of this empire furnished an important lesson to be learned by the seventy-four-year-old United States.

While this view explains Irving's focus, it does not explain his last chapter, which begins with this abrupt sentence, "to return to affairs in Africa." This chapter, which deals hastily with the capture of the last opposing stronghold on the African coast and the preparations for the invasion of Spain, is a discordant ending, quite unlike any of Irving's other well-planned conclusions. Indeed, I suspect that it was written at the last minute, possibly being substituted for the original conclusion. For in this chapter Irving deals again with the treason of Count Julian, previously recorded in *Legends of the Conquest of Spain.* But here, while mentioning the act of treason, Irving gives no further details. And he concludes the volume with a speculation: "whether it will ever be our lot to resume this theme . . . and narrate their memorable conquest of Gothic Spain, is one of those uncertainties of mortal life." Since Irving had already narrated the legends—if not the history—of the conquest of

Spain, this is a most striking statement. Irving had not reprinted the *Legends* in his Author's Revised Edition, and this statement continues to conceal the existence of the earlier work. Why? *Mahomet's Successors* appeared the first week in April 1850. John C. Calhoun, the Count Julian of the *Legends*, died on March 30, 1850. Irving would not speak ill of the dead.

VI Wolfert's Roost

Wolfert's Roost (1855), Irving's last collection of sketches and tales, is just that—a collection. It lacks the unity and sense of sure progression of his earlier volumes, probably because its contents had been published between 1837 and 1841 in various periodicals. Irving collected these sketches and tales, written for the audience of the moment, and presented them to the audience of fifteen years later. If there is any order, any reason why the tales should be read in their order, it is autobiographical; in these tales and sketches we retrace Irving's literary career from his first New York works to his last historical studies. Once more Irving repeats his old themes, but with some intriguing variations.

Collected in this one volume is Irving's variety: fable, legend, chronicle, sketch, tale, criticism, biography, history. In the chronicles that make up the first section, "Wolfert's Roost," we have Knickerbocker's *A History of Sleepy Hollow*—but a mellow, drowsy history of quiet humor, quite unlike his first history. "Sketches in Paris in 1825" is a miniature French *Sketch Book*, while "The Bermudas: A Shakespeareian Research" and "Don Juan: A Spectral Research" add the flavor of literary antiquarianism.

"The Early Experiences of Ralph Ringwood," "The Seminoles," and "The Conspiracy of Neamathla" contribute biography—this of Governor Duval of Florida—and stress again Irving's concern for the Indians. In "A Time of Unexampled Prosperity" and "The Count Van Horn," Irving details histories of the Regency of the duke of Orleans of France. Again, he is drawing lessons from history, giving parallels from the French Regency to events of Van Buren's federal administration (not to the Albany Regency which ruled New York while he was in Washington). These show Irving's unhappiness with that administration, especially with its economic policies. At least one Whig campaign paper reprinted them during the election year of 1840.

Two of the selections from this book that were often reprinted are "The Birds of Spring" and "The Creole Village." The first follows the bobolink in his migrations: first the cheerful spring songster of the north, then the gourmandizing reed bird of the Delaware, finally the sensual rice bird of the Carolinas, hunted for the dinner tables. Irving draws the moral of this fable for little boys: "keep to those refined and intellectual pursuits . . . eschew all tendency to that gross and dissipated indulgence, which brought this mistaken little bird to an untimely end." The moral of "The Creole Village" is more ambiguous. Irving presents the village as a little bit of Europe, where the missionaries of "the almighty dollar" have not yet won devotees, nor yet set up their shrines, the banks, leaving it in contented poverty. But the great man of the village exerts his sway out of "custom and convention, out of deference to his family. Beside, he was worth full fifty thousand dollars." And again Irving states his thesis, first propounded in *Bracebridge Hall*, that the freer a people are, the less merry they are: "the cares of maintaining their rights and liberties, adding to their wealth, and making presidents, engross all their thoughts, and dry up all the moisture of their souls." Irving closes by contrasting the stability, merriment, and poverty of the Creole village with a new American town. It was rich and getting richer, but was torn in pieces by rival papers, rival churches, and rival political doctrines. Irving's sympathies lie most with the merry, fiddling "poor devil"; they are most against the worshippers of the almighty dollar.

In "A Time of Unexampled Prosperity," Irving describes speculation as "the romance of trade [which] casts contempt upon all its sober realities." It is a delusion, a "ruinous delusion." This old theme, that poetry and romance are delusion, is expressed also in his tales, the first and funniest of which is "Mountjoy." The tale is told, in the first person, by Mountjoy, and is a portrait of an ass as a young man. Irving thoroughly enjoys the discomfitures of his hero, all of which arise from his poetic imagination and his metaphysical education. Mountjoy details the early influence on him of story books, his abandoning himself to his romantic imagination, his being tutored by Glencoe, who dreams "of romantic enterprises in morals, and splendid systems for the improvement of society."

But Mountjoy soon tires of philosophy, turns to novels, exists in an "amorous delirium," and falls in love with a footprint.

Then, as in "Dolph Heyliger," comes the voyage, the thunderstorm, and the hero finding himself in the home of a judicious man with an only daughter. On discovering that the daughter made the footprint, Mountjoy falls in love with her, and determines to educate her. Unfortunately, her knowledge surpasses his—in all fields but metaphysics. The father gives Mountjoy sensible advice on his need for an educational system; Mountjoy's pride in himself is temporarily dampened, but only temporarily. Although similar in form to "Dolph Heyliger" and in theme to "Buckthorne," here Irving is openly laughing at his hero and his delusions.

In "The Grand Prior of Minorca: A Veritable Ghost Story," Irving returns to the motif and devices of "The Young Italian." Again the protagonist murders a man who comes between him and his loved one, flees, and is punished by his conscience with dreams of his victim. But instead of painting a portrait of the murdered one, which then seems to come to life, he makes a penitential pilgrimage to the castle of his victim, and there sees portraits of the victim's ancestors come to life, at which he falls senseless. Although he revives, his conscience continues to punish him, and he dies, "the victim of a diseased imagination." "Guests from Gibbet Island" has an equally dire conclusion. A pirate, having returned home after many years abroad, one night daringly calls to three hanged companions, still swinging from their gibbets, to come dine with him. They do, and the pirate dies. In both stories, the evocation of the past leads to death.

"The Adalantado of the Seven Cities" is a variation on the same theme. In it, Don Fernando is commissioned by the Portuguese government to find the Island of the Seven Cities, legendary land of Gothic Christians who left Spain when the Moors invaded. Exchanging pledges of constancy with his betrothed, Serafina, he embarks on his mission, finds the island, and is there welcomed as Adalantado by the people, dressed in ancient garb. He is wined and feted, and pledges his devotion to the bewitching daughter of the alcayde. On his return to his ship, he becomes drowsy and falls asleep. When he awakens, he is on another ship, which carries him to Lisbon. He rushes to Serafina, seeks to embrace her, but is repulsed; it is Serafina's great-granddaughter. Needless to say, Don Fernando, still youthful-looking, is perplexed by this sudden passage of time and by being a stranger in his native city. He is shown his Serafina's tomb, she lying in effigy with her numerous family also depicted: "Don Fernando felt a transient glow of indignation at beholding this monumental proof of the inconstancy of his mistress." Now that Serafina was "nothing but a great-grandmother in marble," he wishes himself back "to that wonderful island, with its anti-quated banquet halls, where he had been so courteously received." But, although he goes to the Canaries to look for it in the west, he can never catch sight of it again; he grows gray and dies in the attempt. Thus, in pursuit of the legendary past, Don Fernando loses his present, and finds himself a stranger in the future. In this tale, Irving extends the story of Rip Van Winkle. Unlike Rip, Don Fernando does not remain contentedly as a storyteller in his home town, but, a stranger there and mocked for his vision, seeks to reattain the ancient past.

The last story of the volume, "The Abencerrage," is more cheerful. In it, the Alcayde of a frontier fortress captures a valorous Moor on his way to visit his secretly wed bride. Hearing of this, the alcayde releases his prisoner on his promise to return within three days. The Moor returns with his bride, the Moorish king persuades the father to forgive the couple, the alcayde releases them and sends back their ransom as a wedding present. Thus, for the first time since *Bracebridge Hall*, Irving ends a volume with a "true" wedding. The happy ending is, however, overshadowed by the greater force of "The Adalantado of the Seven Seas."

Wolfert's Roost is a jumble of various kinds of works thrown together with little regard for the chronological order of their composition or publication. Thus it does not have the impact or unity of Irving's earlier volumes. It does contain, however, in some of its sketches and tales, Irving's reactions to the United States he found after his long absence. Just as the Moors degenerated after their first conquests, as the bird of spring degenerated as it grew older, so the United States had changed, now worshipping luxury and the almighty dollar.

VII   Life of Washington

Washington Irving's last work is a great, five-volume plea that the Union be preserved. Irving is again using history to teach; he uses the life of Washington and the history of the transformation of the colonies into the United States to show that, through intelligence, charity, and perseverance, regional differences and antagonisms had been overcome, that all sections of the country were dependent upon one another, and that, all else failing, Washington's memory binds the states together: "with us his memory remains a national property, where all sympathies throughout our widely extended and diversified empire meet in unison. Under all dissensions and amid all the storms of party, his precepts and example speak to us from the grave with a paternal appeal; and his name—by all revered—forms a universal tie of brotherhood—a watchword of our Union." Irving's plea is not impassioned or sentimental. He avoids, as he says in his preface to his first volume, "all false coloring and exaggeration." He does not wax eloquent over "the father of our country," he does not seek to conceal his defects, but he does reprint, it seems, every letter, every conversation of Washington's that reprobated sectional antagonism. And he takes pains to point out every instance, in the French and Indian War and in the Revolutionary War, when the different colonies, or states, cooperated to relieve one another.

Today, the virtue of Irving's *Washington* is that it is magnificently readable. Irving, even in the early days of the *Analectic*, had been a great reteller of battles. In his *Washington*, he relates the various battles so clearly and vividly that, although most are unaccompanied by maps, we easily comprehend them. In his handling of character he is temperate and evenhanded. (Although Irving is far more lenient than most other historians to his fellow New Yorker, Philip Schuyler, we tolerate this, for Irving convinces us of the worth of his character.) There are few "flat" characters in this history; Irving makes them live believably. He shows us the later petulance of the stolid General Knox, the quiet caution of General Greene, the rash daring of "Old Put," the ambition and intrigue of General Lee, the fury and frustration of Von Steuben, swearing fluently at the troops he was drilling in all languages but English. Irving not only describes actions; he seeks the motivations of the actions. He presents Benedict Arnold not just as a traitor, but as an able officer, just married into a Tory family, who had gotten terribly in debt and had had his pride wounded. Irving does not condone, but understands his treason. His presentation of the Genet affair is one of the clearest of that tangled web of circumstance and personalities; his treatment of the collisions between Hamilton and Jefferson is remarkably fair—again, he gives the motivations for the stands taken by the two. Almost the only instance of name-calling in the volumes is his reference to the "cur Freneau," certainly an uncalled-for epithet.

Irving individualizes and humanizes the British also. Braddock is not the blockhead of legend, André is not the noble hero of sentimental drama. Burgoyne, Gage, Clinton, the Howes—Irving treats them fairly. We sense their growing frustration with having the Continental Army always camped nearby, but always waiting, never putting itself in a position to be signally defeated. And we almost pity Cornwallis, thinking he had subdued the Carolinas, marching north to Virginia, only to find Greene and the local militias driving his Carolina troops back into Charleston, with the northern army between him and New York, and the French squadron cutting off all hopes of reenforcement.

Recollections of the participants or observers add to the description of major events and movements. Irving interweaves letters from Mrs. Adams to her husband, a journal of a young Hessian soldier, memories of Washington's granddaughter, recollections of Baroness Riedesel of General Schuyler's kind hospitality in Albany (even though his guests were responsible for the burning and sacking of his estate), notes made by Jefferson of cabinet meetings, anecdotes from old ladies of what went on at a ball—all work together to make us feel the truth of the time. Major characters, minor characters, all are presented as individuals, all are important. Irving emphasizes this in his conclusion to his fourth volume, when he quotes Lafayette as saying of the war, " 'it was the grandest of causes won by skirmishes of sentinels and outposts.' " Irving refuses to concentrate on the great battles, preferring to detail the privations so long experienced: "it was in the patience and fortitude with which these ills were sustained by a half-disciplined yeomanry, voluntary exiles from their homes, destitute of all the 'pomp and circumstance' of war to excite them, and animated solely by their patriotism, that we read the noblest and most affecting characteristics of that great struggle for human rights."

Irving's *Life of Washington*, as a life of Washington, is uneven and incomplete. We see little of the private man (although Irving does allow him to indulge in unreasonable, violent fits of temper), Irving claiming that he was "eminently a public character." The first volume concerns itself, basically, with the French and Indian

War, the second, third, and fourth are devoted to the Revolutionary War, and the last, briefest volume, details Washington's years as president and in retirement. Thus the biography is obviously out of proportion. But the *Life of Washington* is a history of the founding of the United States, its various strands unified by the presence of George Washington, "for his spirit pervaded and directed the whole." After the war, Washington visited all parts of the new nation, the North, the South, the West: "he knew no divided fidelity, no separate obligation; his most sacred duty to himself was his highest duty to his country and his God."

In these five volumes we have Irving's evocation of a glorious past, glorious not for its wealth, luxury, or romance, but for its hardships endured, for the single-mindedness of those who established the nation. The present might not heed the lesson of this "no divided fidelity," but there was always the future. When told by a friend that he had read the work to his children, Irving exclaimed, " 'that's it: that is what I write it for. I want it so clear that anybody can understand it. I want the action to shine through the style' " [19] Irving's last work was a direct work; he concentrates on the tale, rather than on the way it was told; his message was too important for him to indulge in misdirection.

CHAPTER 5

Summation

WASHINGTON Irving's influence on his own times was great. His main contribution to literature was his style; no matter what he wrote, he generally wrote well. His ability to draw pictures with words and his comic renditions of character were hailed as great. Dickens and Thackery acknowledged their indebtedness to him; in the United States, Melville, Hawthorne, and Poe were indebted. Politically, his influence may have been great, although this is impossible to measure. His exact influence on English positions, as diplomat, author, or propagandist, may never be known; his influence on Spain may have been greater. He was certainly influential enough that governments thought they had to censor his works: *Astoria* was censored in Russia, *A Chronicle of the Conquest of Granada* in Spain, and his play, *Richelieu*, in England. In the United States, he was the confidant of presidents, from Madison to Van Buren.

His production was immense: a collection of his fugitive pieces alone—if they ever could be exactly ascertained—would fill six or seven volumes. His knowledge was immense. He knew French early, he taught himself German, Italian, and Spanish, and there is some indication he may have begun the study of Arabic. He learned the languages, then read the literatures of these languages. He was deeply read in ancient and modern English literature; his knowledge of the drama was especially profound. Above all, he knew contemporary politics and its intrigues. Even in Europe, he kept up with those of the United States; he knew of the inner machinations of the Holy Alliance, of England, of France, of Spain, of Italy. He interested himself in wine, in husbandry, in usury, in the latest African explorations, in metaphysics.

And all is reflected in his writing—although indirectly. A judgment of Irving's influence today is not hard to make, for few read him. Only historians read his Western works; only college students read more than one or two of his tales. Even in his own time, few ever understood him; in his last work, when the urgency of his message was most compelling, he felt he had to cast aside his famous "style" and write so everyone could understand him. Why, until his *Life of Washington* (which also was somewhat of a misdirection), did Irving misdirect his readers, and consequently feel "lack of confidence in myself, and with the public"?

The answer must lie in the security and stability of his first thirty years in New York—where misdirection was expected, where outright libels and slanders were not encouraged, but where wit was. His first acknowledged English work, *The Sketch Book*, has few contemporary political allusions, but his next, *Bracebridge Hall*, abounds with allusion and caricature. Perhaps because Irving was provoked by the reception of *Bracebridge Hall*, he retaliated on the critics and his audience with *Tales of a Traveller*. The American criticism of *Tales* so shocked Irving that he turned to history—history that would please his American audience—his *Columbus. The Conquest of Granada* and its satire was a work he could not help but write—the parallels were so obvious, the disaster of the monarchy so plain. And then, out of Spain, with the success of *Columbus* behind him, he tossed off his *Companions of Columbus*, in his old allusive vein, and also the happy *Alhambra*, in the same vein.

His first work after his return, *The Crayon Miscellany*, was personally and politically allusive; his *Astoria* and *Bonneville* were propaganda. His *Goldsmith* contains many personal allusions and jokes; *Mahomet* is religiously allusive; *Mahomet's Successor* contains politcal allusions. Only in his *Washington* does he refrain from allegory or allusion. In it, he teaches his lesson directly.

The Irving monument near Sunnyside records that he was "Essayist, Poet, Historian, Diplomatist, Soldier," although many other terms could have been added. He was an essayist in the sense of Cotton Mather, in his *Bonifacius*, or Franklin, an "essayist upon the good." He was a poet in two senses: in the sense that he wrote of and for the heart, and in the literal sense—we know he provided the poems for several of Payne's plays. He was undoubtedly an historian; for any contemporary incident, he could find—and use—an historical parallel. While Irving always seemed to be the historian of the past, he also recorded the story of the present in order to aid the historians of the future. In Europe, he was always a diplomat. He may have been attached to the French legation in the same way that Everett attached him to the Spanish; he was secretary to the legation in London, and, for a time, its chargé d'affaires. Finally, he was minister to Spain. And he was a soldier. He was a colonel in the New York Militia; when Tompkins was named commander of the Third Military District in 1815, Irving may then have received a regular army commission. In Europe, he was no longer a soldier (although, if there had been a CIA then—and Jefferson did not invent the most complex cipher machine before World War II merely to exchange observations on cherry blossoms with his friends—Irving would have been an ideal agent). But he served his country well by his writings.

His best works are those that, like Goldsmith's, abound "with pictures of life and touches of nature drawn from his own ob-servation and experience." We follow his own parable of the prodigal son, follow it through most of his books written in Europe, follow it even in one after the return. Indeed, much of Irving's imagery is religious; the "poor devil" author hopes to be transformed into an angel, "with a halo of literary glory." In *Bracebridge Hall*, Irving refers to political creeds as faiths: his was that of the United States; he worshipped in the "temple of true liberty." He uses the Christians and Moors to depict re-publicans and reactionaries, although the parallels are never consistent; sometimes the Christians offer true liberty, sometimes the Moors do. He, himself, always remained a soldier of the Constitution, marching as to war, even when he returned to the United States and saw it lapsing from the faith of the fathers: "his most sacred duty . . . was his highest duty to his country and his God."

Notes and References

Chapter One

1. William Hedges, *Washington Irving: An American Study, 1802–1832* (Baltimore: Johns Hopkins Press, 1965), p. 95.
2. Stanley T. Williams, *The Life of Washington Irving* (1935; reprint ed., New York: Octagon Books, 1971), II, pp. 255–62.
3. See M. A. Weatherspoon, "1815–1819: Prelude to Irving's *Sketch Book*," *American Literature*, 16, no. 4 (1970), 566–71.
4. Dorothie Bobbé, *DeWitt Clinton* (New York: Balch, 1933), pp. 89–91.
5. Martin Roth, *Washington Irving's Contributions to The Corrector* (Minneapolis: University of Minnesota Press, 1968), p. 60.
6. Ibid., p. 11.
7. Ibid., p. 55.
8. Ibid., p. 104.
9. See Bruce Granger and Martha Hartzog, "Assignments of Authorship," in *Oldstyle; Salmagundi,* by Washington Irving (Boston: Twayne Publishers, 1978).
10. H. M. Dickinson, *Robert Fulton* (London: John Lane, 1913), pp. 206–18.
11. George Dangerfield, *Chancellor Robert R. Livingston of New York* (New York: Harcourt, Brace, 1960), pp. 408–9.
12. Pierre M. Irving, *Life and Letters of Washington Irving* (1863; reprint ed., Detroit: Gale Research Company, 1967), I, 210.
13. Compare the engraving of Launcelot Langstaff with the 1808 John Trumbull portrait of Morgan Lewis in the Governors' Room, City Hall, New York. For further information on *Salmagundi,* see M. W. Bowden, "Cocklofts and Slang-whangers: The Historical Sources of Washington Irving's *Salmagundi*." *New York History* (April, 1980), 133–160.
14. *The Weekly Inspector*, February 7, 1807, pt. 1, pp. 277–78.
15. Williams, II, 265.
16. Walter Barrett, pseud., *The Old Merchants of New York City,* 2d ser. (New York: Carleton, 1862), p. 46. Knickerbocker refers to the Goelets as "my highly respected friends" in his *History*, ed. Stanley Williams and Tremaine McDowell (New York: Harcourt, Brace, 1927), p. 103.

17. Williams, I, 82.

18. Compare Alexander Anderson's engraving of "The Little Man in Black" in the second edition (1814) of *Salmagundi* with John Vanderlyn's 1809 portrait of Aaron Burr, owned by the New-York Historical Society. While Anderson gives the little man more hair than Burr had at the time, he gives him Burr's ears, eyes, nose, mouth, and jaw-line, and suggests his side-whiskers.

19. Washington Irving, *Letters*, ed. Ralph M. Aderman, Herbert L. Kleinfield, and Jenifer S. Banks (Boston: Twayne Publishers, 1978), I, 244.

20. "Washington Irving, Esq.," *The Port Folio*, 11 (March, 1821), 231.

21. "New York," in *Encyclopedia Americana* (1972 ed.), XX, 231.

22. David M. Ellis, James A. Frost, Harold C. Syrett, and Harry J. Carman, *A Short History of New York State* (Ithaca: Cornell University Press, 1957), p. 23.

23. Howard Thomas, *Marinus Willett* (Prospect, N. Y.: Prospect Books, 1954), p. 195.

24. Ibid., p. 198.

25. Ibid., p. 211.

26. John Neal, "American Writers, No. IV," Blackwood's *Edinburgh Magazine*, 18 (1825), 58–67.

27. Bobbé, p. 106.

28. Ellis et al., p. 24.

29. Roth, p. 90.

Chapter Two

1. Washington Irving, *Letters*, I, 399.

2. Ibid., I, 435.

3. Ibid., I, 435.

4. Ibid., I, 464–65.

5. Ibid., I, 501.

6. Ben McClary, *Washington Irving and the House of Murray* (Knoxville: University of Tennessee Press, 1969), p. 152, n. 68.

7. Pierre Irving, I, 408–9.

8. Washington Irving, *Letters*, I, 540.

9. Margaret Oliphant, *William Blackwood and His Sons*, vol 1. (New York: Charles Scribner's Sons, 1897), p. 377.

10. Williams, I, 148.

11. Washington Irving, *Bracebridge Hall*, ed. Herbert F. Smith (Boston: Twayne Publishers, 1977), p. xxix.

12. Williams, I, 208.

13. Egbert Benson, *Brief remarks on the "wife" of Washington Irving* (New York: Grattan and Banks, 1817).

14. Pierre Irving, III, 226–27.

15. *The Collected Works of Edgar Allen Poe*, ed. Thomas O. Mabbott (Cambridge: Harvard University Press, Belknap Press, 1978), XIV, 73.

16. "Thomas Young," in *Dictionary of National Biography*, ed. Sir Leslie Stephen and Sir Sidney Lee (London: Oxford University Press, 1921–1922), XXI, 1308–13.

17. J. B. Priestley, *The Prince of Pleasure and His Regency* (New York: Harper and Row, 1969), p. 213.

Chapter Three

1. Washington Irving, *Journals and Notebooks*, vol. 3, ed. Walter A. Reichart (Madison: University of Wisconsin Press, 1970), p. 335.

2. Washington Irving, *Diary: Spain 1828–1829*, ed. Clara L. Penney (New York: Hispanic Society of America, 1926), p. 90.

3. Pierre Irving, II, 226.

4. Williams, I, 346.

5. Ibid., I, 339.

6. H. Butler Clarke, *Modern Spain: 1815–1898* (Cambridge: At the University Press, 1906), p. 33.

7. Ibid., p. 66.

8. Ibid., p. 73.

9. Ibid., p. 77.

10. Williams, I, 332.

11. DeWitt Clinton, *An Account of Abimelech Coody* (New York: 1815), p. 7.

12. Clarke, pp. 84–85.

Chapter Four

1. Pierre Irving, II, 490.

2. Ibid., III, 129.

3. Ibid., III, 179.

4. Ibid., III, 146.

5. Ibid., III, 123.

6. Ibid., III, 198.

7. Ibid., IV, 162.

8. Ibid., III, 65.

9. Washington Irving, *A Tour on the Prairies*, ed. John F. McDermott (Norman: University of Oklahoma Press, 1956), p. 6.

10. Margaret L. Coit, *John C. Calhoun* (Boston: Houghton Mifflin, 1950), p. 123.

11. Ibid., p. 124.

12. Pierre Irving, III, p. 113.

13. Alan Sandy, "Introduction," in *The Adventures of Captain Bonneville*, by Washington Irving, ed. Robert A. Rees and Alan Sandy (Boston: Twayne Publishers, 1977), p. xxxix.

14. "California," in *Encyclopedia Americana* (1972 ed.), V, 211.

15. The Buenaventura River drains into Monterey Bay according to *Mitchell's School Atlas* (Philadelphia: H. Cowperthwait & Company, 1855), map number 5.

16. *California: A Guide to the Golden State*, ed. Harray Hansen (New York: Hastings House, 1967), p. 48.

17. E. N. Feltskog, "Historical Note," in *Mahomet and His Successors*, by Washington Irving, ed. Harry A. Pochmann and E. N. Feltskog (Madison: University of Wisconsin Press, 1970), p. 545.

18. Feltskog, p. 552.

19. Williams, II, 230.

Selected Bibliography

PRIMARY SOURCES

The best bibliography of Washington Irving may be found in Jacob Blanck, *Bibliography of American Literature*, V (New Haven: Yale University Press, 1969). Edwin T. Bowden is preparing a bibliography for the Twayne edition of *The Complete Works of Washington Irving*.

1. Books (listed in order of first appearance)

Letters of Jonathan Oldstyle, Gent.: Salmagundi. Edited by Bruce I. Granger and Martha Hartzog. Boston: Twayne Publishers, 1977.
Washington Irving's Contributions to The Corrector. Edited by Martin Roth. Minneapolis: University of Minnesota Press, 1968.
Diedrich Knickerbocker's A History of New York. Edited by Stanley Williams and Tremaine McDowell. New York: Harcourt, Brace and Company, 1927.
The Sketch Book. Edited by Haskell Springer. Boston: Twayne Publishers, 1977.
Bracebridge Hall. Edited by Herbert F. Smith. Boston: Twayne Publishers, 1977.
Tales of a Traveller. London: John Murray, 1824.
The Life and Voyages of Christopher Columbus. New York: G. P. Putnam, 1863.
A Chronicle of the Conquest of Granada. London: John Murray, 1829; reprint ed., New York: AMS Press, 1970.
The Companions of Columbus. New York: G. P. Putnam, 1863.
The Alhambra. London: Henry Colburn and Richard Bentley, 1832.
A Tour on the Prairies. London: John Murray, 1835.
"Abbotsford" and "Newstead Abbey." In *The Crayon Miscellany*. New York: G. P. Putnam, 1861.
"The Legend of Don Roderick," "Legend of the Subjugation of Spain," "Legend of Count Julian and His Family." In *Spanish Papers*. New York: G. P. Putnam, Hurd and Houghton, 1866.
Astoria. Edited by Richard Dilworth Rust. Boston: Twayne Publishers, 1976.
The Adventures of Captain Bonneville. Edited by Robert A. Rees and Alan Sandy. Boston: Twayne Publishers, 1977.

Biography of the Late Margaret Miller Davidson: Oliver Goldsmith, A Biography. Edited by Elsie Lee West. Boston: Twayne Publishers, 1978.

Mahomet and His Successors. Edited by Henry A. Pochmann and E. N. Feltskog. Madison: University of Wisconsin Press, 1970.

Wolfert's Roost. New York: G. P. Putnam, 1855.

Life of George Washington. New York: G. P. Putnam, 1863.

2. Letters, journals, and notebooks

Letters. Vol. 1. Edited by Ralph Aderman, Herbert Kleinfield, and Jennifer Banks. Boston: Twayne Publishers, 1978.

Journals and Notebooks. Vol 1. Edited by Nathalia Wright. Madison: University of Wisconsin Press, 1969.

Notes While Preparing the Sketch Book &c. Edited by Stanley T. Williams. New Haven: Yale University Press, 1927.

Tour in Scotland, 1817. Edited by Stanley T. Williams. New Haven: Yale University Press, 1927.

Journals and Notebooks. Vol. 3. Edited by Walter A. Reichart. Madison: University of Wisconsin Press, 1970.

Letters of Washington Irving to Henry Brevoort. Edited by George S. Hellman. New York: G. P. Putnam's Sons, 1918.

"Correspondence of Washington Irving and John Howard Payne [1821–1828]." Edited by Thatcher T. Payne Luquer. *Scribner's Magazine,* 48 (1910).

Letters. Vol. 2. Edited by Ralph Aderman, Herbert Kleinfield, and Jennifer Banks. Boston: Twayne Publishers, 1979.

Diary: Spain 1828–1829. Edited by Clara L. Penney. New York: Hispanic Society of America, 1926.

Journal of Washington Irving, 1828. Edited by Stanley T. Williams. New York: American Book Company, 1937.

The Western Journals of Washington Irving. Edited by John F. McDermott. Norman: University of Oklahoma Press, 1944.

Letters from Sunnyside and Spain. Edited by Stanley T. Williams. New Haven: Yale University Press, 1928.

3. Periodicals containing significant contributions (incomplete)

The *Morning Chronicle.* 1802–1805.

The Corrector. 1804.

The Analectic Magazine. 1813–1819.

Blackwood's Edinburgh Magazine. 1817–?

The *Knickerbocker Magazine.* 1839–1841.

SECONDARY SOURCES

1. Works on Irving

BOWERS, CLAUDE G. *The Spanish Adventures of Washington Irving.*
     Boston: Houghton Mifflin, 1940. Gives additional details of
     Irving's years in Spain.
A *Century of Commentary on the Works of Washington Irving.*
     Edited by Andrew B. Myers. Tarrytown, New York: Sleepy
     Hollow Restorations, 1976. Valuable for a range of criticism on
     Irving.
CLARK, LOUIS GAYLORD. "Memorial of Washington Irving." *Knicker-
     bocker Magazine,* 55 (1860), 113–28. A series of reminiscences
     published just after Irving's death.
GREENLAW, EDWIN. "Washington Irving's Comedy of Politics." *Texas
     Review,* 1 (1916), 291–306. Points out the political nature of
     some of Irving's Knickerbocker satire.
HEDGES, WILLIAM L. *Washington Irving: An American Study, 1802–
     1832.* Baltimore: Johns Hopkins Press, 1965. Some good insights
     on some of Irving's works, especially *The Sketch Book* and *Tales
     of a Traveller.*
IRVING, PIERRE M. *The Life and Letters of Washington Irving.* 4 vols.
     New York: G. P. Putnam, 1863; reprint ed., Detroit: Gale Re-
     search Company, 1967. Written with close attention paid to his
     uncle's wishes and reputation.
KIME, WAYNE R. *Pierre M. Irving and Washington Irving: A Col-
     laboration in Life and Letters.* Waterloo, Ontario: Wilfrid Laurier
     University Press, 1977. Extremely detailed account of the rela-
     tionship between Irving and Pierre.
McCLARY, BEN HARRIS. *Washington Irving and the House of Murray.*
     Knoxville: University of Tennessee Press, 1969. Presents, with
     commentary, the letters between Irving and his English pub-
     lisher.
McDERMOTT, JOHN FRANCIS, ed. *A Tour on the Prairies,* by Wash-
     ington Irving. Norman: University of Oklahoma Press, 1956.
     Valuable for presenting, in notes, others' records of the same
     tour.
McELROY, JOHN. "The Integrity of Irving's Columbus." *American
     Literature,* 50, no. 1 (March, 1978), 1–16. Defends Irving
     against old charge of having plagiarized Navarette.
McFARLAND, PHILIP. *Sojourners.* New York: Atheneum, 1979. Biog-
     raphy of Irving interspersed with sketches of his contemporaries.
NEAL, JOHN. "American Writers. No. IV." *Blackwood's Edinburgh
     Magazine,* 17 (1825), 57–67. An interesting and somewhat
     tongue-in-cheek evaluation by a contemporary.

REICHART, WALTER A. *Washington Irving and Germany.* Boston: Houghton Mifflin, 1940. Valuable for information collected in Germany before World War II.

ROTH, MARTIN. *Comedy and America: The Lost World of Washington Irving.* Port Washington, N.Y.: Kennikat Press, 1976. Provocative.

WILLIAMS, STANLEY T. *The Life of Washington Irving.* 2 vols. New York: Oxford University Press, 1935; reprint ed., New York: Octagon Books, 1971. Contains a mass of facts. Its opinions are biased by Williams's hatred of Irving.

2. Works offering historical background

ADERMAN, RALPH, ed. *Letters of James Kirke Paulding.* Madison: University of Wisconsin Press, 1962. Correspondence of Irving's early collaborator.

BARRET, WALTER, pseud. *The Old Merchants of New York City.* New York: Carleton, 1862. Anecdotes of merchants of Irving's time.

BOBBÉ, DOROTHIE. *De Witt Clinton.* New York: Minton, Balch, 1933. Brief biography of the complex Clinton.

CLARKE, H. BUTLER. *Modern Spain 1815–1898.* Cambridge: University Press, 1906. Somewhat slanted, but detailed.

[CLINTON, DEWITT.] *An Account of Abimelech Coody.* New York: 1815. Gives satirical portraits of Donald Fraser, John Treat Irving, Washington Irving, James K. Paulding, Guilian Verplanck, and one other.

COIT, MARGARET L. *John C. Calhoun.* Boston: Houghton Mifflin, 1950. Detailed biography.

DANGERFIELD, GEORGE. *Chancellor Robert R. Livingston of New York 1746–1813.* New York: Harcourt, Brace, 1960. Contains much information on the Livingstons.

Dictionary of National Biography. Edited by Sir Leslie Stephen and Sir Sidney Lee. London: Oxford University Press, 1921–1922. Valuable for the careers of Irving's contemporaries.

ELLIS, DAVID M., FROST, JAMES A., SYRETT, HAROLD C., and CARMAN, HARRY J. *A Short History of New York State.* Ithaca: Cornell University Press, 1957.

Encyclopedia Americana. New York: Americana Corp., 1972. Necessary for tracing Irving's references and allusions.

FRANCIS, JOHN W. *Old New York.* New York: W. J. Middleton, 1866. Anecdotes and reminiscences.

HELLMAN, GEORGE S., ed. *Letters of Henry Brevoort to Washington Irving.* New York: G. P. Putnam's Sons, 1916. Correspondence of Irving's best friend.

JAMES, MARQUIS. *The Life of Andrew Jackson.* New York: Bobbs-

Merrill, 1938. Readable biography of the president that intrigued Irving.

[LAMBERT, JOHN.] *Letters from London*. London: 1816. Gives conditions in London in Irving's early years there.

Minutes of the Common Council of the City of New York. Vol. 5. 1808–1809. New York: The City of New York, 1917.

[MITCHELL, SAMUEL L.] *The Picture of New-York*. New York: I. Riley, 1807. Describes contemporary New York.

PARTON, JAMES. *The Life and Times of Aaron Burr*. Boston: Houghton, Mifflin, 1888. Contains personal recollections of Burr.

PRIESTLEY, J. B. *The Prince of Pleasure and His Regency 1811–1820*. New York: Harper, 1969. A beautifully done book giving the various aspects of the times.

RICHARDSON, JOANNA. *George the Magnificent*. New York: Harcourt, Brace & World, 1966. More detailed biography of George IV.

SPAULDING, GEORGE F., ed. *On the Western Tour with Washington Irving: The Journal and Letters of Count de Pourtalès*. Translated by Seymour Foiler. Norman: University of Oklahoma Press, 1968. Charming.

THOMAS, HOWARD. *Marinus Willett*. Prospect, N.Y.: Prospect Books, 1954. Adequate biography of the mayor.

WILLIAMS, STANLEY T., and SIMISON, BARBARA D., eds. *Washington Irving on the Prairie or a Narrative of a Tour of the Southwest in the Year 1832*, by Henry L. Ellsworth. New York: American Book Company, 1937.

Index